The Belt Road and Beyond

From 1998 to 2018, China had three political–economic crises, resulting in bureaucratic paralysis. It was at such junctures that China's leadership launched initiatives, like the Western Development Program, which mobilized state and market actors to expedite globalization and revive economic growth. In *The Belt Road and Beyond*, Min Ye reevaluates the common tendency to attribute China's Belt and Road to individual leaders' strategic ambitions, using state-mobilized globalization as a comparative framework and investigative tool to understand Chinese capitalism. State-mobilized globalization has helped sustain China's high-growth economy and social–political stability, while also sparking some political backlash. In order to succeed in globalization, the author argues, China's state mobilization must readapt to global circumstances. She sheds light on the tactics China used to spring from a crisis-stricken middle economy to a formidable global power, implicating not only China, but also the world.

Min Ye is Associate Professor of International Relations at the Frederick S. Pardee School of Global Studies at Boston University and the recipient of fellowships from Princeton University, Harvard University, the National Committee on United States-China Relations (NCUSCR) and institutions in Japan, South Korea, and Singapore. Her books include *Diasporas and Foreign Direct Investment in China and India* (2014) and *The Making of Northeast Asia* (2010).

The Belt Road and Beyond

State-Mobilized Globalization in China: 1998–2018

MIN YE
Boston University

CAMBRIDGE
UNIVERSITY PRESS

CAMBRIDGE
UNIVERSITY PRESS

University Printing House, Cambridge CB2 8BS, United Kingdom

One Liberty Plaza, 20th Floor, New York, NY 10006, USA

477 Williamstown Road, Port Melbourne, VIC 3207, Australia

314–321, 3rd Floor, Plot 3, Splendor Forum, Jasola District Centre, New Delhi – 110025, India

79 Anson Road, #06-04/06, Singapore 079906

Cambridge University Press is part of the University of Cambridge.

It furthers the University's mission by disseminating knowledge in the pursuit of education, learning, and research at the highest international levels of excellence.

www.cambridge.org
Information on this title: www.cambridge.org/9781108479561
DOI: 10.1017/9781108855389

First published 2020

A catalogue record for this publication is available from the British Library.

ISBN 978-1-108-47956-1 Hardback

To Claire and Sophia
with Love

Contents

Figures

Map

Tables

Prologue: Encountering the Silk Road in Urumqi

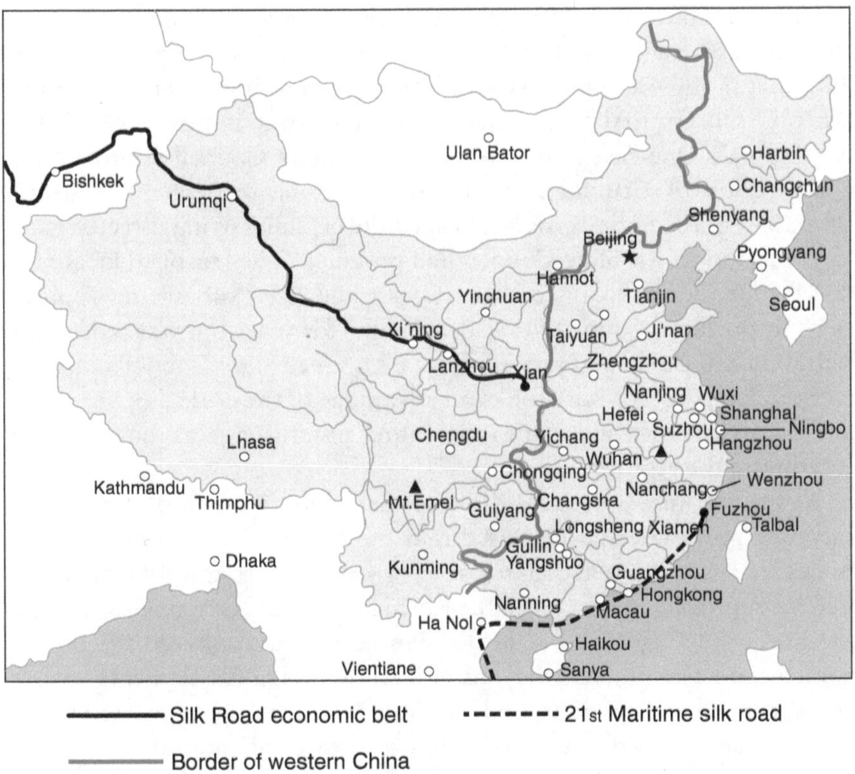

MAP Belt and Road Initiative *inside* China. *Source:* drawn by author.

In August 2017, the All China Association of Geographers and Resources held its annual international conference in the capital city of Xinjiang, Urumqi, featuring the Belt and Road Strategy. Over the course of three days, various government units in Xinjiang presented their plans and proposals to implement the Belt and Road Initiative (BRI). The hosting unit – Xinjiang's Earth and Resources Research Institute – also arranged for conference attendees a private peek into the revamped Heavenly Mountain [*tianshan*] – a stunning natural wonder that now has modern infrastructure – and a five-hour cultural feast presented by Uyghur performers and acrobats from central Asia. My personal favorite, however, was a specially arranged tour to Urumqi's New Tariff-Free Zone, accompanied by the director of the Urumqi City Development Bureau and a visiting delegation from the Erdos government in Inner Mongolia, Xinjiang's eastward neighbor.

The tour started at the zone's brand-new Grand Hall, a massive five-story structure with a red front; inside, a series of posters with narratives and images showcase the city's ambitious plan to implement the BRI in central Asia. The first poster opens with "In order to implement President Xi Jinping's One Belt and One Road, the State Council approved the construction of Urumqi New Tariff-Free Zone in September 2015." Interested in the policy process, I asked the accompanying director what kind of support the State Council had provided. The seasoned local official grinned. He explained that the city had been submitting applications to the State Council for a special zone for years but was repeatedly rejected until the inauguration of the BRI. Once State Council approval came in late 2015, the city took full advantage of the critical opportunity and constructed the new zone in just three months, against harsh winter weather in the region!

At the working lunch, the director then elaborated on the process of the zone proposal, and disclosed that the city government and market forces had worked together for several years before the BRI. In 2010, Beijing approved and financed the Kashigar special economic zone along the border of China and central Asian nations and offered the border zone the most favorable policy incentives, such as tax abatements for five years, concessionary loans, and free land to companies registered there. In the ensuing years, many companies – state, private, and foreign – registered in the zone but operated out of their Urumqi offices in order to access markets, skilled labor, and urban infrastructure. These investors persistently pushed for a special zone in the city itself, and with the BRI, their calls were answered.

Apart from my interest in the policy-making process, the Erdos government delegation probed the director on specific policies and incentives provided by Urumqi city to attract firms to the new zone; they were clearly interested in which policies and incentives might be applicable in their own city and which might not. For the remainder of the tour, we were bused to the zone's checkpoints, shipment storage locations, and vast construction sites planned for the zone. Every spot featured professionally designed images and narratives related to upcoming projects. The Erdos delegation was extremely attentive and asked many questions about the consulting teams that Urumqi city had hired to do the design and planning. It turned out that Erdos was in the midst of leveraging the BRI strategy as they proposed a new zone to the State Council; the consulting teams Erdos government was working with were the same experts that had helped design the Urumqi zone.

Urumqi was the tail end of my research on the BRI in China that lasted for more than four years. It strongly confirms the state-mobilized globalization paradigm I formulated and investigate in this book. Urumqi's new zone shows how a nationalist strategy, launched by a political leader to cope with economic challenges, mobilized subnational governments into growth-generating projects and programs. The BRI's local implementation expanded the scope and depth of economic globalization *inside* China, by building more special zones and providing more incentives to companies, including foreign ones. The pattern in Urumqi is likely to be applied to Erdos city, although the success rate may differ. Similar patterns have been practiced in Chongqing, Ningbo, and Wenzhou, although the leading actors and concrete projects have varied across the cities.

My four years of research in and about China reveals that state-mobilized globalization also occurred during the Western Development Program and China Goes Global strategy launched at the turn of the century. This book is about unpacking the origins and characteristics of these nationalist strategies, mapping out the processes and patterns of implementation by Chinese commercial actors, and explaining the political and economic consequences of state-mobilized globalization, implications of which are critical to China and to the world.

Acknowledgments

This book was supported by two granting institutions: the Smith Richardson Foundation, which financed the eight field trips in China and Boston University's Frederick S. Pardee Center for the Study of Longer-Range Future, which organized and financed three annual conferences that brought together domestic and international scholars on China's outward globalization. I particularly appreciate their flexibility in allowing me to diverge and shift focus as I encountered new information (and new challenges) in conducting fieldwork in China. Just as important, the capable staff at the Pardee Center made organization of the international conferences and intellectual exchanges effortless on my part.

In the United States and in China, the book benefited from supportive and vibrant scholarly communities who work on China, specialize in economics and globalization, and/or care about US–China relations. In those communities, I gave talks, exchanged ideas, and received feedback during different stages of the book. They are the Public Intellectual Program fellowships (PIP) of the National Committee on US–China Relations; the China and the World Program (CWP) at Princeton University and then Columbia University; Boston University's Global Development Policy Research Center; Zhejiang University's China Western Development Academy; and the Institute of Geographic Sciences and Natural Resources Research at the Chinese Academy of Sciences.

The following scholars have all read and/or given comments that helped improve and revise parts of the book: Deborah Brautigam, Kent Calder, Ling Chen, Gregory Chin, Thomas Christensen, Jacques deLisle, Joshua Eisenman, Joseph Fewsmith, Kevin Gallagher, Mary Gallagher, Bonnie Glaser, William Grimes, Yinan He, Junda Jin, Iain Johnston,

Miles Kahler, Atul Kohli, Bo Kong, Jonathan Krishner, Margaret Pearson, John Ravenhill, Joshua Shifrinson, Ezra Vogel, Yuhua Wang, Audrye Wong, Lynn White, Haitao Yin, and Suisheng Zhao. In China, special thanks go to my research collaborators (Dong Xuebing and Liu Weidong), former visiting scholars at the Pardee Center (Dong He, Xu Feibiao, Zhang Hongju, and Zhang Shu), and my college friends (Cai Jianqun, Dong Guanpeng, Dong Shuhui, and Zhang Yin). Many more scholars and colleagues with whom I have exchanged ideas – Chinese scholars, corporate personnel and government officials who were generous and earnest in taking my interviews, and the two anonymous reviewers at Cambridge University Press – deserve special, although nameless, thanks and gratitude. Senior editor Robert Dreesen at Cambridge University Press was an expert as well as efficient during the book's review and production.

And last, but not least, I would like to thank my family for supporting my scholarly pursuit and for being an integral part of this book's creation. My husband and two daughters have accompanied me on many trips to China, making those research travels so much more enjoyable and filled with exciting adventures. Back in Boston, my daughters have been a persistent motivator for me to work harder and to challenge myself. They are also my writing buddies during summers. When I write, they are engrossed in their favorite books. When I need a break, they are my joyful distraction. This book is dedicated to them.

A Note on Conventions

As per mainland China's convention, for all Chinese names in this book, I use the pinyin system, with exception of well-recognized names, such as Sun Yat-sen, which has conventionally used the Wades–Giles system. For Chinese scholars, officials, and other individuals who are based in China, the book follows the Chinese convention, that is, with the surname followed by the given name, in reversal of standard Western practice. For Chinese scholars who are based in the United States and other Western societies, their names are spelled following the Western practice, that is, the first name is followed by the surname. This convention is used in footnotes and bibliography as well.

PART I

THE THEORY

1

The Mobilization State: Belt, Road, and Beyond

> The One Belt and One Road are the two wings of the China Roc (中国大鹏, a mythical bird). Once they are constructed, the China Roc can fly higher and farther.
>
> —Xi Jinping[1]

In 2012–2013, the Chinese state was in a state of crisis. It had just experienced a political storm in relation to the abrupt downfall of political giant Bo Xilai, who had built a formidable power base and political movement in western China. Newly minted president Xi Jinping forced an aggressive anticorruption campaign that targeted incumbent state officials. There were widespread economic troubles, with shrinking exports, loss-making state-owned enterprises (SOEs), and industrial overcapacities. On top of all this, America's diplomatic "encirclement" of China was succeeding – the US-led Trans-Pacific Partnership (TPP) had signatures from twelve major economies in the Asia Pacific region, and China was being excluded. Facing these challenges, Chinese officials and state-affiliated researchers were concerned and gloomy.[2] They had workable proposals to address these challenges; but none of them, in 2012–2013, gained enough traction to rally cross-agency support and societal approval.[3]

[1] Xi Jinping's speech to Ministerial and Provincial Leaders of the Communist Party, November 2014.

[2] For a cross-agency study, of this period see Min Ye, "Competing Cooperation in Asia Pacific: TPP, RCEP, and the New Silk Road," *Asian Security*, 11(3), 2015, pp. 206–224.

[3] For a detailed introduction of the proposals, see Min Ye, "Domestic Politics of China's Belt and Road," *Journal of Contemporary China*, 2019, doi:10.1080/10670564.2019.1580428.

In September 2013, Xi Jinping visited Kazakhstan and made a speech titled "Work Together to Build the Silk Road Economic Belt." Calling it "a great undertaking benefitting the people of all countries along the route," Xi proposed to build infrastructure connectivity with substantial Chinese investment.[4] A month later, in October 2013, Xi visited Indonesia and announced the proposal for "the 21st-century Maritime Silk Road." In it, Xi proposed the establishment of the Asian Infrastructure Investment Bank (AIIB) to invest in infrastructure development in southeast Asia and other countries in the region.[5] Both speeches contained traditional Chinese visions and ideas for regional cooperation and friendship; they did not make immediate splashes outside China.

Yet internally, One Belt and One Road (subsequently called the Belt and Road Initiative, BRI) rapidly became a "perfect storm" that swept up actors in Beijing.[6] Officials and researchers in different parts of the state came out to explain, support, and propose policies to consolidate and expand the initiative. Quickly, print, broadcast, and online media was stormed with ideas, projects, and events related to the BRI. In 2014, policy actors and key agencies – representing diplomacy, economic functions, and foreign strategy – all claimed to be the initial proposers behind President Xi's Belt and Road.[7] In a mere two years, the Chinese state was like a paralyzed man full of worries in 2012 suddenly coming fully to life in 2014, with bustling activities on the BRI. If nothing else, such transformation of the state was mesmerizing.

The outside world, particularly across the Pacific Ocean, was not stirred by the bubbling currents in China, until November 2014 when Beijing announced the $40 billion Silk Road Fund at the Asian-Pacific Economic Cooperation (APEC) Summit, followed by the $20 billion Maritime Silk Road Fund announced a month later in Indonesia, and a $46 billion pledge in early 2015 to construct the China-Pakistan Economic Corridor (CPEC), a flagship program of the BRI. It is clear that foreign attention to the strategy was largely driven by the amount of money that Beijing pledged to commit to the BRI. Along with heightened

[4] Xi Jinping, "Work Together to Build the Silk Road Economic Belt," in *Xi Jinping: The Governance of China*. Beijing: Foreign Language Press, 2014, pp. 317–318.

[5] Xi Jinping, "Work Together to Build a 21st-Century Maritime Silk Road," in *Xi Jinping: The Governance of China*. Beijing: Foreign Language Press, 2014, pp. 320–324.

[6] The Chinese materials are too numerous to be cited here. For reference, see documentary analysis in Ye, "Competing Cooperation in Asia Pacific."

[7] Interviews with 15 senior scholars and central bureaucrats in Beijing in 2014.

attention, foreign observers came to view the Belt and Road as the "centerpiece" foreign policy of the Xi Jinping era to project Chinese power abroad. From late 2014 to 2018, countless volumes were produced on the Belt and Road, the vast majority focusing on its external strategic implications and exploring how the BRI would lead to the emergence of the "Chinese empire" on the global stage.[8]

In 1953, historians John Gallagher and Ronald Robinson wrote an influential article on economic empire, observing that "the conventional interpretation of the nineteenth-century empire continues to rest upon study of the formal empire alone, which is rather like judging the size and character of icebergs solely from the parts above the water-line."[9] Fast-forward to discourses on today's Belt and Road, and the focus on the strategy's external expansion alone is also like "judging the size and character of icebergs from the parts above the water-line." It is not wrong, but it is woefully incomplete. It ignores domestic political–economic conditions that have driven the formation of the strategy and significant fragmentation and commercial tendencies in its implementation. The nature of domestic conditions and their potential changes are likely to hold the key to the rise of China and China's global impacts. Therefore, this book investigates the strategy from the enduring logic of Chinese domestic politics and policy dynamics of China's globalization since the late 1990s. It seeks to reveal the movements and shapes of "icebergs" in the sea.

THE ARGUMENT

The starting questions here are *why* autocratic leaders launch nationalist strategies and *how* subnational and commercial actors interpret and implement such strategies. The process of tracing the BRI strategy results in formulation of the state-mobilized globalization framework (SMG). First, economic crisis and state fragmentation have together given rise to autocratic intervention with nationalist strategies such as the BRI. Second, the strategy amounts to a mobilization campaign that is marked

[8] See, for example, Tom Miller, *China's Asian Dream*. London: Zed, 2017; Robert Kaplan, *The Return of Marco Polo's World: War, Strategy, and American Interests in the Twenty-First Century*. New York: Random House, 2018; Elizabeth Economy, *The Third Revolution: Xi Jinping and the New Chinese State*. New York: Oxford University Press, 2018.

[9] John Gallagher and Ronald Robinson, "The Imperialism of Free Trade," *Economic History Review*, 6(1), 1953, pp. 1–15 (p. 1).

by ambitious political rhetoric and ambiguous policy measures. Thus, all state actors are called upon to act without being given specific instructions. Finally, fragmented state actors self-interpret and reinterpret the strategy in proposing and implementing programs and projects in their power and interest. The process demonstrates a cycle in which an autocratic leader coordinates a fragmented state through announcing and promoting a seemingly cohesive "strategy," yet implementation refragments the strategy to facilitate the expansion of a globalized market.

The Belt and Road Initiative is still young. The underlying political logic of SMG has a long standing in China. The state system – autocratic leader, fragmented state, and powerful subnational units – has roots in early reforms.[10] Similarly, the policy process – an ambitious and ambiguous strategy reinterpreted by subnational implementers that eventually facilitate local development – was available in the early periods, too.[11] In the past two decades, which have been marked by intense globalization, discourse on global China has focused on either an expectation of "convergence" or a unique "China model,"[12] without seriously tracing how China has adapted to challenges from globalization and how the Chinese state system changed from 1998 to 2018.

This book fills in the gaps and formulates the SMG to investigate the BRI and the process and implementation of the Western Development Program (WDP) and China Goes Global policy (CGG), two nationalist strategies that were launched at the turn of the century and are continuing today. Like today's BRI, the WDP and CGG were controversial and critiqued by foreign observers; they were also important to China's growth and globalization in the past two decades.

The empirical investigation here reveals remarkable parallels among the three nationalist strategies. They were all announced by political autocrats in the heat of economic crises, they relied on political mobilization based on ambitious rhetoric and ambiguous measures, and they

[10] See Kenneth Lieberthal, Michael Oksenberg, and David Lampton, *Policy Making in China: Leaders, Structures, and Processes*. Princeton, NJ: Princeton University Press, 1988; Kenneth Lieberthal and David Lampton (eds.), *Bureaucracy, Politics, and Decision Making in Post-Mao China*. Berkeley: California University Press, 1992; Andrew Mertha, "Fragmented Authoritarianism 2.0: Political Pluralization in Chinese Policy Process," *The China Quarterly*, 200, 2009, pp. 995–1012.

[11] Yuen Yuen Ang, *How China Escaped the Poverty Trap*. Ithaca, NY: Cornell University Press, 2016; Ling Chen, *Manipulating Globalization: The Influence of Bureaucrats on Business in China*. Stanford, CA: Stanford University Press, 2018.

[12] For a good synthesis on the divided debates, see Jeffrey Wassestrom, "China & Globalization," *Daedalus*, 143(2), 2013, pp. 157–169.

all experienced fragmented implementation that precipitated globalization and market expansion inside China. The WDP and CGG have longer histories than the BRI and overlap with key components of the latter. Specifically, the WDP coverage overlaps with the land-based Belt inside China, and the CGG roughly overlaps with the maritime-based Road outside China. The BRI strives to systematically integrate domestic and foreign policy priorities. With China being a "major power" and Xi Jinping being a strong leader, the BRI has broader global implications and also faces stricter scrutiny abroad. In this book, studying these strategies together provides longer timeframes, establishes the consistency and robustness of the SMG, and contributes to discussions of long-term mechanisms and effects of globalization *by* China.

More importantly, state-mobilized globalization in China from 1998 to 2018 sheds light on the nature, characteristics, strengths, and relationships in the Chinese state system.[13] The system consists of different authority structures and power centers – political leadership, central agencies, state capital, and local governments. There is considerable fragmentation and negotiation between the leadership and the agencies, between the state and state capital, and between the center and local governments. There are also complicated interest groups and functional separations inside the political authority, across different state agencies, across SOEs, and across local governments. In short, in contrast to the image of a coercive and effective authoritarian system, the Chinese state system is structurally fragmented.

The SMG also demonstrates reasonably cohesive ideology and organization that anchor the "mobilization state" in China. At the highest order of ideology, it is nationalism – the rise and modernization of the Chinese nation. At the next level, it is the overriding priority given to rapid economic growth, because growth enhances the ruling legitimacy and brings resources necessary for tackling social and political challenges. Further down, general consensus in the state system is that high growth is most likely with market expansion and globalization. Such *layered* ideological cohesion is not any individual or agency's design or direction, but *accumulated* ideas and preferences rooted in four decades of reform and have become more explicit in the past two decades, the period of state-mobilized globalization.

[13] For the idea of state as a system, see Robert Gilpin, "Economic Evolution of National Systems," *International Studies Quarterly*, 40, 1996, pp. 441–431; Vivien Schmidt, "Putting the Political Back into Political Economy by Bringing the State Back in Yet Again," *World Politics*, 61(3), 2009, pp. 516–546.

While the above state consensus and layered ideology were forged during reform and globalization, the SMG analysis reveals that the instruments of organizing state authority and intervention in the economy in China are much older. For example, the leadership relies on the party's organizational power to rein in agents of the state; the ruling party controls information and media to enforce cohesive messaging and uses intraparty interactions to induce preferred behaviors among the ruling elites; the state depends on the state capital – banks, producers, and lower governments – to achieve development goals. In countering recurrent economic crises, the state system consistently uses three old practices – nationalist rhetoric for political mobilization, state-controlled messaging to induce conformity, and policy ambiguity that incentivizes commercial actors.

All these elements of the Chinese state and how they interact among themselves and with market forces are extremely complex and remarkably different from other well-studied capitalist economies. The main scholarly agenda here is to construct a parsimonious enough framework to capture the complexities and to explain policy outcomes in China. In the following text, the literature section first draws on earlier scholarship in the China field, which provides the theoretical foundation for the SMG framework, and then places the SMG in comparative capitalism literature, focusing on sharpening the similarities and differences between the SMG and the more familiar developmental state model in East Asia.

EXPLAINING STATE-MOBILIZED GLOBALIZATION

The China Literature

State-mobilized globalization offers a robust framework to capture the drivers, processes, and outcomes of China's nationalist strategies in the past two decades. Its theoretical foundations comprise long-term scholarship on Chinese state and domestic political mobilization. Going beyond earlier scholarship, the SMG offers new insights and theoretical values. First, it integrates analysis of central and local governments, along with political, bureaucratic, and commercial actors comprising the state system, rather than focusing on one element or another. Second, it is an explanatory framework that can be used to establish causes and consequences of major policies in China, not only descriptive characterization of Chinese state and political institutions. Finally, the SMG expands the analysis of the Chinese state to external policies and speaks more directly to debates in comparative and international political economy beyond the China field.

On the Chinese state, Kenneth Lieberthal, Michael Oksenberg, and David Lampton have conceptualized the power and policy interactions between the political leadership and economic bureaucracies as "fragmented authoritarianism."[14] Susan Shirk captured the relationship between the political center and its ruling power base – provincial leaders, heads of national agencies and large companies, and representatives of the military and others – as "reciprocal accountability."[15] Jean Oi explained how at the local government level, national policy change incentivized lower governments to become "local corporatist states" that played critical roles in helping local economies.[16] These are lasting insights on the Chinese state and its instruments of economic growth promotion. However, they also tacitly and explicitly argued that such a state system was a "transitional model" that was to be phased out as political–economic development progressed in China.

Also focusing on the Chinese state, Lynn White's writing was much more flexible.[17] He observed that the Chinese state, although being extremely important, cannot be explained with Weberian state literature that defines the state as bureaucracies and measures state strength with the ability to penetrate or overpower society. Rather, the state needs to be defined via behavior. According to White, "In China the state seems to include preeminent leader, the few elders who second guess his policies, ministry heads, and other leaders of major agencies in Beijing. The state often extends fairly far beyond this group, but there is some evidence that local officials as high as provincial governors have views that differ from the central mainstream. At lower administrative levels, the state can become a now-you-can-see-it-now-you-don't organization."[18]

More recently, scholars have examined how state fragmentation has interacted and been reinforced by authoritarian institutions in China.

[14] Lieberthal, Oksenberg, and Lampton, *Policy Making in China*.

[15] Susan Shirk, *The Political Logic of Economic Reform in China*. Berkeley: University of California Press, 1993.

[16] Jean Oi, "The Role of the Local State in China's Transition Economy," *The China Quarterly*, 178, 1995, pp. 467–487.

[17] Lynn White, *Unstately Power: Volume I. Local Causes of China's Economic Reforms*. Armonk, NY: M.E. Sharpe, 1998, p. 17.

[18] Ibid., p. 27.

Victor Shih observes that as an autocracy, there is lack of an institutionalized policy authority, or clear indicator of power. Political leaders thus rely on cultivating personal support, rather than rule-based authority, to demand compliance from subordinates.[19] Furthermore, the party-state, not just authoritarianism, adds new divisions and conflation between power and policy authorities, making intrastate relationships and policy outcomes even less transparent and predictable because positions in the state may translate into different power in the party organization, and vice versa.[20] Speaking on burgeoning social protests, Elizabeth Perry has argued that Chinese leaders enhance legitimacy by heeding social outcries and how protestors in turn use their rhetoric and actions to resist lower-level governments by "playing by the rule."[21]

From 1998 to 2018, it also appears that rapid globalization reinforced state fragmentation, making cohesive policy and uniform law-making more difficult. For example, corporations and capital investment used to be more effectively regulated by economic bureaucracies; they now have "unregulated" externalities in security and diplomacy. Take a Chinese SOE building a hydropower plant in a neighbor country as an example. The project has the potential to improve or impair China's relationship with this country; yet the state organs that deal with China's external relations – Ministry of Foreign Affairs (MFA) and Ministry of Commerce (MOFCOM) – have little power over the corporation or the project in question. The SOE reports to State Assets Supervision and Administration Council (SASAC), its project is subject to the power of National Development and Reform Council (NDRC), and its funding comes from the state banks. Neither MFA nor MOFCOM have sway over SASAC, NDRC, or Chinese banks whose priorities are domestic and economic in nature.

In the fragmented system, coordination and consensus are still possible, but they often require crisis-induced autocratic intervention, as well as flexibility during implementation that incentivizes different groups in the state system. Lieberthal and Oksenberg observed in 1988 that for a Chinese leader to promote a new policy, "a consensus must be sought

[19] Victor Shih, *Factions and Finance in China: Elite Conflict and Inflation*. New York: Cambridge University Press, 2008, p. 4.

[20] Arthur Kroeber, *China's Economy: What Everyone Needs to Know*. New York: Oxford University Press, 2016.

[21] Elizabeth Perry, "Playing by the Rule," in *China Today, China Tomorrow*, edited by Joseph Fewmith. New York: Routledge, 2008.

both vertically and horizontally in the system. Lower-level units have important resources they can bring to bear, and wide-ranging efforts are therefore made to permit each major actor to support an effort or project with some enthusiasm."[22] Crisis, coordination, and mobilization indeed have comprised important elements in the process of the SMG framework.

In recent decades, bureaucratic discord has been frequent and unyielding in normal circumstances. Yet when economic and political crises erupt and demand quick responses, decisive leadership does seem to emerge, as in the origins of the WDP, CGG, and BRI.[23] However, given fragmented interests and ideas, a policy response to deal with a crisis is often framed in politically ambitious terms so that it could mobilize broader coalitions against specific oppositions. For example, in the WDP (see Chapter 3), justification to create jobs was rejected by functional reasoning based on efficiency; in the CGG (see Chapter 4), encouraging companies to find overseas market was immediately resisted due to fear of capital flight; in the BRI (see Chapter 5), the proposal to finance overcapacity industries going global was countered with politically charged accusation of "wasting money abroad." As nationalist strategies strive to enhance the "rise of China" in the world, they are able to mobilize different interests and groups to implement them, while following their own preferred measures.

In short, in the state-mobilized globalization formula, the state is central, but it is the system that consists of political leaders, national bureaucracies, local governments, and SOEs in a complex and interactive web of roles and relationships. The political autocrats speak to national ambition and uplift economic growth to the level of achieving ruling elites' power aspirations. The autocrats refrain from making concrete policy guidelines; thus, autocratic programs tend to help national agencies and local governments pursue their desired policies and programs. By nominally answering the calls of the political leaders, implementation by the state and commercial actors boosts the authority of the political leader. By improvising their own approaches, the implementers simultaneously intensifies fragmentation in the state system.

The second key theoretical component of the SMG framework is political mobilization. State mobilization has two logical connotations. In the

[22] Lieberthal, Oksenberg, and Lampton, *Policy Making in China*, p. 23.

[23] Calder and Ye formulate a critical juncture logic to explain how crises generate political leadership. See Kent Calder and Min Ye, *Making of Northeast Asia*. Stanford, CA: Stanford University Press, 2010.

first, the state mobilizes market and economic forces to pursue state-defined goals and agendas. State-mobilized globalization in this sense has similarities to other state-directed development models, except that the SMG uses political campaigns and movements rather than policy guidelines or economic incentives.[24] In the second logical connotation, the state is mobilized to action. That is, the state has divisions, and each division can be inactive and paralyzed. Under specific circumstances, the political leadership mobilizes different state actors to action and accomplishes a set of goals.

In the three nationalist strategies, the second logical connotation – the state being mobilized – is salient, but the first logic – the state mobilizing market actors – also exists. More importantly, the process analysis reveals that political mobilization accomplishes "actions" by the state, but not "cohesion" into an overarching behavior. For example, the state actors can be mobilized to carry out a national strategy; how they do it is up for interpretation and improvisation. With regard to the effects on market forces, mobilization signals cohesive messaging and policy coalitions from the state but leaves whether and how to participate in the strategy to be decided by the market actors themselves.

In short, mobilization in the SMG employs nationalist rhetoric but allows fragmentation and implementation based on incentives. Such "soft" mobilization differs from more coercive authoritarian contexts in which the political autocrat promotes programs through "fiat" or through setting up "enemies" to be targeted during mobilization.[25] Operating under the soft political mobilization, subnational and market actors have ample freedom to "choose" whether and how to interpret and implement the nationalist strategy. Such "choices" are then based on localized incentives and instruments.

The last component in the SMG is globalization, which has emerged as an important mechanism of implementation in the WDP, CGG, and BRI. Globalization covers inflows and outflows of capital, import and export of goods and services, and partnership and technology sharing with multinational corporations. During the WDP, although the political leadership did not urge globalization as a top-down mandate, state implementers

[24] Atul Kohli, *State-Directed Development: Political Power and Industrialization in the Global Periphery*. New York: Cambridge University Press, 2004; Stephan Haggard, *The Developmental States*. New York: Cambridge University Press, 2018.

[25] In class struggle sessions in the Maoist era, demonizing/dehumanizing the targets of class struggle was key to the mobilization. See Elizabeth Perry, "Moving the Masses: Emotion Work in the Chinese Revolution," *Mobilization: An International Quarterly*, 17 (2), 2002, pp. 111–128.

prevalently adopted measures that facilitated globalization and were quite successful in enhancing inflows of technology and capital. The CGG openly urged Chinese companies to "go global," yet in reality, companies conducted just as much, if not more, "attracting" of foreign capital and technology. Furthermore, local governments conducted sweeping changes to attract foreign investment to their localities. The BRI has rhetoric and mobilization to expand China externally – developing international influence and global presence. Yet, the domestic connection and priority to promote "internal growth" remains essential. Much of what was practiced in the WDP and CGG is being continued in local jurisdictions and by similar implementers.

In other words, when Chinese leadership urged "globalization" in the top-down mobilization and promotion of a nationalist strategy, the domestic audience – different state and capital actors – can do many different things. The state agencies can free (or even tighten) controls over capital; local governments establish preferential zones to attract foreign investment or support Chinese companies going global; companies can transfer foreign technology and form equity partnerships inside China or outside. Even when the strategy (the CGG), urges companies to expand global footprints, it is often inbound globalization – attracting foreign capital, for example – that proceeds more quickly than outward globalization. Empirical investigation of the strategies reveals that the domestic networks of globalization – state financiers, SOEs, local governments – continue to prevail as Chinese capital goes global.

In summary, state-mobilized globalization focuses on conceptual and empirical analysis of the Chinese state, political mobilization, and economic globalization that together defined and shaped the emergence of China as a middle power in 1998 to a superpower in 2018. The SMG's theoretical foundation thus includes lasting scholarship in the China field, especially the various versions of "fragmented authoritarianism" and political mobilization. The theory, and the Chinese framework of globalization, can also be understood more sharply by comparing it to other frameworks in comparative capitalism: liberal economy (LE), coordinate markets (CM), developmental state (DS), and state capitalism (SC).

Comparative Frameworks

The SMG, unpacking policy drivers and implementation of the three nationalist strategies, reveals and underscores a wide array of experiences of globalization *in* and *by* China. The diverse experiences of Chinese globalization, however, have generated heated debates in comparative and international political economy in recent years. To explain China's rapid internal growth, Barry Naughton and Kellee Tsai, focusing on SOEs, portray the Chinese system through lens of state penetration and domination.[26] By contrast, focusing on private business, Nicholas Lardy establishes that the market is in command and nonstate companies are the drivers of China's success.[27] With regard to China's external implications, Ian Bremmer depicts alarming images of Chinese capital and its global reach,[28] while Christopher McNally offers a favorable description of Sino-capitalism that embodies "top-down state-led development with bottom-up entrepreneurial private capital accumulation."[29]

These debates and publications have drawn on different "elements" of China and undoubtedly have explained some aspects well, but as a whole, they are decidedly incomplete. State-mobilized globalization offers a *wholistic* capitalist framework that both complements and contrasts with other frameworks in comparative capitalism.

When seen through a comparative lens, the SMG demonstrates *who* comprises the Chinese state, *what* the dominant political–economic institutions in China are, and *how* the Chinese state influences market behaviors. These questions are important not only to China studies but also to studies of other emerging and established countries in the world. Furthermore, a holistic and comparative understanding of Chinese capitalism has been generally lacking. For example, a book that covers economic growth in multiple countries in Latin America, East Asia, and Eastern Europe leaves China out.[30] An extensive volume on developmental states, which includes historical and comparative discussions of states and politics of economic policies, also fails to include China.[31]

[26] Barry Naughton and Kellee Tsai (eds.), *State Capitalism, Institutional Adaptation, and the Chinese Miracle*. New York: Cambridge University Press, 2015.

[27] Nicholas Lardy, *Markets over Mao: The Rise of Private Business in China*. Washington, DC: Peterson Institute for International Economics, 2014.

[28] Ian Bremmer, *The End of the Free Market: Who Wins the War between States and Corporations?* New York: Portfolio, 2010.

[29] Christopher McNally, "Sino-Capitalism: China's Reemergence and the International Political Economy," *World Politics*, 64(4), 2012, pp. 741–776 (p. 744).

[30] Stephan Haggard and Robert Kaufman, *Development, Democracy, and Welfare States: Latin America, East Asia, and East Europe*. Princeton, NJ: Princeton University Press, 2008.

[31] Haggard, *Developmental States*.

TABLE 1.1. *Comparative frameworks of capitalism and globalization*

	Key actors	Mechanisms	Norms
Liberal market model	Private corporations	Competition; efficiency; profits	Liberalism
Developmental state	Economic bureaucracies	Price distortion; industry policy	Protectionism
Coordinated markets	Large corporations; associations	Coordination; collective bargains	Corporatism
State capitalism	State-owned enterprises	Monopoly; political control	Socialism
State-mobilized globalization	Leadership; local governments; SOEs	Mobilization; market responses	Nationalism/ growth-orientation

Source: Made by the Author.

In Table 1.1, the SMG is placed alongside with other capitalist frameworks, the liberal market economy (LE), coordinated markets (CE), developmental states (DS), and state capitalism (SC), and focuses on their key actors, mechanisms, and underlying norms. To be sure, the frameworks cover ideal types and do not capture nuanced experiences in various countries that gave rise to the capitalist systems. In the LE framework, for example, the United Kingdom and the United States are the most representative countries, but they each have experienced periods of protectionism. Free trade they have promoted has historically been viewed as an "instrument" of their economic empires.[32] Similarly, the DS literature originated with a Japanese economic miracle, but the Japanese system could also be called "a cooperative market."[33] And much of its growth and globalization experiences evokes similarities to the SMG pattern. Furthermore, SC has varied considerably across writings by Ian Bremmer, Christopher McNally, and Barry Naughton and Kellee Tsai.[34]

With the caveats and nuances noted above, the SMG here presents a conceptually different framework compared to the other ideal types.

[32] Haggard, *Developmental States*; Gallagher and Robinson, "The Imperialism of Free Trade."

[33] Kent Calder, *Circles of Compensation: Economic Growth and the Globalization of Japan*. Stanford, CA: Stanford University Press, 2017.

[34] Bremmer, *The End of the Free Market*; McNally, "Sino-Capitalism"; Naughton and Tsai, *State Capitalism, Institutional Adaptation, and the Chinese Economic Miracle*.

To elaborate, in Table 1.1, the LE framework prioritizes strong companies and minimal states.[35] Its market mechanism emphasizes competition, profits, and efficiency. Because of its emphasis on a minimal state and strong society, the ideological tendency is toward liberalism. The two countries in the LE paradigm are economic empires of modern history – the United Kingdom and the United States – thus elevating the LE model as the "mainstream" paradigm. Peter Evans has critiqued it as the "Anglo-American ideology," with other frameworks being presented as "revisionist."[36]

The DS literature, growing from economic miracles in Japan, South Korea, and Taiwan from the 1960s to the 1980s, has had significant impacts on development studies in the comparative discipline.[37] The state centrality and political mobilization in the SMG also have parallels to the former developmental states. Yet, originating in different historical periods and different domestic contexts, the DS cannot capture the state, politics, and economic policies in the SMG framework. The DS, to be specific, underscores national bureaucracies that devise industrial policies through price distortion and infant industry protection. Underlying these economic practices is protectionism, as the DS consistently showed bureaucracies' deep mistrust of foreign capital.

In the revisionist camp, CM was posited by the variety of capitalism literature born to European experiences.[38] The literature argues that national institutions shape comparative advantage across different economies. When facing similar global stimuli, different capitalist economies adopt

[35] Gilpin, "Economic Evolution of National Systems"; Kathleen Thelen, "The American Precariat: U.S. Capitalism in Comparative Perspective," *Perspectives on Politics*, 17(11), 2019, pp. 5–27.

[36] Peter Evans, "The Eclipse of the State: Reflections on Stateness in an Era of Globalization," *World Politics*, 50(1), 1997, pp. 62–87 (p. 65).

[37] Chalmers Johnson, *MITI and the Japanese Miracle: The Growth of Industrial Policy, 1925–1975*. Stanford, CA: Stanford University Press, 1982; Alice Amsden, *Asia's Next Giant: South Korea and Late Industrialization*. New York: Oxford University Press, 1989; Robert Wade, *Governing the Market: Economic Theory and the Role of Government in East Asian Industrialization*. Princeton, NJ: Princeton University Press, 1990; Peter Evans, *Embedded Autonomy: States and Industrial Transformation*. Princeton, NJ: Princeton University Press, 1995; Stephan Haggard, *Pathways from the Periphery: The Politics of Growth in the Newly Industrializing Countries*. Ithaca, NY: Cornell University Press, 1991.

[38] Peter Hall and David Soskice (eds.), *Varieties of Capitalism: The Institutional Foundations of Comparative Advantage*. New York: Oxford University Press, 2001; Schmidt, "Putting the Political Back into Political Economy by Bringing the State Back in Yet Again"; Grant Wyn and Graham Wilson (eds.), *Consequences of the Global Financial Crisis: The Rhetoric of Reform and Regulation*. New York: Oxford University Press, 2012; Calder, *Circles of Compensation*.

diverse national instruments and responses.[39] In a CM framework, large companies and industrial associations are the key actors, and their collective bargaining with the state shapes industrial development and market behaviors. In Table 1.1, the underlying ideology is called "corporatism." Finally, the state capitalism perspective (SC) examines economies with dominant SOEs, a category that has recently become salient due to the rise of China. The literature typically emphasizes the state's anti-market tendency and political control in the economy, albeit internal debates.[40]

The SMG is a framework that embodies elements from the liberal market economy, developmental states, and state capitalism, but as a whole it differs from them all. In the SMG, political campaigns and state involvement are often observed; yet in the meantime, commercial concerns have shaped decision making and state behaviors in relation to the economy. As shown in the WDP, CGG, and BRI, despite political rhetoric, Chinese actors, with very few exceptions, prioritize profits, competition, and business expansion. Across two decades, it has become clear that a globalizing China has shown dominance and superiority of market mechanisms in driving national economic growth, confirming Nicholas Lardy's argument that "market, not Mao" has been the source of the economic miracle in China.[41]

Yet, the Chinese state has also been central to development, decisions, and changes in society. Therefore, although the SMG exhibits a preference to market mechanisms in economic decisions, it is quite different from the liberal economy model. In China, national policies – in particular nationalist strategies – influence corporate behaviors, not only the behavior of state capital but also private companies. Furthermore, subnational governments have such a strong role to play in the local economy that they can directly approve infrastructure, attract investors, and make plans for economic zones. In short, between market and state, the liberal economy prioritizes the market; the revisionists stress state intervention. In China's SMG, a strong and multilevel state promotes and expands market globalization.

To summarize the theoretical discussion, in the SMG, the state is a much bigger and more complex *system* than any of the other frameworks,

[39] The idea of global "stimuli" is from Etel Solingen, *Regional Orders at Century's Dawn: Global and Domestic Influences on Grand Strategy*. Princeton, NJ: Princeton University Press, 1998.

[40] Naughton and Tsai, *State Capitalism, Institutional Adaptation, and the Chinese Miracle*; Joshua Kurlantizick, *State Capitalism: How the Return of Statism Is Transforming the World*. New York: Oxford University Press, 2016.

[41] Lardy, *Market over Mao*, p. 2.

including the DS. The state system is comprised of powerful political leadership, national agencies, influential local governments, and state capital. However, compared to the DS literature, separation across and differences within these state clusters make the system fragmented and difficult to coordinate when facing policy challenges. As a whole, the common perception of the Chinese state as a unitary and strategic actor, or a stronger version of DS, is incorrect.

More importantly, over a longer period, the SMG does demonstrate consistent ideology and organization that differ from other comparative frameworks as well. In terms of ideology, the SMG displays nationalism and growth priority at the political level, and underneath this, particularly among companies and local governments, market mechanisms and globalization are broadly accepted as the best means to achieving high growth. In terms of instruments to coordinate between the state and market and inside the state system, the SMG shows standard measures from the toolkits afforded by the ruling Communist party: the party organization, control over information and flows, and decentralized mobilization based on incentives.

HOW TO USE THE BOOK: CHAPTER OUTLINES

The concept of state-mobilized globalization (SMG) formulated in this book combines a strong state and strong market; it offers a framework to capture the process and conditions of China's rapid rise and globalization in the past two decades. The SMG is also policy analysis that explains the drivers and outcomes of the nationalist strategies and provides novel investigative tools for studying major development policies in China. Therefore, Chapter 2 spells out the conditions, variables, and processes of the SMG, explaining why and how this framework works in China. Then the chapter provides a preliminary account of the WDP, CGG, and BRI as empirical demonstration of the SMG analysis. Together, Chapters 1 and 2 comprise of Part I *The Theory* in this book.

In Part II *The Strategies*, three empirical chapters demonstrate how the SMG dynamics work at the national level. In Part III *Subnational Actors*, two more empirical chapters show how SMG applies to local governments and comparative companies. Each of the chapter deals with an important subject of study in the China field. In addition to the SMG analysis, each chapter incorporates earlier research and presents the subject's major dynamics. For scholars with an interest in specific subjects, these empirical chapters can be read and used individually and separately.

In Part II, *The Strategies*, Chapter 3 employs the SMG framework to investigate the drivers, processes, and implementation of the WDP from 1998 to 2012. It evaluates economic transformation in western China and the role of state-market forces. The chapter reveals that the nationalist strategy, announced in times of deep economic crises, has profoundly changed the Chinese state by reinforcing regional development planning in China and spreading high growth and industrialization across the nation.[42] More importantly, by investigating specific policies and market behaviors in different stages of the WDP, the chapter establishes that the nationalist strategy has precipitated industrialization and globalization in western China and that it has done so through mutual enhancement of both state and market.

Chapter 4 focuses on the political economy of China's outbound investment. It first unpacks the policy making and implementation of the CGG from the late 1990s to 2015 and establishes the strategy's autocratic origin, fragmented implementation, and enhanced globalization inside China. Second, it compiles official documents on China's outbound investment and analyzes patterns of change in the regulatory framework. Finally, the chapter presents comprehensive statistics and comparative cases, and it studies trends, distributions, and problems of outward investment from China, across regions and sectors. Since policies and statistical materials have been updated since the BRI, the patterns can reveal whether and to what extent the BRI strategy has shifted policy and capital movement in China.

Chapter 5 focuses on formation and implementation of the Belt and Road and conducts three analyses. First, because of the newness of the strategy, the BRI analysis maps out preexisting state fragmentation and prior practices in detail and therefore provides stronger evidence of the motivating contexts of nationalist strategies. Second, thanks to the emergence of new information sources and technologies, there was considerable reporting on the activities and actors of the BRI. Drawing on such unprecedented rich materials, the chapter details the characteristics and nature of political mobilization in China. Finally, while the WDP and CGG demonstrate patterns of implementation over a decade, a real-time analysis of BRI's implementation establishes the complex interaction and fragmentation among an autocratic leader, national agencies, and subnational actors in shaping the national strategy in China and abroad.

42 See also Sebastian Heilmann and Oliver Melton, "The Reinvention of Development Planning in China, 1993–2012," *Modern China*, 39(6), 2013, pp. 580–628.

In Part III *Subnational Actors*, Chapter 6 selects three different cities in China to illustrate the patterns of subnational interpretation of nationalist strategies and their effects on local development. Local governments are among the key actors in the Chinese state system; they have driven successful economic growth and globalization in China. Yet, they are not part of international negotiations, and their behaviors are not well understood by foreign observers. In this chapter, the research captures how the three cities interpret and implement nationalist strategies and powerfully establish market-based implementation at the local level. The three cities have different economic structures and local state powers: The first of them represents the state capitalism; the second is close to the developmental state; and the third is closest to the liberal market economy. Comparatively, they demonstrate how different political–economic conditions generate diverse programs and mechanisms in implementation, though they are subject to the same political dynamics from the top.[43]

Chapter 7 investigates the growth and globalization of Chinese companies. Different companies have different political power, government relationships, and policy preferences. For example, companies with differing ownership (state-owned or private) and industrial sectors (e.g., heavy machinery or light consumer goods) display different relations with global market and the home government. They improvise and interpret the nationalist strategies in rather different ways. Interviews at these companies add information on the ideas, limitations, and experiences of corporate elites in China. Furthermore, as the analyzed companies have been involved in globalization and experienced different relationships with global markets and foreign capital, the chapter sheds light on how globalization – even when it is a wealth-generating process – challenges domestic politics and drives pro-autocracy nationalism in the corporate circles, internal variations notwithstanding.

The concluding chapter synthesizes the theoretical and empirical analyses of the earlier chapters and reflects on findings important to key economic debates regarding China, state–market roles in historical cases, and rising China's impact on global developments and shifting power. On China, the chapter speaks to its political future related to Communism and the rise of Xi Jinping in the Chinese state system.

[43] See Eric Thun, *Changing Lanes in China: Foreign Direct Investment, Local Governments, and Auto Sector Development*. New York: Cambridge University Press, 2008; Ang, *How China Escaped the Poverty Trap*; Chen, *Manipulating Globalization*.

Going beyond China, the chapter stresses, first, the importance of both state and market for economies to succeed in today's globalization. Second, it covers concerns in world development and shifting power as a result of globalization *by* China. The chapter concludes with a discussion of the Belt and Road and points to different implementation pathways and potential roadblocks in China and beyond.

A NOTE ON RESEARCH IN CHINA

China is a difficult place to conduct empirical research on policy making, and it has become harder in the recent years. Although more Chinese materials are available online, the demand on researchers' ability to distinguish valuable information from a great deal of noise is extremely high. Research on the three nationalist strategies discussed in this text lasted from 2014 to 2018. It consisted of eight round trips to China, during which I conducted structured and open-ended interviews with policy communities in Beijing and in various localities. Back in the United States, I collected archival materials and analyzed official policies, journals and scholarly publications, online reporting, and economic statistics. This note is a reflection of this process and hope to be instrumental to other students and scholars of China.

For policy questions such as why autocratic leaders launch nationalist strategies and how subnational and commercial actors interpret such strategies, the most useful and direct information came from open-ended interviews with Chinese policy actors. Those interviewed – scholars, as well as state and commercial actors – have all worked and lived through the processes of policy debate, policy making, and implementation. Those experiences and reflections are usually not available in print. In Beijing, interviews were arranged with individuals representing different agencies and perspectives in the central government (see Appendix 1).

In the localities, I carried out interviews with state and commercial actors at the local level, ranging from coastal port Ningbo to western heavyweight Chongqing to border hotspot Urumqi. Key informants in Beijing and the localities were interviewed multiple times to confirm and expand on the findings. In addition, through attending conferences and workshops in different parts of China, I was able to speak to many actors without conducting prearranged interviews. These informal conversations were useful to verify findings from the structured interviews and archival sources.

To make interviews more informative, I made efforts to ensure reasonable openness and honesty on the part of the interviewees. Most interviewed government officials are retired or deputy chiefs with 10–20 years of work experience. Scholars typically occupy the senior ranks in their fields. These individuals, having more international exposure and professional experience, were more willing to share and had more to share than many junior scholars and officials. Incumbent senior officials, on the other hand, were less accessible to exchanges with scholars.

Field research in the localities was both complicated and extremely rewarding. The quality and availability of key informants depend on the right channels that this researcher was able to find. In some places, personal ties and informal conversations among friends were essential; in other places, top-down introductions were necessary. In still other places, relationships with well-connected local academics go a long way. All researchers need to be cognizant of different political-economic contexts to solicit the right channels.

A researcher also needs to be adaptive and versatile in arranging interviews. On the one hand, the timing and subject matter are important. The field research for this book started in 2014, when Chinese central actors were reasonably eager to share their experience and association with the newly announced Belt and Road. By late 2015, the BRI had become so debated in Beijing that serious conversation had become infeasible. Then I shifted the research focus to subnational interpretation and implementation. The timing of the shift was propitious because local actors were just becoming eager to share their thoughts and solicit expert advice in implementing the new strategy.

In arranging interviews in the localities, local knowledge and contacts inside China helped significantly. I relied on three channels to arrange interviews: (1) contacts in the central government, (2) local academic networks, and (3) personal friends. I called on all channels in the selected localities: Chongqing, Ningbo, Wenzhou, Shanghai, and Urumqi. It was clear that different channels worked differently in the various localities.

In more politicized localities, such as Chongqing and Urumqi, local academic leaders were not as useful and personal friends could not provide much relevant information; on the other hand, relatively formal introductions from influential agencies/actors in Beijing worked the best. In Chongqing, with an introduction from a supervising agency in the central state, I was scheduled to interview more than a dozen companies and officials in depth. Academic linkages and personal friends, by contrast, had minimal effect.

In Ningbo, where the policy community was professional and aspirational, an introduction from a local academic leader helped arrange three days of packed interviews and site visits. The interviews were framed as being with a trusted expert from the United States who wanted to know what the city was doing and wanted to help the city globalize. Top-down introduction, on the other hand, did not help much; personal friends generally were not able to provide the necessary information.

Finally, in Shanghai and Wenzhou, neither top-down introduction nor academic contacts worked well. The most useful instrument was friends who put me in touch with their colleagues and friends in government and companies. Here, many of the interviews were conducted in an informal capacity and nonwork setting. The requests for interviews were made as personal favors for a scholar friend.

Interviews provided firsthand information on the policy processes that help draw interactive roadmaps for archival collection and statistics. For example, regarding the BRI's origins, diplomats alerted me to prior infrastructure proposals, technocrats called attention to the Chinese Marshall Plan, and strategists underscored the China Goes West proposal. Then, using Chinese archival database CNKI and Chinese-language newspapers, I was able to find journals and newspaper articles covering these issues and trace their contents and main advocates (see Appendix 2).

On mobilization, I combined CNKI with Chinese search engines to find, step-by-step in a time sequence, conferences, speeches, and participants related to various relevant agencies and commercial actors. The State Council think tank Development and Reform Center (DRC) compiled archival reports on BRI implementation, and the CNKI provided academic writings and analysis. For corporate cases, I relied on interviews at representative companies, publications online and in print, and particularly the two leading economic magazines in China: *Caijing* (*Finance and Economics Magazine*) and *Caixin* (*Finance and News Magazine*) from 2001 to 2015.

The Chinese government is an important source for information on economic policies and economic indicators. Different depositories in the State Council collected hundreds of relevant policy documents from 1992 to 2018. However, fully and accurately locating these documents requires deep knowledge of the government system. I relied on extremely capable researchers who had done considerable studies on Chinese government policies. Instead of asking them or using computer software to analyze the materials, I personally read all the documents and analyzed them to create the policy dynamics and track changes in the state system. This took an enormous amount of time and required deep linguistic skills, but alternative methods would not have worked in this case. As a trial, a content analysis with software not only buried useful knowledge in information overload but also presented a distorted pattern of state–market interactions. Other researchers, even those who were extremely capable of collecting materials, could not tease out state dynamics and mobilization underpinning the nationalist strategies.

CONCLUSION

The Belt and Road Initiative has generated numerous publications in China and abroad. These publications predominantly view the BRI as China's strategy to project power in the region and in the world. This book takes a different focus. Rooted in enduring domestic political logic, state-mobilized globalization demonstrates two important processes that are overlooked by power-projection perspectives. First, the BRI was forged not in the "strike of a pen" – two sudden speeches by the leader in late 2013; rather, there were well-practiced and justified proposals before the autocratic announcement, and concerted mobilization was necessary before it emerged as a nationalist strategy. Behind this formation process were dual contexts of political–economic crises and bureaucratic paralysis confronting the Chinese state.

Second, the autocratic strategy was ambitious and ambiguous; different agencies and commercial actors could interpret and implement it in diverse and divergent ways from the official rhetoric. Behind such fragmentation is a shared imperative to reinvigorate the economy inside the state system. Thus, although specific measures differed across different implementers, this growth priority has worked to enhance both market and globalization trends in China.

More importantly, by studying the WDP, CGG, and BRI together, this book opens up the Chinese state system and finds that there are different authority structures and power centers – political leadership, central agencies, state capital, and local governments. There is considerable fragmentation across and inside these power centers, but over a long period is also shown cohesion in the ideology and organization that anchor "the mobilization state" in China.

At the highest order of ideology, it is nationalism – the rise and modernization of the Chinese nation. At the next level, it is the overriding priority given to rapid economic growth; further down, it is a general consensus in the state system that high growth is most likely with market expansion and globalization. In terms of organization, the leadership relies on the party's political power to rein in agents of the state; the ruling party controls information and media to enforce cohesive messaging; the state depends on state capital – banks, producers, and lower government – to achieve development goals.

In summary, the SMG framework, drawing on earlier scholarship in Chinese politics, provides a heuristic device to clarify the drivers, processes, and outcomes of the three nationalist strategies in China; it offers a wholistic tool that explains behaviors by Chinese central agencies, local governments, and companies in the context of political mobilization and market globalization. The politics and policies revealed in the SMG set the Chinese state apart from the regulatory framework in the liberal economies, or technocratic planning in the developmental states, or top-down fiat in other coercive regimes. Mechanisms in the SMG may not travel outside China, but they comprise a conceptually distinct capitalist framework in the comparative and international political economy. Furthermore, tactics employed in China to achieve high growth and social stability may be instrumental to other globalizing nations and are worthy to study beyond China.

2

State-Mobilized Globalization as Policy Analysis

> Globalization has increased the risks for domestic economy and politics; in a certain sense, the era of globalization ushers in the end of an era of stability. Therefore, from Deng Xiaoping to Jiang Zemin and Hu Jintao, China's leaders have emphasized incrementalism and gradualism, aiming for a "soft landing" in both politics and economics.
>
> —Yu Keping[1]

China has an authoritarian political system, with the political leadership concentrating major powers at the apex of the regime. China also has a state-controlled economic system, in which the state owns the financial resources and largest companies, as well as powerful local governments. Under this political–economic system, when a political leader announces an ambitious strategy to expand Chinese influence abroad, it is natural for observers to conclude that this strategy will cohesively pursue the autocrat's expansionist aims.

The SMG framework departs from this popular portrayal of the BRI. It establishes that crises, along with national agencies' inability to handle them, have compelled and enabled the political leadership to announce the BRI; since its announcement, the strategy has incorporated and empowered national agencies to pursue their preexisting policy ideas; and most important, SOEs and local governments have implemented the BRI largely in line with their market needs and commercial interests. In

[1] Yu Keping, *Globalization and Changes in China's Governance*. Leiden: Brill, 2008, pp. 31–32.

short, top-down political mobilization and bottom-up market implementation have worked to stabilize and revive economic growth inside China.

In Chapter 1, I explain how the SMG sets up a capitalist framework that is different from other comparative capitalist systems, such as the liberal economy, the coordinated markets, the developmental states, and state capitalism. In this chapter, I focus on the configuration of the SMG as a policy-investigative tool that can be potentially applied to other policy issues in China. First, the chapter maps out the policy process of the SMG – a multistep cycle with two stages – and different causal/contextual conditions that drive the process. Second, it explains the fiscal and institutional sources for the SMG. Since the fiscal and institutional structures are the macro foundation of the Chinese system, it is feasible to envision the SMG policy dynamic as being applicable to other issues. Finally, the chapter conducts an empirical demonstration of the SMG using the WDP, CGG, and BRI. The close fit of the SMG with these strategies, across two decades, establishes the robustness and consistency of the SMG as a general policy framework in China.

THE POLICY CYCLE AND CONDITIONS

Conceptually, state-mobilized globalization comprises of two fundamental mechanisms involving the state. The first refers to the state (the state system as a whole) utilizing political mobilization to promote market actors to more actively and more freely pursue growth-stimulating measures and globalization. The second refers to the process in which intrastate fragmentation compels the political leadership to intervene and mobilize different state agencies and lower-level units to more cohesively pursue growth and globalization. The full process of SMG analysis would establish both the state as *mobilizer* of market forces and the state as the *mobilized* in the political system.

Figure 2.1 draws the policy cycle of a nationalist strategy and spells out variables and mechanisms that drive the progression of the cycle. In the complete cycle, there are two stages and six steps. In the policy-making stage, economic pressure prompts political leadership into intervention with a nationalist strategy. After the leadership's announcement, the strategy enters the implementation stage, in which commercial actors lead the process and focus primarily on market expansion and globalization. Market-based globalization conducted by commercial actors helps them realize their economic agendas and as a whole helps the country combat the motivating economic pressure and revive the high-growth economy.

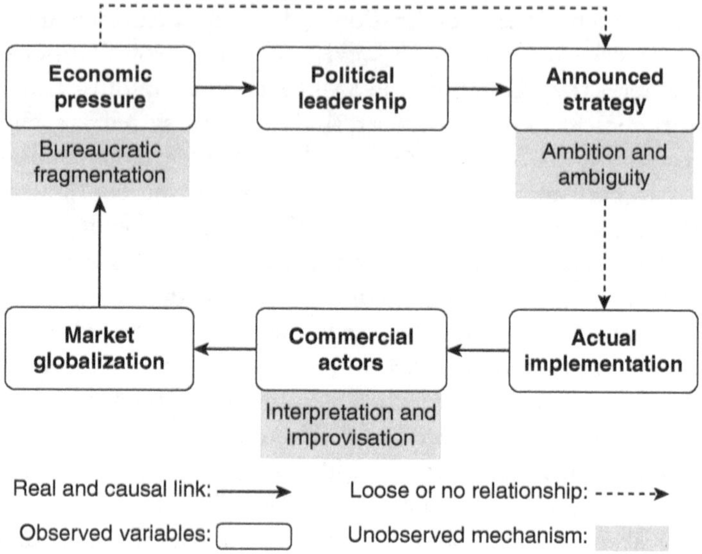

FIGURE 2.1. The policy cycle of state-mobilized globalization. *Source:* Made by the author.

In the policy cycle, there are two types of relationships connecting various conditions, represented by different lines. The first is observed influence, represented by the solid lines from economic pressure to political leadership and then to the announced strategy. The other relationship is deduced and loose, represented by the dashed lines. In other words, these conditions are "decoupled."[2] For example, on the surface, the domestic economic pressure and the announced foreign policy strategy do not demonstrate close causation. Furthermore, wide gaps exist between the ambitious wording and nationalist rhetoric in the announced strategy and more limited and typically economic-oriented implementation of the strategy, in particular in the early phases. Both observed and deduced linkages are important to driving and shaping state-mobilized globalization in China and abroad.

Framed differently, the SMG cycle in Figure 2.1 consists of *observed* variables, such as economic pressure, leadership actions, new policies, implementation projects, and substate actors, and *unobserved* mechanisms, such

[2] The idea of decoupling is borrowed from Patricia Bromley and Walter Powell, "From Smoke and Mirrors to Walking the Talk: Decoupling in the Contemporary World," *Academy of Management Annals*, 10, 2012, pp. 1–48.

as "bureaucratic fragmentation" that prompts the autocrat to use ambitious nationalist strategies to counter economic crises rather than technocrats to devise economic adjustment programs. Furthermore, "ambition and ambiguity" – the two characteristics of the strategy – are essential to the formation and implementation of the strategy. Nationalist ambition – the highest-order ideology driving the ruling elites – helps the state overcome fragmentation in the state system; ambiguity simultaneously allows different interest groups to interpret and implement the strategy according to their practical needs on the ground. Thus, the commercial actors implement the strategy through "interpretation and improvisation" – self-interpreting the strategy and focusing on their own business opportunities.

As a policy analysis, the SMG presents an explanation for a nationalist strategy that is deeply rooted in domestic politics and is motivated to continue rapid internal growth. It differs from various explanations based on external power-projection motivations. However, domestic development and power projection are not mutually exclusive. Decision makers/political leadership choose to promote a major policy, or a major policy emerges, typically due to confluence or a multitude of interests and drivers. The SMG's heuristic strength lies in its staged and layered causal mechanism, in which it spells out *when* and *how* power projection and internal growth play parts in pushing policy formation, implementation, and outcomes. By analyzing the complete cycle, it becomes clear that internal growth motivation predominates other factors in driving the emergence and shaping the outcomes of a nationalist strategy, as shown in the case studies of the WDP, CGG, and BRI in this chapter. Strategic motivation and nationalist rhetoric, on the other hand, facilitate political mobilization and amplify the development effect in China.

FISCAL AND INSTITUTIONAL UNDERPINNINGS

The SMG framework is posited on two underlying political–economic conditions in China. First, fiscally, internal growth in China and reasonably high gross domestic product (GDP) rates are paramount to political stability and serve as the governing foundation of the ruling system. Second, institutionally, the state system is large, important, and functionally separated in its organizational structure. Authority relations inside the state system are complex and negotiable.

Maintaining reasonably high growth is critical to the ruling regime in China for three reasons. First, the reform-era regime has drawn considerable legitimacy from economic performance, even though the economy

TABLE 2.1. *Sources of revenue in China in 2016 (%)*

Tax Revenue	82%
Valued-added tax (VAT)	26%
Corporate income tax	18%
Business and services tax	10%
Individual income tax	6%
Stamp and contract duties	5%
Land and resources	3%
Trade	2%
Non-tax revenue	18%

Source: Author's computation based on raw data from China National Statistical Bureau, *China Statistical Yearbook 2017*, available at http://stats.gov.cn.

is not the sole source of legitimacy. Second, high growth has become the most important indicator of the ruling party's efficacy and hence the source of public trust in the state; again, it is not the only indicator. Third, and most directly related to policy making, the majority of the government's annual budgetary revenue comes from the high-growth economy, as the fiscal system is based on taxing "the growth," not the people. In other words, stagnant economic growth not only suggests the declining competence of the ruling party but also forebodes a direct decline in revenues in the government coffers.

As shown in Table 2.1, in 2016, Chinese direct tax on personal income accounted for only 6 percent of its total revenue. The other revenue streams were all, one way or another, collected from the results of the high economic growth. Among the sources of tax revenue, value-added tax (VAT) was the highest, at 26 percent, followed by corporate income tax at 18 percent and business and services tax at 10 percent. There is no property tax in China – the other kind of direct tax.

Closely associated with this fiscal system is the importance of state-owned companies. SOEs are not only useful instruments of the state to carry out industrial policy and control over the market economy, but just as important, they have been the key source of revenues for the government in the past two decades. Shown in Chapter 7 (Table 7.1), in 2010, the number of SOEs was only 1/10 of private companies, but SOEs contributed just as much industrial output and revenue to the government as private companies did. In 2015, the ratio of the number of SOEs and private firms stayed at 1/10, but SOEs' industrial output and revenue contributions to the state went down to 2/3 of those of private firms.

This change in fiscal contribution between SOEs and private firms, on the one hand, reduced the importance of SOEs in Beijing's fiscal calculation and on the other hand, made it imperative to stop further revenue declines in the state sector.

From 1998 to 2018, as the empirical chapters of this book demonstrate, in the formation stages of nationalist strategies (WDP, CGG, and BRI), industrial overcapacities, slowing growth rates, and sliding performance in SOEs were the common stimuli and harbingers of economic crises and presented crises-induced critical junctures for autocratic intervention.[3]

In short, the Chinese fiscal system, or the underlying "social contract" between the rulers and ruled in China, is to tax economic growth, not tax the people. In the past two decades, while central revenues have grown exponentially, central expenditures have also increased, at an even faster pace than revenue growth. Economic downturns in such a fiscal system mean not only challenges for specific technocrats to address but also grave dangers to the stability and operation of the government as a whole; hence, the whole political system needs to be mobilized to respond.

Recently, in particular, as the Chinese state increased social welfare expenditures and rolled out aggressive antipoverty programs, the imperative to ensure stable revenue sources and relatively high growth has intensified even further. During an interview in Beijing in 2015, a seasoned foreign policy expert from a party-affiliated think tank explained that the driver for the Belt and Road was President Xi's pledge to eliminate poverty throughout the population by 2030 because for budgetary allocations for that target to be met, the Chinese economy has to maintain annual growth rates above 6 percent. For the economy to maintain reasonably high growth, strong doses of government intervention, such as the BRI, are necessary.

The SMG policy analysis establishes that economic pressures prompt the political leadership to announce a nationalist strategy because given the Chinese fiscal structure and ruling imperative, economic downward pressures amount to major crises that the regime faces in peacetime. In fact, because Chinese borders are reasonably secure and social uprisings are not prominent (insecure borders and social uprisings are two common causes of regime downfall), economic stagnation that could freeze

[3] On the roles of crises, see also Peter Gourevitch, *Politics in Hard Times: Politics of Response to International Economic Crisis*. Ithaca, NY: Cornell University Press, 1986; Stephan Haggard and Sylvia Webb, "What Do We Know about the Political Economy of Economic Policy Reform?" *World Bank Research Observer*, 8(2), pp. 143–168.

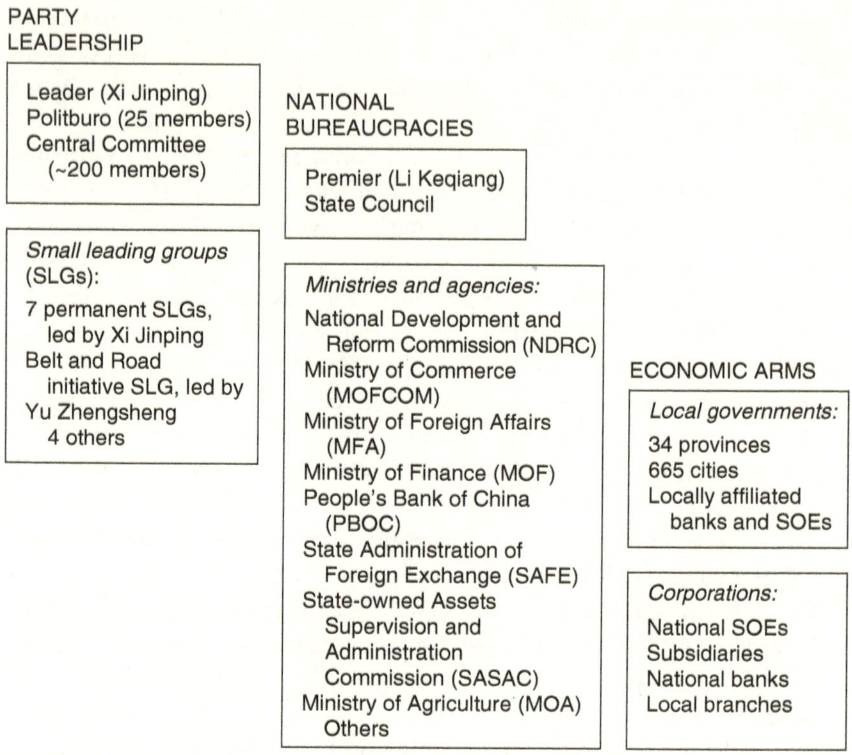

FIGURE 2.2. The tri-block state system over China's globalization: The party, bureaucracies, and economic actors. *Note:* Made by author, based on the party–state structure before the 2018 restructuring.

state revenues and compel the government to cut major civilian and social expenditures is arguably the gravest danger the Chinese regime has experienced in the recent past and will likely experience in the foreseeable future.

Now let us move to the institutional underpinning of the SMG framework and the question of why state intervention to revive the high-growth economy has to be accomplished by the political leadership through nationalist strategies. The Chinese state system is broadly overarching and all inclusive of political, bureaucratic, and commercial (economic) elites in China; it is also deeply divided in terms of formal structures and fragmented in terms of informal practices. Figure 2.2 draws the tri-block structure of the state system and illustrates the institutional fragmentation in the economic governance of China.

The first block is the Communist Party leadership structure led by the political leader, 25 Politburo standing and alternative members, and around 200 members in the Central Committee. Inside the Party structure, there are leading small groups that oversee state efforts on major development, globalization and foreign policy priorities.

The second block is the structure of the national bureaucracy, with the State Council headed by the premier at the top. Underneath the State Council are dozens of ministries and agencies that lead policy making and core functions in the state apparatus. The third block can be called the state's economic arms. They are local governments, state banks, and SOEs. As important elements of the state system, these economic arms, in particular local governments, also have noneconomic mandates at all times. Yet compared to the other two blocks, actors in this block are consistently the main executors of China's high-growth and globalization agendas in the reform era.

Because of separated functions and powers in the party, bureaucracies, and economic actors, the state system as described above can be extremely complex and fragmented. Many "leaks" happen in interactions between agencies and commercial units; many checks also exist across the blocks and within the blocks. Thus, in normal circumstances, major policy changes are difficult to effect in this tri-block structure. What really integrates the tri-block system are the ideology and organization provided by the ruling party. For example, almost all heads of government agencies and commercial units are party members, who are subject to the appointment and promotion power of the party system. Party leadership also controls ideological training, messaging, and information throughout the country, but more important, it has control over the 89 million party members who staff the huge government apparatus throughout China.

Again, under normal circumstances, the scale and separation of the tri-block structure make decisive, nationwide policy changes very difficult. When major economic crises occur, the state system is compelled to react, and the response is possible only with autocrat-led political mobilization in which party-affiliated instruments can move quickly and concertedly, thus helping coordinate state behavior toward reviving internal growth. As globalization has been an important means to achieving internal growth, such political mobilization has the potential to expand and expedite economic globalization in China.

To summarize the discussion above, the SMG, with its policy cycle and deduced causal mechanisms, is useful to show *how* the state and market interact in China, how the two mutually reinforce each other, and how the state changes in the context of a changing economy. It illuminates three processes and mechanisms. First, the origins of a nationalist strategy support structural fragmentation among key elements of the Chinese state. Second, the formation of a strategy shows autocratic adaptation to major economic pressures. Finally, refragmented implementation of the strategy reveals market expansion and growth of the national economy.

Putting these processes together, the Chinese state can be described as a "coordinated-capitalist" state, with a distinct ideology and organizational underpinnings. This ideology, first introduced in Chapter 1, consists of three tiers – nationalism as the highest order, economic growth as a middle-level priority, and capitalist markets as the prevailing, preferred instruments.[4]

Coordination of such a complex state system over a continental-size economy is difficult and has been helped by political institutions and organizational tools in the ruling party: Top-down messaging, controlled media, and incentive-based mobilization are all familiar playbooks that the Communist regime has been adept at utilizing.

EMPIRICAL DEMONSTRATION

The SMG analysis seeks to capture how the Chinese state reacts to crises that are typically induced or aggravated by globalization, and how different components of the Communist state implement the adopted strategies that facilitate the growth of Chinese capital. The framework focuses on investigating the *steps* of the policy cycles and *interactive* mechanisms of the state and markets. In other words, the analysis seeks to reveal *how* the state system reinforces the market forces in China, while it is simultaneously being transformed and strengthened by growth and globalization. As an empirical demonstration, this section employs the SMG framework to present the process, causes, and outcomes of WDP, CGG, and BRI.

In summary, Table 2.2 shows that first, these strategies were in response to major economic crises during China's globalization. Second, the rhetoric surrounding them was ambitious and ambiguous, focusing on the rise of China on the world stage and speaking to security, economic, and diplomatic priorities simultaneously. Finally, during implementation, commercial actors reinterpreted and improvised the nationalist strategies to help achieve economic growth. To that end, SOE reforms,

4 The relationship between external ambition and economic efficiency, see Miles Kahler, "External Ambition and Economic Performance," *World Politics*, 40(4), 1988, pp. 419–451.

TABLE 2.2. *Summary of nationalist strategies*

	Contexts and drivers	Ambition and ambiguity	Interpretation and improvisation
Western Development Program (1999)	Industrial overcapacity; declining exports; failing SOEs	Rise of China; border security; domestic stability	National infrastructure to integrate the national economy; provincial governments to attract major multinational corporations (MNCs); grassroots governments to recruit private manufacturers to expand inland
China Goes Global (2000)	Industrial overcapacity; failing SOEs; the World Trade Organization (WTO) pressure	Rise of China; global competition market expansion	Major SOEs to conduct self-reform to attract foreign equity; provincial government to conduct bottom-up deregulation; private companies to enhance inbound and outbound FDI
Belt and Road (2013)	Economic downturn; industrial overcapacity; TPP pressure	Rise of China; economic integration; regional stability	Local governments to carry out industrial planning; SOEs to expand commerce inside and outside China; private companies to strengthen inbound and outbound investment

Source: Made by the author, based on interviews, archival research, and policy documents.

open market access, and deregulation were conducted in the name of nationalist strategies. Inbound and outbound foreign direct investment (FDI), imports, and exports all gained significantly. Furthermore, the WDP also helped integrate industrial bases in the western region into the national economy, thereby expanding globalization and marketization all over the country. The BRI, due to China's increased economic power, is incorporating more markets in the world but also faces stricter scrutiny and stronger collective opposition.

Table 2.2 is based on multiple sources of material and types of research. To find the context and drivers for the launch of the strategies, I rely on two types of research: one, interviews with central actors, scholars, and local actors, and two, document analysis of economic magazines, official policies, and memoirs of senior and retired leaders. To demonstrate the characteristics of the strategies – ambition and ambiguity – I compile and analyze remarks by political leaders and policy publications by the central agencies with regard to the strategies. Finally, in terms of interpretation and improvisation, I draw on structured interviews with government officials and companies in the localities, as well as online reports and archival materials that support or refine the interview findings.

Western Developmental Program

Western China is a weighty political–economic region in the country. Of the nation's thirty-four provincial units, the region occupies twelve, making it a substantial player in the ruling bodies in Beijing: the CCP Central Committee, the CCP Party Congress, and the National People's Congress. With 19 percent of the country's population and 20 percent of GDP, western China occupies 71 percent territory and the vast majority of national resources. Modern Chinese leaders, from Sun Yat-sen to Mao Zedong, and generations of national economic planners emphasized the importance of western development.

During the period of economic reform since 1979, the political leader Deng Xiaoping (and the state) adopted a coastal development strategy and privileged infrastructure, industry, and investment in the coastal region. The development of western China was delayed and slowed down. To mollify dissatisfied western interests, Deng "promised" them that once China's economy reached a sufficient level, central government would provide them with preferential support.[5]

Deng's successor Jiang Zemin, who rose to power in Shanghai, was committed to the coastal regions. However, after he consolidated power in 1995, Jiang faced strong pressure from western China to reduce the huge development gaps between the western and coastal regions in the country. At the National People's Congress in 1996, Jiang bowed to this pressure and pledged to address the gap in regional development. Despite this

[5] Zeng Peiyan, *Xibu dakaifa juece huigu* [Reflections on the Process of Western Development Program Policy Making]. Beijing: Zhonggong dangshi chubanshe, 2010, p. 3.

pledge, Jiang's economic policy over the following three years was largely pro-Shanghai and pro–coastal China. It was only in March 1999 that he talked about large-scale development of the western region. On this occasion, he pushed strongly for the "large-scale development of the western region [...] otherwise how are we to modernize the whole country?"[6]

At the time, the economic crisis was an overwhelming concern in Beijing. Industrial overcapacity had been building up since 1996. Following the 1997–1998 Asian financial crisis, exports almost dried up; SOEs were in deep trouble.[7] China badly needed alternative sources of growth and markets. It was against this backdrop that Jiang began to seriously consider western development as a means to expand domestic consumption and generate significant numbers of jobs. Although this rationale was clear to national economic planners, it was hard to achieve consensus across government agencies. National bureaucracies could not agree on the timing or the necessity of the WDP. In early 1999, the State Planning Commission (SPC, the predecessor to the NDRC[8]) convened several meetings with other ministries and provincial governments to discuss the development of the western region. The opposition made their voices heard loud and clear. Some questioned the effectiveness of state intervention in the WDP; others opposed the policy for reasons of efficiency – investment in the coastal regions would bring better returns.[9]

Despite the SPC's best efforts at economic rationale, highlighting the creation of jobs and increased consumption in western China, opponents of the WDP remained unconvinced. In the ensuing stalemate, President Jiang stepped in and justified the WDP based on nationalist ambitions – the rise of China on the world stage. He referred multiple times to the rise of the United States, and the importance of US expansion into its western region. He stated flatly: "If there is no western development, how can China become an economically strong country? Had there been no western development in the United States, how could it have developed to today's level?"[10]

[6] Jiang Zemin. "Seize the Opportunity to Implement the Strategy of Large-Scale Development of the West," June 17, in *Selected Works of Jiang Zemin*, Volume 2. Beijing: Foreign Languages Press, [1999] 2010, p. 332.

[7] Nicholas Lardy, "China and the Asian Contagion," *Foreign Affairs*, 77(4), July 1, 1998, pp. 78–88.

[8] NDRC was officially structured and named in 2003.

[9] Zeng, *Xibu dakaifa juece huigu*, pp. 9–10.

[10] Zeng, *Xibu dakaifa juece huigu*, p. 8.

In 2000, the government passed its official document on the WDP, urging that "implementing the great development of western China and expediting economic growth in interior regions are important components of our modernization strategy [*xiandaihua zhanlüe de zhongyao bufen*], a major decision by the party leadership for the new century, and a strategic move to enhance ethnic unity [*minzu tuanjie*] and border security [*bianjiang anquan*]." In one policy, it speaks to economic growth in western China, political and security needs in the border areas, and overall modernization of the nation. The WDP's official launch resulted in publication of many documents; none, however, provided specific blueprints or action plans for subnational actors.

From 1999 to 2008, the implementation of the WDP frequently called upon market-based calculations. Central agencies favored three infrastructure projects: the Tibetan-Qinghai Railway, the West to East Gas Pipeline, and the West to East National Grid. These infrastructure projects had a threefold purpose: first, they involved significant investment that could increase GDP growth right away; second, they helped expand the Chinese domestic market and economic scale; and third, they helped bring in foreign capital and mobilize grassroots market actors. The Tibetan-Qinghai Railway, for example, had been studied for decades and in 2000, it was deemed feasible. Furthermore, the length of and sites for the railway were chosen based on cost efficiency. The West to East Gas Pipeline sought to transport abundant gas resources in western China to large consumer markets on the coast, and foreign energy players, such as British Petroleum (BP), Royal Dutch's Shell, and the Russian Gas Company, were invited to participate. The National Grid was able to revamp and unify a formerly fragmented national electricity system, allowing for the transfer of surplus hydropower in western China to coastal cities.

At the subnational level, the ambiguous and ambitious WDP has facilitated local actors' market-based implementation. Local governments and SOEs in western China, initially looking to cash in on central budgets, realized that the central government did not provide special subsidies for the WDP but instead fostered a permissive and encouraging environment for them to pursue economic growth.[11] Such an environment encouraged grassroots governments in western China to attract private investment from the coast by providing concessionary land, preferential taxes, and tariff waivers. Light industry manufacturers from

[11] Interviews in Chongqing; see also Chapters 3 and 6.

Zhejiang and Guangdong were indeed attracted to these cities, building infrastructure and factories for manufacturing.[12] While these new production facilities in western China did not replace manufacturing in coastal China, they did expand the companies' sales networks into interior regions. Using concessionary land, the market actors helped and benefited from new real-estate markets in interior cities.

Provincial governments in western China were supportive of the grassroots governments' efforts, while focusing on attracting large foreign MNCs to establish manufacturing in their industrial cities. Chongqing, a provincial city, constructed electronics industrial parks and provided incentives to Hewlett Packard (HP) and its major supplier Foxconn. Because HP's global distribution center was in Germany, the Chongqing government launched and constructed the Chongqing-Europe railway, allegedly the predecessor to today's Silk Road Economic Belt. To help Ford establish an assembly line in its capital city Chengdu, the Sichuan government constructed highways and an industrial zone specifically to serve Ford and its suppliers. As production costs and labor shortages rose in coastal China in recent years, these industries have grown rapidly in western China – Chongqing and Sichuan have been the largest manufacturing sites for automobiles and electronics by volume.

To summarize the analysis of the WDP, three observations can be made. First, globalization led to political cleavage in the country, a cleavage that was less about the division between exporters and producers[13] than between wealthier regions and poorer ones. Furthermore, losing provinces battled *not* for protection, but for more openness in their region. Second, fragmentation persisted across bureaucratic agencies and between central planning and local interests. While the central planners were interested in balanced nationwide development and therefore argued for preferential investment in western China, resistance from coastal regions – the early industrializers – to such preferential investment was strong. Moreover, the political leadership was generally more driven to boost economic growth. Economic crises enhanced the power of autocratic leaders, who were able to rally diverse groups around a nationalist

[12] Interviews with factories in Zhejiang, confirmed with investment data in localities in Chongqing.

[13] See Helen Milner, *Resisting Protectionism: Global Industries and the Politics of International Trade*. Princeton, NJ: Princeton University Press, 1988 Ronald Rogowski, *Coalition and Commerce: How Trade Affects Domestic Political Alignments*. Princeton, NJ: Princeton University Press, 1989.

strategy. Third, through implementation of the ambitious strategy, local governments' economic power was both strengthened and mobilized to seek growth-generating programs. Subnational actors improvised and designed their own development programs in accordance with their local economic conditions: Machine-making localities sought partners with foreign electronics and automakers, light-manufacturing localities chased private manufacturers from the coastal region, and localities with natural beauty embraced the potential of tourism. Ambiguity in the WDP allowed bottom-up market implementation.

China Goes Global

The CGG came about in the same climate of economic crisis as the WDP. It pertained mostly to SOEs. In China, SOEs are the main sources of revenue and employment; they also constitute important political power in the autocracy. Like provincial governors, the heads of large SOEs are often members of the CCP Central Committee. With deepening reform and openness in the 1990s, SOEs faced mounting problems: Overcapacities were severe, and nonperforming loans were substantial. In 1996, Jiang traveled to Africa to meet SOE representatives there. Desperate for new markets to make up for losses in advanced economies, Jiang was eager to tap into the market potential of less-developed countries. On his return, Jiang espoused the idea of China Goes Global (CGG) and urged struggling SOEs to expand markets and seek financing abroad. As economic pressure intensified at the end of the 1990s, Jiang made a stronger push for the CGG. In 2000, he officially elevated the CGG to a nationalist strategy and argued that it was critical to China's overall development and future destiny.[14]

It is clear that the CGG – seeking foreign financing and expanding exports – was driven by economic needs in China. Why was it then justified on nationalist ambitions? The underlying reasons were similar to the drivers of the WDP and BRI. First, political leadership, concerned about stability, did not want to alarm the society about economic troubles. Second, economic debate and resistance to globalization were

[14] Jiang Zemin, "Hold the Initiative in Fierce International Competition," January 25, in *Selected Works of Jiang Zemin* 3, Beijing: Foreign Languages Press, [2002] 2013, pp. 439, 444.

intense in Beijing. Inside state sectors, there were clear discontents who blamed globalization for outcompeting SOEs in China. Third, more liberal thinkers, on the other hand, were skeptical of any policy that promoted SOEs to go global out of fear; they were concerned that such promotion would become conduits for bailing out SOEs at the expense of market efficiency.[15] Finally, national bureaucracies regulating SOEs and capital accounts were wary of capital flight should SOEs be encouraged to go global in the form of the CGG.

Despite these concerns, once the CGG was announced by the political leadership as a national strategy [*guoce*] that was necessary to achieve China's great power status, no opposition groups could veto it openly. To promote the CGG, President Jiang remarked, "In the long run, to compete more effectively internationally, we must create a large number of large internationally competitive enterprises and multinationals.... All enterprises that have the capability and the conditions, including SOEs as well as enterprises in other sectors, should boldly go global...through equal and mutually beneficial international cooperation.... I have thought about this matter for a long time, mainly for the sake of the future development of our country and the welfare of future generations of the Chinese nation."[16]

The CGG was also ambiguous and did not provide concrete policy guidelines. In the first stage, there was no formal loosening of government controls over outbound investments.[17] Rather, the national agencies imposed clear restrictions on access to foreign exchange and tightened the approval for outbound investment projects. To be specific, companies wishing to invest abroad were required to gain preapproval with multiple central agencies and secure prior business contracts and foreign partner agreements. The regulation also imposed stringent control over foreign exchange used for overseas investment. In 2001, the government allowed home country financing for SOEs' overseas projects but demanded the borrowers repatriate foreign exchange earnings within six months. Only in 2003, when the internal economy was stabilized and there was surplus foreign exchange, did State Administration of Foreign Exchange (SAFE) allow

15 For the array of debates on SOE reforms, see Min Ye, *Diasporas and Foreign Direct Investment in China and India*. New York: Cambridge University Press, 2014, pp. 111–112.

16 Zemin, "Hold the Initiative in Fierce International Competition."

17 See a detailed two-series report in Li Shufeng and Huang Peijian, "Jingwai touzi waihui guanli gaige chushi shenshou" [Outward Investment Foreign Exchange Experimental Reforms], *Caijing*, No. 3, 2003.

selected localities to self-approve requests for the use of foreign exchange, but not in excess of $3 million. In short, at a national level, despite the political mobilization on behalf of the CGG, the strategy did not liberalize China's formal regulation over outbound FDI in the first period.

Yet beyond formal rules, the CGG enabled local government to improvise and implement *de facto* liberalization that facilitated outgoing companies. In 2000, Zhejiang province made a decision to expedite implementation of the CGG strategy. The local government quickly recognized the problem in the national regulation that placed foreign exchange and outbound-investment approval in the hands of central agencies. Local government sent a team to inspect its subordinate cities and held conferences with local companies and grassroots officials. The team issued a report that criticized national foreign-exchange regulations and argued that in order to implement President Jiang's CGG, companies should have easier access to foreign exchange. The team asked SAFE to designate Zhejiang as an experimental site for more liberal foreign-exchange approval.[18]

In May 2000, when SAFE held a work meeting in the province, the local government persuaded the central agency to authorize a special foreign-exchange policy for the province, without changing the national regulation. Zhejiang's special treatment led other coastal cities to lobby for similar foreign-exchange liberalization, also drawing on the CGG. By 2004, almost all coastal cities had received special foreign-exchange treatment, effectively putting an end to stringent national regulations.[19]

Chinese private companies also successfully leveraged the CGG to launch outbound globalization efforts. In 1999, for example, Zhejiang province's Hua Li, the world's largest manufacturer of digital watches at the time, planned to set up a subsidiary in the United States.[20] It spent eight months gaining the required foreign-exchange approvals from central agencies (SPC, Ministry of Foreign Trade and Economic Cooperation [MOFTEC], Ministry of Foreign Affairs [MFA], and SAFE). The company's application was significantly strengthened by its appeal to a goal in the new CGG policy: to raise funds in foreign markets. After the company entered the United States, it did not raise funds; rather, it

[18] Li and Huang, "Jingwai touzi waihui guanli gaige chushi shenshou."

[19] Ibid.

[20] The case is drawn from an investigative report in Huang Peijian, "Hua Li: chuanyue waihui guanzhi pingjing" [HuaLi, Overcoming Foreign Exchange Restriction Bottleneck], *Caijing*, No. 4, 2003.

used its foreign exchange to purchase two high-tech companies. When it needed more foreign exchange, it filed another application with the regulators, this time relying on another CGG goal – access to advanced technology – and receiving approval only following intervention by the Ministry of Industry and Information Technology (MIIT).

It is clear from the CGG's launch that the immediate driver was to incentivize SOEs to undertake reform, seek foreign financing, and expand international markets.[21] Its launch pressured major SOEs to conduct self-restructuring and then go abroad to raise funds. SOEs going global, however, had mixed results. China National Petroleum Corporations (CNPC) was a good example. Under the CGG, CNPC changed its governance structure, laid off massive numbers of workers, and restructured its nonperforming loans. With a streamlined corporate structure in place, CNPC went abroad. During CNPC's three weeks of roadshow, chasing global capital markets in thirty-two cities, the company was rejected everywhere except for a small offering on the Hong Kong Stock Exchange. Other state-owned companies also did not succeed in the global capital market.[22] In Boston, CNPC even caused some public outcry as a Chinese state-owned company.[23]

Like the WDP, the analysis of CGG supports the policy process and mechanisms of state-mobilized globalization, but it is clear that the CGG's domestic components had more success in that local governments managed to conduct *de facto* liberalization, private companies gained more latitude to invest abroad, and SOEs were pressured to restructure business in order to go global. The external side of the CGG, by contrast, was less successful. When SOEs – the main target of the CGG – went global, the international market received them with little enthusiasm. Despite autocratic mobilization, the CGG could not make SOEs a success abroad. Its domestic effects, however, helped revive industrialization and growth momentum. With a revived Chinese economy, restructured SOEs – now with leaner corporate structures, better human capital, and more financial resources – came to be an important player in the world market.

[21] In Jiang Zemin's speeches to promote the CGG, SOE reform was always emphasized.

[22] The case on CNPC and other SOEs' CGG draws on an investigative report, Zhang Jiwei, "Zhongguo shiyou: guoqi qijian nan xiashui" [China Petroleum: Flagship SOE Had Difficulty in Going Global], *Caijing*, No. 5, 2000.

[23] Ibid.

The Belt and Road

Now fast-forward to late 2013, and Chinese power looked fearsome abroad – the world's second largest economy had escaped the 2008 global financial crisis with enormous power gains[24]; it was, however, extremely fragile inside.[25] The central government faced real challenges that the state was too divided to combat.[26] On the external front, the U.S-led TPP expanded key members in 2012, including Japan, raising the prospect of economic encirclement against China.[27] Global recession was piling pressure on China: Inbound FDI was stagnating and exports were in decline. Internally, GDP growth rates had continued to slide, corporate performance was in trouble, and industrial overcapacities were widespread. President Xi's earlier anticorruption campaign had further dampened local development drives.

These economic pressure points provoked a sense of urgency – the state had to respond and respond quickly. Unfortunately, central bureaucracies were too divided to devise coordinated programs to tackle these challenges effectively. Proposals by economic technocrats could not gain support from other government agencies, nor from societal groups.[28] The China goes west idea, whose strategic implications aligned well with the Silk Road Economic Belt, could not reach beyond the security specialists and agents. A sense of impasse was clearly observed and experienced in Beijing in 2012–2013.

It was against this background of crises and state paralysis that the BRI was launched. The rhetoric of the initiative focused on the rise of the nation

[24] Thomas Christensen, *The China Challenge: Shaping the Choices of Rising Power.* New York: W.W. Norton & Company, 2015.

[25] Susan Shirk, *China Fragile Superpower.* New York: Oxford University Press, 2007.

[26] On Chinese policy elites' sense of crisis, see Guo Shuyong, "Lun heping fazhan dazhanluexia de guoji jingji yu guoji anquan xietiao" [On International Economic and Security Coordination under the Peaceful Development Grand Strategy], *Shehui kexue* [Social Sciences], No. 12, 2008, pp. 17–22; Lin Yifu, "Yong xinjegou jingjixue kan weilai quanqiu he zhongguo de jingji zengzhang" [Use New Structural Economics to Examine the Future Growth in China and in the World], *Xin jinrong pinglun* [New Financial Commentary], No. 2, 2012, pp. 1–17; Li Xiangyang, "Lun haishang sichou zhilu de duoyuanhua hezuo jizhi" [On Multilateral Cooperation Mechanisms of the Maritime Silk Road], *Shijie jingji yu zhengzhi* [World Economics and Politics], 2014; Zeng Peiyan, "Yazhou jichu sheshi hulian hutong shizai bixing" [Asian Infrastructure Mutual Connectivity Has to Be Done], Boao Review, October 13, 2013, pp. 38–40.

[27] Min Ye, "Competing Cooperation in Asia Pacific: TPP, RCEP, and the New Silk Road," *Asian Security*, 11(3), 2015, pp. 206–224.

[28] For the debates on the Chinese Marshall Plan, see Jin Zhongxia, "Zhongguo de maxieer jihua tantao zhongguo duiwai jichu jianshe touzi zhanlue" [China's Marshall Plan: Discussing the Strategy to Promote Outward Investment], *Guoji jingji pinglun* [International Economic Review], No. 6, 2012, pp. 57–65.

and simultaneously tackled security, diplomatic, and economic challenges. The BRI rapidly became a nationalist strategy that mobilized key actors and groups in the state system. The political leadership, via launching the strategy, broadened this coalitional support. Key interests and agencies in the state also latched onto the strategy to promote their own policies and preferences. Being so ambitious and ambiguous, how can the BRI indicate what the subnational actors can do and who should be in charge?

Research on subnational actors reveals disconnects between what they said and what they did in relation to the BRI. Chinese companies and local states were keen to praise the top-down program; in practice, they displayed widely spread deviation from the bottom up.[29] In one city, local SOEs implemented BRI projects that tried to make money from imported goods. In another city, local technocrats used the BRI to conduct industrial planning that sought to boost the city's international profile, upgrade local industries, and attract "high-tech" inbound FDI. In yet another city, the projects were improvised and financed by private entrepreneurs who intended to expand their traditional markets in Western Europe. Such diverse approaches reflect different economic structures and local market conditions. Clearly, the top-down strategy did not lead to uniform compliance by local agents.[30]

Furthermore, enormous diversities of approach were observed across different companies and they can diverse significantly from the leaders' remarks. Among SOEs, despite state ownership, they have interpreted the BRI differently; many chose not to act upon the strategy. For example, President Xi signed CPEC and called the Gwadar Port in Pakistan a "flagship" of the BRI. SOEs approached by the state could decide not to invest in the Port.[31] The leadership prioritized political relations with Pakistan. SOEs, however, could prefer expanding business in India, a chief opponent of the BRI. The BRI claimed to expand China's manufacturing exports to markets in Eastern Europe. Local SOEs, on the contrary, had used the strategy to expedite imports of consumer goods from Western Europe.[32]

[29] Chapter 5, focusing on early implementation of the BRI, presents detailed cases of subnational interpretation and deviations.

[30] Explanation of city selection and different local interpretation is detailed in Chapter 6.

[31] China Investment Group invited major port groups and funds to participate in construction of the Gwadar Port. Most of them declined because the term of returns is too long. The Shanghai Port Group agreed to participate in the downstream operation. Interviews in Shanghai and Zhejiang.

[32] Interviews in Chongqing.

Such divergence between actions and words was not simply due to principle–agent problems that emerged because of misinformation or asymmetric information between the principle and the agents. Here, research in Beijing and localities shows that top-down and bottom-up information and communication were frequent. The divergent implementation of the BRI was likely rooted in the institutional design and the process mapped out in the SMG, not due to "blocked" or distorted information flows between the center and the localities.

During interviews, large SOEs explained that they had consulted central actors such as China Development Bank (CDB), China Ex-Im Bank (CEIB), AIIB, and Silk Road Fund (SRF) to inquire about financing and found that little "soft" money was available – financiers were only interested in funding "bankable" projects. Large private companies had also been active in soliciting guidelines and information at provincial-level governments and ministries in Beijing. In Beijing and other places, central agencies – MOFCOM in particular – held workshops and summer courses for business representatives on investing abroad (or not) in the context of BRI.

Local governments also had effective communications with central agencies in Beijing. Among the researched cities, one served as an important venue for many national conferences on the BRI, attended by central economic planners and think tanks. Another sent regular delegations to Beijing to gain information and lobby for its BRI projects. It also hosted experts' conferences and workshops on the BRI, involving scholars and practitioners from Beijing and abroad. In the third city with a dominant private economy, the BRI projects were led by private entrepreneurs, but nonetheless had extensive endorsements from national bureaucracies. In those top-down and bottom-up interactions, it became clear that the lower units' main priority was to find growth opportunities, not to "sacrifice" their financial prudence in implementing the BRI.

Working in such an informational and institutional environment, the subnational actors, SOEs and local governments, proactively latched onto the BRI strategy to pursue their own opportunities and interests. In the name of the BRI, in recent years, a variety of new zones, production sites, projects, and programs emerged or were expanded in China. Through divergence and reinterpretation, the BRI and business reinforce each other, helping revive the Chinese economy as a whole.

To recap the SMG cycle in the BRI, President Xi, facing economic pressure and a divided state, announced the nationalist strategy to mobilize and coordinate diverse state and commercial actors to more actively seek growth opportunities and embrace economic globalization. The two puzzling (and most criticized) characteristics of the nationalist strategy – ambition and ambiguity – were vital to state mobilization in order to counter economic challenges. Nationalist ambition pushed by the political leadership overcame state fragmentation and mobilized diverse state and commercial actors into action. Instrumental ambiguity then allowed state and commercial actors to improvise programs based on markets and business calculations. Together, ambition and ambiguity in the BRI helped the country overcome recession and revive the high-growth economy. Outside China, BRI-related projects also display commercial motivations and close ties with domestic priorities.

In investigating the process of BRI formation, several causal links are deduced, not observed. For example, what (or who) were the immediate drivers behind President Xi's speeches in late 2013? Interviews with senior scholars and mid-level officials could not establish that black-box decision; they only established the plausible links. For example, agencies in charge of diplomacy, the economy, and security had practiced and proposed policy ideas that were similar to the BRI, such as infrastructure diplomacy, industrial capacities going global, and strategic reorientation to the Eurasian continent. And these agencies had fed such ideas to policy advisers, even speech writers, of the political leadership. Furthermore, for the numerous projects and programs in the name of the BRI, we cannot pin down whether external ambitions or domestic priorities were a more salient driver; both considerations were presented as explanations for BRI projects. Finally, it is too soon to tell the long-term impacts of China's BRI. The data so far establish that BRI implementation worked to stabilize the domestic economy and expand Chinese economic influence abroad. Specifics about how far and how much remain contingent.

Finding answers to these questions is infeasible at this point, and perhaps is immaterial to understanding BRI policy and politics. The SMG model has established that (1) irrespective of the "direct" causes of the leadership decision, the BRI had solid preexisting policy practices and proposals and when it was announced, the national agencies came out to promote it with their own interests and preferences; (2) irrespective of different justifications and rationalizations for the BRI by these agencies, the strategy has empowered state actors with resources to bring to the implementation and helped them expand markets and globalization; and (3) while it is still too soon to determine the long-term impacts, in the short-term, subnational and commercial actors are driven to combat economic downturns. Reinvigoration of the national economy, however, is likely to increase China's global linkages and involvement because domestic markets are saturated, and outbound globalization is becoming a necessity for Chinese producers and builders.

In summary, the analysis of WDP, CGG, and BRI processes here establish what constitute the main actors in the state, how they interact among themselves and with market forces, and what are the short-term and longer-term impacts on China and abroad. From 1998 to 2018, the basics of the Chinese state system have been persistent. First, the state system has dual imperatives – high growth and political stability – and the central leadership is adamant about achieving both, even when measures required for one priority can be in tension with the other. Second, there is clear separation between the autocratic leader and national bureaucracies, as well as deep divisions inside the state apparatus. Such fragmentation makes coordination difficult during normal times, but also enables autocratic intervention during critical junctures, as state agencies have a hard time waging collective opposition, in particular when they can exploit autocratic interventions to their own advantage. Finally, significant disjuncture and flexibility exist at the lower levels of the government and across different units. Lower-level actors can exploit strategies to improvise and implement projects and programs in their own economic interests.

CONCLUSION

Major policies usually come about because of the confluence of different interests and drivers. That was the case with the WDP launched in 1999, the CGG in 2000, and the BRI in 2013. Behind each strategy's formation, the empirical process demonstrates a critical juncture opened up by economic crisis, pressing domestic development imperatives, and nationalist external ambition. In this chapter, the SMG analysis maps out the complete cycle that includes policy-making and implementation stages and explicates variables and conditions at different steps of the cycle. It is able to demonstrate which drivers – internal development or external expansion – are more important and in what way.

The SMG framework prioritizes internal development as an important motivating factor for China's nationalist strategies and reviving high economic growth as an important outcome of each strategy's implementation in China. In explicating and applying the SMG framework, the chapter presents the fiscal and institutional foundations of the Chinese state.

On the fiscal side, the state budget is almost entirely financed by revenues collected from rapid economic growth. Therefore, economic downturns amount to regime-threatening crises that mobilize the state system into action. On the institutional side, the Chinese state consists of a tri-block system: the ruling party, government, and commercial actors. There is enormous fragmentation across and within the blocks; systemwide coordination is therefore difficult. When the state is compelled to react, it typically comes from an autocratic leader launching an ambitious and ambiguous strategy.

The nature and organization of the Chinese state are difficult to define in any one episodic moment, or in specific sectors or in particular areas of governance. The SMG's complete cycles, in particular the long-term study of globalization from 1998 to 2018, demonstrate a "coordinated-capitalist" state in the PRC because, among competing issues and priorities facing the state, economic development has served both as a dominant driver and a key outcome of the SMG. In the meantime, the Communist organization and information control help produce "coordinated" images and voices that are important to mobilize fragmented state groups to support and implement the strategy in a reasonably cohesive direction, that is, the imperative to revive and expand the Chinese capital in China and abroad.

PART II

THE STRATEGIES

3

The Development of Western China

> Deepening [the] Western development program is [our] important means to cope with the global financial crisis while maintaining stable economic growth in China. It is a must-make choice to expand domestic consumption, safeguard sustainable development, improve [our] living standards, and ensure ethnic unity and border security.
>
> —Zeng Peiyan[1]

The SMG analysis has established that the WDP, like the BRI and CGG, was launched by the political leadership, who were facing economic recession and other challenges, and then mobilized subnational and commercial actors to improvise growth-reviving endeavors in their own purviews. This chapter focuses on three tasks: First, it presents the reform-era developmental history of western China and captures how the WDP and globalization have interacted in this region; second, it elaborates on the process and phases of WDP implementation and explains how state roles have adapted to different periods of developmental challenges in the country; and finally, it uses three large infrastructure projects in the WDP as examples to illustrate that, while expanding globalization, the WDP's implementation has also intensified centralization and political penetration by the ruling party into inland China.

Empirically, the chapter builds on three sets of research materials for analysis of the sources and processes of western development in China. First, it compiles and analyzes official documents to show whether and what political priorities and guidance the state promulgated under the WDP. Second, it uses economic statistics to capture development trends

[1] Zeng, *Xibu dakaifa juece huigu*, p. 443.

in western China and how it was compared to the coastal region, where industrialization and globalization had taken place earlier. Finally, I use interviews at local governments and companies to verify and crystallize how these actors have experienced the WDP during recent decades. As a whole, the chapter elucidates to what extent state behaviors, as revealed in the process of the WDP, are antimarket or ahead of market and in what areas the state makes conscious efforts to facilitate market actors operating in the western region.

A SKETCH OF WESTERN CHINA

China's economic reform is four decades old, and economic growth across regions has been uneven. In the first two decades (1978–1998), the coastal region experienced rapid growth by exploiting the influx of foreign direct investment (FDI) and the rapid increase in international trade. By contrast, the western part of China, with limited exposure to global capital and foreign trade, experienced markedly worse economic performance. The western region served primarily as a source of cheap labor and natural resources for coastal China and thus went through terrible social and ecological degradation. By the end of the 1990s, people in western China were enduring not only a lower standard of living but also lower esteem in Chinese society than coastal residents. Many of them had to migrate to coastal cities and worked as manual labor and domestic help. In short, China's reform and openness in the first two decades resulted in a deeply divided and unequal country.

On the other hand, the western region possessed the majority of territory, natural resources, and national borders. It was strategically and politically important to China. In 1922, Sun Yat-sen argued for preferential investment and construction of infrastructure in western China.[2] Mao Zedong launched the Third-Front industrialization strategy to relocate technology, experts, and industrial equipment to western China in the 1960s.[3] Although the Third-Front strategy was largely unsuccessful, it left a long legacy of relationships between the region and economic planners in Beijing. Many central bureaucrats had personal and professional experiences in western China.

[2] Sun Yat-sen, *The International Development of China*. New York & London: G.P. Putnam's Sons, 1922.

[3] Heike Holbig, "The Emergence of the Campaign to Open Up the West: Ideological Formation, Central Decision-Making and the Role of the Provinces." *The China Quarterly*, 178, 2004, pp. 335–357.

Reform-era leader Deng Xiaoping privileged coastal development but promised the western region that Beijing would shift toward pro-western development over time.[4] Pressure to narrow development gaps between the west and the coast was persistent. Jiang Zemin, Deng's successor, announced in his famous 1995 speech that fostering economic growth in western China and narrowing the gap between western and coastal China were among the top priorities of Chinese socialist modernization.[5] In short, there had been sustained political pressure on the central leadership to develop western China. The question was when and how would this be achieved?

Figure 3.1 shows western China geography and growth data. There are twelve provincial units in the region, divided into three categories. First, the border provinces connect China with Russia, Mongolia, Central Asia, South Asia, and Southeast Asia. The border economies

Types	*GDP (2014)*	*GDP Growth (2013–14)*
Border provinces		
Inner Mongolia	17,770	5%
Guangxi	15,673	8.5%
Yunnan	12,815	8.3%
Xinjiang	9,273	9.8%
Tibet	921	12.9%
Interior provinces		
Sichuan	28,537	8.1%
Shaanxi	17,690	9.2%
Guizhou	9,266	14.6%
Gansu	6,837	8.0%
Ningxia	2,752	6.8%
Qinghai	2,303	8.5%
Provincial city		
Chongqing	14,263	11.6%

FIGURE 3.1. Western China: Geography and growth. *Source:* Author, based on raw data from the National Bureau of Statistics of China, database on Provincial Statistical Yearbooks, annual editions, see data.statistics.gov.cn. *Note:* The unit of provincial GDP is RMB¥100 million.

4 Zeng, *Xibu dakaifa juece huigu*, p. 3.

5 Jiang Zemin, "Zhengque chuli shehui zhuyi xiandaihua jianshezhong de ruogan zhongda guanxi," speech at the Fifth Plenum of the Fourteenth Party Congress, September 28, 1995. Central Committee Compilation Office, *Jiang Zemin Selected Works*. Beijing: People's Publisher, 2006, p. 466.

vary significantly in size, ranging from the economically weighty Inner Mongolia to Tibet's small economy. Guangxi and Yunnan, deeply embedded in trade and investment between China and Southeast Asia, have sizable economies. Second, there are six provinces that constitute the middle provinces of western China, connecting the border provinces with the coastal region. Economic sizes of the middle provinces also vary, ranging from the populous and well-industrialized Sichuan to sparse and undeveloped Qinghai. Last, there is a provincial city, Chongqing, on par with Beijing, Shanghai, and Tianjin in coastal China. Originally a major industry city in Sichuan, Chongqing was made the provincial city in 1997. It is currently the fifth largest economy in western China and plays an important role in leading development in the region.

Figure 3.1 shows the provinces of western China and their diverse GDP growth rates, though there was generally higher growth than the national average rate in recent years. Statistics show that in 2013–2014, China's overall growth rates were declining conspicuously. Yet in western China, Guizhou province enjoyed a growth rate of 14.6 percent, Tibet grew at 12.9 percent, and Xinjiang grew at 9.8 percent. With the exception of Inner Mongolia, whose resource-dependent economy suffered major losses, all of the western provinces achieved much higher growth than the national growth rate of 6.8 percent. Furthermore, several provinces in the western region had large economies and industries. The high growth rates were important to counter economic recession and stabilize sliding growth rates in China in recent years.

To summarize, it has long been an aspiration of modern Chinese leaders to industrialize and develop the vast territory of western China. By better integrating natural resources, the labor force, and consumer markets in the region into the fast-growing and export-dependent coastal region, the Chinese economic boom has become more pronounced and more sustainable in the recent past. Arguably, the WDP strategy, launched in 1999, has contributed to industrial transformation in western China. Several important questions ensue: Under what circumstances did the Chinese leadership launch the WDP? To what extent did state intervention contribute to development in western China? How did the state and market interact during the WDP? Was state behavior in WDP implementation primarily antimarket or ahead of market?

PAST DISCOURSES

When the WDP was officially launched in 1999, Beijing was eager to solicit global capital and technology. Vice Premier Zeng Peiyan held meetings with business representatives from Hong Kong, with hedge fund billionaire Richard Lee among those to whom strong overtures were made. Lee hired renowned economist Jeffrey Sachs to conduct research on the WDP's feasibility and report back to the Chinese official. Six months later, Sachs's report concluded that worldwide, economic growth has taken place within 200 miles of major seaports. The WDP trying to industrialize and globalize inland China was like "directing water from low grounds to high grounds ... It is against the law of physics."[6]

Nonetheless, China went ahead with the WDP strategy, although the head of the WDP Small Leading Group took Sachs's report seriously and underscored the importance of market mechanisms in implementation of the strategy.[7]

Within China, there were thousands of publications on the WDP from 2000 to 2012. But most of them offered easy and repetitive praise, while others paid attention to shortcomings in local implementation only. These Chinese archives demonstrate political mobilization on behalf of the WDP but have little use in explaining the drivers or effects of the WDP. Among the numerous archives, the most authoritative and most useful research on the WDP was done by famous scholar Hu Angang and his team at Tsinghua University; it provided the strongest positive appraisal of the strategy.[8] Using a difference-in-difference (DiD) statistical model and provincial data from 1987 to 2007, Hu's team found that the WDP since 2000 has boosted GDP growth in western China by an average of 1.5 percent annually, thus helping narrow the development gap between western and coastal China.

The problems of this DiD analysis are clear. While the WDP was statistically shown to correlate with western development, it failed to explain *how* the WDP had worked. Had it worked primarily because of top-down political fiat, or state investment, or market mechanisms? Granted, the WDP was important, but to what extent had the state incorporated, or followed, market forces in implementing it?

6 Zeng, *Xibu dakaifa juece huigu*, p. 80.

7 Ibid.

8 Hu Angang, Liu Shenglong, and Wang Yahua, "Xibu dakaifa chengxiao yu zhongguo jingji shoulian" [The Effects of Western Development Program and the Chinese Economic Contraction], *Jingji yanjiu* [Economic Research], No. 9. 2009, pp. 94–105.

Contrary to Chinese praise, foreign observers of the WDP were generally critical. Political scientist Victor Shih, for example, stressed the ulterior motives behind President Jiang's decision to launch the strategy. Shih believed that Jiang used the WDP not as a development program to industrialize inland China but rather as a political plot to weaken his rival and successor Hu Jintao, whose main power base had been in western China.[9] Development specialists, on the other hand, underscore that under the WDP, inequality within western China increased, and key WDP projects paradoxically benefited the coastal region more than the western region, aggravating the development gap across regions.[10] Other scholars highlight how, due to interprovincial pipelines constructed under the WDP, national oversight of the energy sector was further weakened. Failing to rein in powerful interests under unified national regulation, the sector was made even more fragmented by the WDP.[11]

Criticisms against the WDP also include concerns about the strategic implications for, and deleterious impact on, ethnic minorities in western China. Foreign policy specialist John Garver warned the US government against rapid infrastructure linkages between China and South Asia, which in his opinion amounted to "a quantum leap in China's west-oriented transportation infrastructure."[12] Canada-based scholars Yuchao Zhu and Dongyan Blanchford point out how economic expansion and marketization under the WDP have undermined ethnic minorities in Xinjiang and Tibet, which they strongly argue has contributed to rising ethnic violence in China in recent years.[13]

These past scholarly analyses get important aspects of the WDP right, yet they neglect a holistic study of the strategy. None of them

[9] Victor Shih, "Development, the Second Time Around: The Political Logic of Developing Western China," *Journal of East Asian Studies*, 4(3), 2004, pp. 427–451.

[10] David Goodman, "The Campaign to Open Up the West: National, Provincial-Level and Local Perspectives," *The China Quarterly*, 178, 2004, pp. 317–334; Christopher McNally, "Sichuan: Driving The Capitalist Development Westward," *The China Quarterly*, 178, 2004, pp. 426–447; Tim Oaks, "Building a Southern Dynamo The Guizhou and State Power," *The China Quarterly*, 178, 2004, pp. 467–487.

[11] Here, the center is narrowly defined as the top regulator and the weakening is concluded by the strengthening of corporate and local governments' roles in energy sectors. Darrin Magee, "Powershed Politics: Yunnan Hydropower under Great Western Development," *The China Quarterly*, 185, 2006, pp. 23–41.

[12] John Garver, "The Development of China's Overland Transportation Links with Central, South-West and South Asia," *The China Quarterly*, 185, 2006, p. 18.

[13] Yuchao Zhu and Dongyan The Blachford, "Economic Expansion, Marketization, and Their Social Impact on China's Ethnic Minorities in Xinjiang and Tibet," *Asian Survey*, 52(4), 2012, pp. 714–733.

pay attention to the process of birthing, dynamics of implementation, reinforcement between the state and market, and interactions of central and local actors. For an important strategy like the WDP, a focus on one component is likely to miss others. For example, if we focus only on the political motives of the WDP, we neglect to consider the economic crisis that had driven its birthing and implementation. Were we only to focus on the foreign policy implications, we would be unable to gauge domestic momentum created by the WDP. Furthermore, the initial motivators of the strategy were less important than the patterns of implementation in determining the long-term effects of the nationalist strategy.

PROCESS TRACING

Roots in Globalization

The WDP, seemingly going against market principles and globalization, was actually rooted in and shaped by China's globalization experience since the 1980s. Structurally, globalization had created large and politically unsustainable income inequalities across regions in China. In particular, the celebrated global production networks produced a new class of entrepreneurs in coastal China, while the western region became a main supplier of cheap labor and natural resources. Such regional and class cleavages were particularly problematic for Communist China, whose ruling ideology presumably represents the whole nation and primarily the working class.

In addition to cross-regional inequality and political cleavages, globalization also created business cycles that resulted in economic recessions and even crises. In the early 1990s, during the global expansion, China rapidly increased industrial capacities, but by the end of the decade, as recession settled in advanced economies, China faced severe overcapacities and economic slowdown. Large-scale industrial shutdown and social turmoil were looming in decision makers' minds.[14] In 1999, it was against this volatile backdrop that the WDP was born, although the strategy's roots were planted earlier and in the very process of globalization throughout the decade.

Globalization also played a positive role in western development. In 1992, after Deng Xiaoping made his famous Southern Tour, coastal China expedited reform and openness. At that time, the central

[14] Zeng, *Xibu dakaifa juece huigu.*

government urged western China to reform as well. The SPC held a multi-day conference involving provincial representatives in western China and pushed for expedited development in this part of the country.[15] At the conference, the SPC made four points: First, economic growth in inland China was important to the national economy; second, development in the western region should follow market principles and prioritize trade and investment from the coastal region; third, the national government would provide preferential policies to inland China and allocate low-interest loans from international organizations there; and last, western development should focus on hydropower, transportation, and energy.[16]

How coastal China achieved its growth through globalization also shaped the *preferred* measures for state intervention in western China. In a planning document on western development, the State Council urged western provinces to "liberate thoughts and adopt new ideas, and based on socialist market economy, deepen reform and openness and expedite transition from the old [economic] system to a new one."[17] To help with western China, the SPC suggested five prioritized areas: infrastructure; foreign capital; special economic zones in key industrial cities; favorable policies in investment, financing, funding, lending, and international credits; and border trade and openness to foreign capital. Four of the prioritized areas were about liberalizing the economy and embracing global capital. The SPC urged, "In order to narrow the gap between interior and coastal China," the western region needed to "actively participate in international division of labor and use foreign capital, resources, technology, and experiences" in a "whole-round openness platform" [*quanfangwei de duiwai kaifang geju*].[18]

Table 3.1 summarizes the developmental gaps between the coastal and western regions, measured by four indicators – nominal GDP, industrial output, foreign direct investment, and foreign trade. It shows that in 1993, after coastal reforms from 1978 to 1992, the coastal region – ten provinces – accumulated considerable development advantages over the western region. In nominal GDP, the ratio between the coastal region and

[15] State Council, "Guojia jiwei guanyu xibei diqu jingji guihua wenti baogao" [SPC's Report on Difficulties in Economic Planning in the Northwestern Region], No. 19, March 1993, www.gov.cn/zhengce/content/2010-12/30/content_2152.htm.

[16] Ibid.

[17] State Council, "Guojia jiwei guanyu xinan he huanan bufen shengqu quyu guihua gangyao de tongzhi" [The SPC Notice on Regional Planning with Regard to Some Provinces in Southwestern and Southern China], State Council Circular #56, 1996.

[18] Ibid.

TABLE 3.1. *Development gaps between western and coastal China, unit = times*

Coastal China divided by Western China	1993	1997
Nominal GDP	3.86	3.61
Industrial output	7.93	7.9
Foreign capital	16.52	23.92
Foreign trade	42.9	40.83

Source: Author, based on raw data from the National Bureau of Statistics of China database on Provincial Statistical Yearbooks, annual editions, see data.statistics.gov.cn.

the western region was 3.86 times higher; in industrial output, the coastal region had 7.93 times that of the western region; in foreign capital, the coastal region had 16.52 times that of the amount in western China; and in foreign trade, the coastal region had 42.9 times the volume of western China.

It is hard to gauge how and how forceful were the central state's efforts to help western China catch up in the 1990s. Table 3.1 shows that the large gaps between the two regions in terms of GDP, industrial outputs, foreign investment, and foreign trade had been largely intact, with slight narrowing in three indicators and a clear widening in the foreign capital indicator. To be sure, considering rapid growth and globalization in coastal China during the period, western China's economic performance over the decade, as a whole, was impressive, despite remaining behind coastal performance.

The late 1990s saw a severe economic crisis and the new pressure from WTO, which together intensified the central state's efforts to expedite growth in western China and culminated in the launch of WDP in 1999. The first major blow came from the Asian financial crisis (AFC) of 1997–1998. China had already accumulated severe industrial overcapacities in the mid-1990s; the AFC hastily transformed what was an economic downturn into a full-blown crisis. The second pressure came from China's expected entry into the WTO, which intensified the imperative to conduct SOE reforms. SOEs dominated industries and employment in the western region; thus, SOE reform in this region was particularly burdensome and difficult to execute. The AFC and WTO membership clearly shaped President Jiang's WDP policy decisions and the messages he emphasized during this period.

Throughout this period, Jiang was deeply concerned about SOEs' economic performance and how to reform SOEs effectively. During his visit to

Africa in June 1996, he met with SOE representatives and urged them to find new export markets. In July 1996, Jiang met representatives of SOEs in Hebei province and used the opportunity to once again urge SOEs to restructure themselves. In December 1997, at the National Foreign Investment Promotion conference (chaired by Jiang), the president took every opportunity to emphasize China's "new challenges" and stress how foreign companies could help China cope with economic crises.[19]

In March 1999, Jiang spoke to key members of the national government: "The central leadership has explicitly decided to expedite development in western China and to expand domestic consumption as a means to expedite economic growth [in the country]."[20] Three months later, Jiang officially announced the WDP, characterizing the strategy as being essential to achieving the rise of China on the world stage. Jiang urged, "Were there no western development, how could China become an economically strong country? Were there no western development in America, how could the United States have developed to today's level?"[21]

The WDP's launch, and Jiang's tireless promotion of it, gave the central planners more authority to coordinate cross-agency projects and mobilize compliance from local governments. Indeed, the SPC had been pushing for western development since the 1990s; now acting on behalf of the political leadership, the SPC published the primary document on the WDP in January 2000, in which it spelled out the central government's ideas, proposed tasks, and general measures. In this central document, the agendas were ambitious, the tasks were extremely broad, and the policy measures were rather vague.[22]

Careful analysis of central documents, as in the next section, establishes that the central state gave *directives* to lower units, but not establish clear *obligations*. Both market-oriented reforms and globalization

[19] Jiang Zemin, "Shishi yinjinlai he zouchuqu xiangjiehe de kaifang zhanlue" [Realize the Strategy to "Attract In and Go Out" Together], *Jiang Zemin Selected Works*, 2001, pp. 91–94.

[20] Zeng, *Xibu dakaifa juece huigu*, p. 7.

[21] See Jiang Zemin's speech at the SOE Reform in Western China Workshop on June 17, 1999. Communist Central Compilation Committee, "Bushi shiji de shishi xibu dakaifa zhanlue" [Do Not Lose Momentum to Implement the Western Development Program Strategy], *Jiang Zemin's Selected Works*. Beijing: People's Publisher, 2006, pp. 340–347.

[22] State Council, "Guowuyuan guanyu shishi xibu dakaifa ruogan zhengce cuoshi de tongzhi" [Notice on Policies Implementing the Great Development of Western Region], State Council Circular #33, 2000, www.gov.cn/gongbao/content/2001/content_60854.htm.

appeared saliently in the central documents. Only by unpacking the stages and priorities during the WDP's implementation are we able to understand the state's role and how the state interacts with market forces in driving growth and globalization in western China.

Stages of Implementation

From 1999 to 2012, WDP implementation can be divided into three phases, each of which reflects different economic conditions and priorities in China.[23] The top priority during the first phase was to address the economic crisis and China's WTO membership. Thus, the WDP exhibited top-down mobilization and the launch of three flagship infrastructure projects. These efforts aimed to increase economic growth as quickly as possible. And by the second phase, the Chinese economy was relatively stable and steadily growing. Furthermore, with a new president, the WDP-Second stage reflected a shift toward social and environmental issues. In the localities, however, governments and companies enthusiastically embraced industrialization and globalization. The third phase was marked by two traumas – the global financial crisis and the disastrous earthquake in Sichuan province in western China. These two crises led to a massive stimulus plan, making the WDP a conduit for state capital that profited from reconstruction of western China over this period.

The first stage began in 1999, when the central government ushered in the WDP with political fanfare and publicity. Focusing on top-down mobilization, the WDP's launching documents did not set out explicit obligatory targets to central agencies or local governments. In a speech in 1999, "Seizing the Opportunity to Implement the Great Western Development Strategy," Jiang underscored the importance of the WDP to the maintenance of China's high-growth economy and to China's rise on the world stage. In terms of policy, Jiang's goal was to mobilize central agencies and local governments to organize "bolder openness and deepen reform and development" in western China.[24] The SPC was also involved in rallying actions by local governments and other industrial bureaucracies in Beijing. Premier Zhu Rongji personally led delegations to provinces in western China to drum up support for the WDP and collect information on the ground.[25]

[23] The WDP still existed after 2012, but its importance has been replaced by the BRI.

[24] CCP Central Compilation Office (ed.), *Jiang Zemin's Selected Works*, Beijing: Renmin Publisher, 2006, p. 342.

[25] Zeng, *Xibu dakaifa juece huigu*, pp. 13–16.

After all these mobilization efforts, in 2000, the State Council published a comprehensive WDP report.[26] While the guidelines in the report was long and exhaustive, none of them stipulated explicit, obligatory measures. The inherent ambiguity was such that *almost anybody was allowed to do almost anything.* As shown in Table 3.2, the report includes general principles and priorities that were both contradictory and comprehensive. For example, the wording simultaneously emphasizes the urgency and the long-term nature of the plan, and the stipulated mechanisms emphasize both market principles and macro state planning. Local activism and national direction were also simultaneously stressed. The two characteristics – ambition and ambiguity – were clear in that, in the document, all sectors and all regions in western China were prioritized in the WDP.

In terms of financing, the report suggested preferential, but not patrimonial, financing arrangement in the WDP and stated that all projects should follow sound loan conditions and market principles. While presenting the WDP as a development strategy, the report stipulated that central transfers be primarily allocated to rural, social, and environmental issues.

As is also clear in Table 3.2, market-oriented reform and globalization were strongly emphasized. For example, the WDP report stipulated that SOE reforms be conducted and government project approvals be simplified. Furthermore, the central government designated especially preferential policies to investors in western China, including 15 percent corporate tax to all domestic and foreign firms; and more favorable land and resources policies than those for the coastal region. Moreover, the central government provided more support for globalization in western China than the coastal region. Special provisions include (1) new sectors to open to FDI, (2) new formats for FDI entry, and (3) new kinds of trade promotion in the region.

In terms of state investment in the region, during the first period, transfer funds from Beijing were limited to the few major national projects.

[26] State Council. "Notice on Policies Implementing the Great Development of Western Region," State Council Circular #33. 2000. www.gov.cn/gongbao/content/2001/content_60854.htm.

TABLE 3.2. *The WDP report: Direction, not obligation*

General principles and priorities: contradictory and comprehensive
Identification of WDP: urgency and long-term project
Driving mechanisms: market principles and macro regulation
Operation: local government initiatives and national integration
"Prioritized" sectors: infrastructure, environment, agriculture, industry, education, and health
"Prioritized" localities: Chongqing, Sichuan, Guizhou, Yunnan, Xizhang, Shaanxi, Gansu, Ningxia, Qinghai, Xinjiang, Inner Mongolia, Guangxi
Financing: preferential, not patrimonial
Crediting: policy loans, international aid, and corporate investments.
Sectors: hydropower, transportation, environment, high-tech, & R&D, in accordance of loans conditions
Transfers: used in agriculture, social provision, education, health, and environment
Bank loans: railways, highways, electricity, oil and gas, agriculture, environment, and rural electrification
Market-oriented reforms
Deepen SOE reforms
Open more sectors to foreign and private investments
Except for government projects, simplify approvals for factories and businesses
Specially preferential policies: apply to all domestic and foreign firms, 15 percent corporate tax; special-provision firms enjoy regular reduction and waver of taxes; environmental and agricultural investments enjoy 10-year fee waiver; qualified companies enjoy duty-free capital goods imports; more favorable land and resources policies; market-based pricing for electricity and utilities
Globalization
Sectors to FDI: agriculture, hydropower, environment, transportation, energy, R&D, high-tech; banking; retail; Chinese currency; insurance; accounting; legal services; and engineering and design
Formats of FDI entry: wholly foreign; Build-Operate-Transfer (BOT); joint stocks; joint bonds; joint venture banks
Trade: easy licensing; contractual labors; tariff-waved machinery import
Human capital
Flexible wages; Hukou reform; establishing research institutions; overseas education; and training of cadres

Source: Author, based on analysis of State Council, "Notice on Politics Implementing the Great Development of Western Region," State Council Circular #33, 2000.

TABLE 3.3. *Continual gap between coastal and western China, unit = times*

Coastal divided by Western region ratio/times	2000	2001	2002	2003
Nominal GDP	3.83	3.86	3.88	3.99
Industrial output	8.54	8.67	8.66	10.24
Foreign capital	26.98	26.25	26.82	32.7
International trade	52.97	57.12	60.95	57.21

Source: Author; raw data are from National Bureau of Statistics of China, Statistical Database, Provincial Statistical Yearbooks, annual editions, data.statistics.gov.cn.

Private capital took time to come to western China. By contrast, in the coastal region, global economic expansion resulted in rapid investment and trade growth. Hence, despite political rhetoric and mobilization on behalf of the WDP, the development gaps between the two regions widened over the period 2000–2003.

Table 3.3 shows that in nominal GDP, the gap between coastal and western China increased from 3.83 times to almost 4 times; in industrial output, the ratio increased from 8.54 times to 10.24 times; in foreign capital, the ratio rose from 26.98 times to 32.7 times; in international trade, the gap increased from 52.97 times to 57.21 times.

Rising economic inequalities between western and coastal regions in the early 2000s created a dilemma for the backers of the WDP. Inside the region, critics bemoaned the lack of real investment and commitment from the central government; from the outside, the argument was that state programs simply did not work. In fact, neither of these arguments was true. Rather, the WDP was designed by the central government to integrate the western region into the national economy and introduce pro-market policies gradually on par with coastal China. Enlarged development gaps in the early 2000s arguably had more to do with the market mechanism than with state intervention because state intervention had been focused on bolstering market forces.

In the second phase, 2004–2008, President Hu Jintao succeeded President Jiang Zemin. The political and economic climate over this period differed from the earlier period. Clearly, there was no imminent crisis that warranted top-down mobilization as part of a nationalist strategy. Furthermore, President Hu had a different set of political priorities from those of his predecessor. Nonetheless, Hu continued the WDP yet reoriented the strategy's central direction to address social issues rather than economic ones. In short, President Jiang's WDP was continued by President Hu but took on different state priorities.

In this period, market reform and globalization that were started earlier now began to bear fruit in the localities. Local economies began to take off. Apparently, the ambiguity inherent in the WDP enabled the strategy to survive both the change of leadership and the change in economic circumstances. Furthermore, the ambiguity allowed markets, not politics, to take the lead in the localities. Therefore, although the political leadership shifted priorities in the WDP, local implementation was continuous and consistent with market circumstances.

The WDP's second phase overlapped with the 11th Five Year Plan (FYP) being publicized in 2004. President Hu Jintao was more interested than his predecessor in poverty and rural issues, and the rhetoric surrounding the WDP reflected these new political priorities.[27] Nevertheless, the policy guidelines made by the SPC and the extent of their implementation in the localities remained largely the same. The announced large projects and their supporting infrastructure projects, including highways, railways, and power plants, were all the same as those of the earlier period. In 2006, Premier Wen Jiabao endorsed 36 projects, costing RMB ¥600 billion, but those were the same projects endorsed by former Premier Zhu Rongji.[28]

Economically, phase 2 policies more strongly reflected efforts to attract FDI from coastal China to the western region, which coincided with coastal China's efforts to upgrade to high-tech manufacturing and high-value exports. Clearly, the central planners envisioned the WDP as being complementary to their national industrial planning. As coastal China was bracing itself for high-tech industries, local governments there provided exceptional incentives to high-tech FDI in order to

[27] State Council, "Guanyu jinyibu xibu dakaifa de ruogan yijian" [Some Opinions on Further Implementing the Western Development Program], State Council Circular #6, 2004; State Council, "Guanyu xibu diqu liangjian gongjian jihua de tongzhi" [Notice on Two Basic Plans in Western China], State Council Circular #20, 2004.

[28] Zhu Rongji, "Zhengfu gongzuo baogao" [Government Work Report], at the Tenth People's Congress, March 5, 2003; Wen Jiabao, "Zhengfu gongzuo baogao" [Government Work Report], Fourth Plenum of the Tenth People's Congress, March 5, 2006.

establish high-tech development zones; low-tech manufacturing and labor-intensive FDI began to be pushed out. Central planners and local governments in western China maintained that the WDP should help improve policies specifically toward FDI in coastal China, revise the guidelines for foreign-invested companies, and attract FDI from coastal China into the region.[29] Despite differences in content, the new WDP planning document, just like its 2000 counterpart, provided directional and nonobligatory provisions that enabled local governments to flexibly interpret and improvise economic programs in their localities. This shift was facilitated by producers that were seeking cheaper sites than the coastal region, and, thanks to the WDP, western China appeared to be a feasible alternative site.

Furthermore, in phase 2, the WDP embraced the mission of helping ethnic politics and border security, human capital, and education, as well as cross-regional collaboration between local governments in the coastal and western regions. Environmental concerns, in particular, were to the fore in the central documents on the WDP. For example, in 2005, the State Council twice made decisions on deforestation and water controls; in 2007, it asked local governments to revert agricultural land to forest.[30] In terms of economic planning, the National Development and Reform Council (NDRC) refrained from espousing liberal policies as the SPC had done in 2000, instead directing local governments in western China to cooperate and coordinate with the coastal region to best use comparative advantage and achieve win–win development. Comparing the 2005 planning with the 2000 WDP report, it becomes clear that market conditions in western China had improved that decentralized cross-regional economic linkages were now possible.

To summarize, from phase 1 to phase 2, the inherent ambiguity in the WDP enabled the central government to reorient its policy preferences and shift its planning goals in accordance with national priorities and prevailing market conditions in the region. The first phase

[29] State Council, *Xibu dakaifa 11 wu guihua* [Western Development Program 11th Five Year Plan].

[30] State Council, "Guanyu weihe liuyu zhili guihua de pifu" [Approval of Wei River clean-up plan], State Council Circular #99, 2005; State Council, "Guanyu jinyibu fangsha zhisha gongzuo de jueding" [Decision on Further Sand prevention and Sand control], State Council Circular #29, 2005; State Council, "Guanyu wanshan tuigeng huanlin zhengce de tongzhi" [Notice on Improving the policy of Returning Agriculture land to Forestry], State Council Circular #6, 2007.

was marked by the imperative to overcome economic recession and conduct SOE reforms. Via the WDP, political mobilization and policy incentives were provided to western China. As the national economy stabilized in phase 2, the central government began to disengage from direct economic intervention. The central budgetary allocation to WDP implementation was spent mostly on education, the environment, and poverty alleviation. Furthermore, the central government decentralized more economic autonomy to western China and urged local governments to facilitate market forces and collaborate with their coastal counterparts.

This market-led trend would have continued were it not for the 2008 global financial crisis. Unlike in 1999, when President Jiang promoted the WDP but provided limited subsidies and transfers to localities in western China, in 2008, the Chinese leadership rolled out a massive stimulus plan (RMB ¥4 trillion, equivalent to US $600 billion). The political rhetoric behind the stimulus plan was not as ambitious; it narrowly framed the allocation as an emergency rescue package for earthquake relief in western China. Furthermore, stimulated by central policy, easy credit from the banking sector swept all China, with local stimulus plans being estimated to reach over RMB ¥9 trillion in a mere two years.[31] The WDP received unprecedented financial injections, and western China experienced rapid infrastructure construction and urbanization dominated by state capital (state banks, state construction companies, and local governments).

In western China, and across the other regions, surging credit – an estimated US $2 trillion in about two years – led to extensive industrial overcapacities, massive debt in the localities and companies, as well as risky overseas projects that caused diplomatic friction. The specters of major economic and political crises hovered menacingly over China.

The WDP's phase 3 revealed intensified decentralization of the Chinese economy. On the one hand, after years of reform and openness, local governments in western China now became active economic agents and, similar to their coastal counterparts in the earlier periods, drove up development initiatives and industrial areas. The easy credit from the stimulus plan enabled this trend. On the other hand, in order to

[31] Barry Naughton, "Understanding the Chinese Stimulus Package," *China Leadership Monitor*, 28, 2009, www.hoover.org/research/understanding-chinese-stimulus-package.

boost domestic demand after the 2008 global recession, central regulators looked favorably upon local development initiatives.[32] For example, responding to Ningxia province's request, the State Council quickly approved an aggressive plan to "actively prepare for industrial relocation from coastal China," which entailed more infrastructure construction and public expenditure in this poor province.[33] Responding to Guangxi province, the State Council readily agreed that the underdeveloped province should seek to integrate with its more developed neighbor province Guangdong by establishing major manufacturing clusters to receive investment from Guangdong itself.[34]

Shifting from its stance against "repetitive industrialization" in phase 1 and from the focus on environmental and social issues in phase 2, the central government used the WDP in phase 3 to mobilize local governments to propose development initiatives. In September 2009, in the State Council's circular "Respond to Global Financial Crisis, Keep Steady Growth in Western Region," Beijing asked provinces, ministries, and other agencies to expedite and enhance implementation of the WDP. With more state funding to be spent under the stimulus plan, the WDP was implemented with aggressive measures such as infrastructure construction, major environmental projects, industrial policy that enhanced manufacturing upgrades, and guiding "capital, technology, skills, [and] management to western regions, setting up experimental zones for industrial transfers and relocation of sunset industries from coastal China, massive social welfare, education, health plans, and incentives for FDI and outbound investment in the western region."[35]

Compared to phases 1 and 2, during phase 3, state intervention related to industries was significant. In 2010, a State Council circular explicitly promoted industrial relocation from coastal to western regions in China.

[32] State Council, "Guanyu zhichi yunnansheng jiakuai jianshe mianxiang xinan kaifang zhongyao qiaotoubao de yijian" [Opinions on Supporting the Expedition of Yunnan Province's Openness to the Southwest], State Council Circular #11, 2011, www.gov.cn/zwgk/2011-11/03/content_1985444.htm.

[33] State Council, "Guanyu jinyibu cujin ningxia jingji shehui fazhan de ruogan yijian" [Opinions on Further Development of Ningxia Province's Economy and Society], State Council Circular #29, 2008, www.gov.cn/zwgk/2008-09/12/content_1094001.htm.

[34] State Council, "Guanyu jinyibu cujin guangxi jingji shehui fazhan de ruogan yijian" [Opinions on Further Development of Guangxi Economy and Society], State Council Circular #42, 2009, http://politics.people.com.cn/GB/1026/10565718.html.

[35] State Council, "Guanyu yingdui guoji jinrong weiji baochi xibu diqu jingji pingwen jiaokuai fazhan de yijian" [Opinions on Maintaining Reasonably High Growth in Western China in Order to Respond to the Global Financial Crisis], State Council Circular #55, 2009.

The document said, "We need to step up transferring of manufacturing from eastern coast to central and western China, where natural resources, and labor are more available," it continued to say that such relocation "not only helps industrialize and urbanize interior China but also helps update economic structure in eastern China."[36] In the circular, the government simultaneously underscored that such industrial relocation should follow market principles and aim for a win–win scenario between the two regions. It applied a wide range of industrial policies, including new incentives for foreign capital, plans to set up economic zones and industrial parks, and programs to train human capital and labor. To incentivize investors, the central government allowed the region to offer tax benefits, provided central budgetary transfers and concessionary loans, and approved new border-free trade zones.[37]

During this period, the border provinces began to effectively propose major projects and justify them on national security grounds. By connecting development with security, their proposals were approved at the level of the national government. For instance, in 2009, the central government approved Guangxi's special economic policy on the grounds that Guangxi province was critical to "defend national security and border stability in Southeastern China."[38] In 2010, the central government approved Gansu province's special status because of its strategic mission "to defend national stability and security."[39] In 2011, in support of Inner Mongolia, the central government argued that the vast border province was China's "defense wall in the North" and the "frontier of opening to Russia and Mongolia."[40] Similarly, Yunnan province, which borders Vietnam, Laos, and Myanmar, received support in WDP documents in which the central government stressed the province's important strategic role in managing ethnic politics and relations with Southeast Asian nations.

[36] State Council, "Guanyu zhongxibu diqu chengjie chanye zhuanyi de zhidao yijian" [The Guiding Opinions on Western China to Receive Industrial Relocation from the Coastal Region], State Council Circular #28, 2010, www.gov.cn/gongbao/content/2010/content_1702211.htm.

[37] Ibid.

[38] State Council, "Guanyu jinyibu cujin guangxi jingji shehui fazhan de ruogan yijian."

[39] State Council, "Guanyu jinyibu zhichi gansu jingji shehui fazhan de ruogan yijian" [Opinions on Further Development of Gansu Economy and Society], State Council Circular #29, 2010.

[40] State Council, "Guanyu jinyibu cujin neimenggu jingji shehui youhao youkuai de ruogan yijian" [Opinions on Developing Inner Mongolia's Economy and Society Better and Faster], State Council Circular #21, 2011.

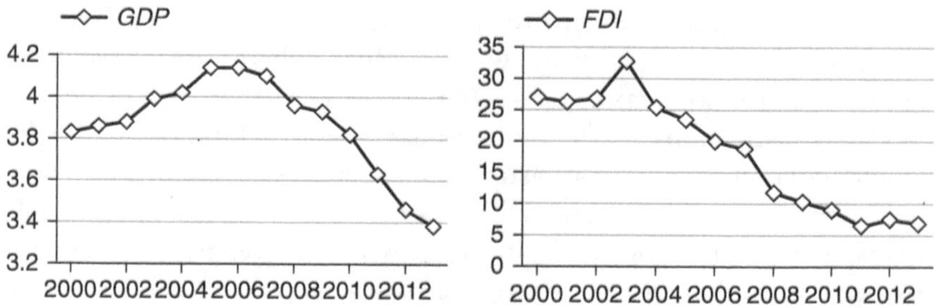

FIGURE 3.2. Closing development gaps between the coastal and western regions. *Source:* Author; based on raw data from National Bureau of Statistics of China, Provincial Statistical Yearbooks database, annual editions, data.statistics.gov.cn.

To all these border provinces, the government allocated special policies for resources extraction and preferential incentives to promote industrialization and globalization in the localities. Yunnan, in particular, benefitted from the WDP and received approval to construct multicity railways, highways, airports, hydropower plants, and dams.[41]

Under the WDP (2000–2012), although growth and globalization in western China were still behind the coastal region, the gaps were indeed reduced. In Figure 3.2, the graphic to the left captures the reduction in GDP between the western and coastal regions; the graphic to the right captures the shrinking gap in FDI inflows between the two regions. The across-regional GDP gap peaked in 2005–2006 and then started to narrow quickly, although in 2013, coastal China's GDP was still more than three times that of western China. The gap between FDI inflow to the coast and western China reached its highest point of thirty-seven times in 2003, after which it sharply declined. In 2011, it had been reduced to a little over six times.

It is important to bear in mind that in this period coastal China was among the fastest growing regions in the world. Growth rates there often exceeded 10 percent annually, so the fact that the gaps between western China and the coastal region continued to narrow was no small achievement. The ability to incorporate previously backward localities into a high-growing capital economy has been critical to China's economic success in recent decades. The following pages will synthesize how a *combination* of state intervention and market forces has achieved this success.

[41] State Council, "Guanyu zhichi yunnansheng jiakuai jianshe mianxiang xinan kaifang zhongyao qiaotoubao de yijian" [Opinions on Supporting the Expedition of Yunnan Province's Openness to the Southwest], State Council Circular #11, 2011, www.gov.cn/zwgk/2011-11/03/content_1985444.htm.

The Tri-block State Revisited

Cross-time archival research on the WDP uncovers active and adaptive states that shaped economic development in western China. The state itself, as shown in Chapter 2, is not unitary but consists of the tri-block system. Nor is it static; different components of the tri-block state took on different importance and interactions at different points of time. The evolving state roles produced important effects in the market, and changed market conditions also impacted state intervention – who are doing intervention and what instruments they use.

During phase 1 (1999–2003), for example, the leadership and central agencies were the main state actors promoting the WDP. President Jiang launched the ambitious and ambiguous strategy; and the central bureaucracy set its agenda and direction. While Jiang's speeches asked western provinces to conduct SOE reforms as a means of achieving western development, the central policy guidelines offered economic freedom and preferential policies to do that. In short, via the WDP strategy, the political leadership and the state bureaucracy – block 1 and block 2 in Figure 2.2 – were in "cohesion."

During phase 2 (2004–2007), after succeeding President Jiang, President Hu reoriented the rhetoric surrounding the WDP to focus on social and rural issues. However, the central bureaucracy more or less continued with the former pro-market agenda. A bifurcation in the central leadership emerged. Furthermore, provincial governments in western China started to play prominent roles, proposed local development initiatives, and built infrastructure to attract FDI. From the perspective of economic growth, the state was still important, but it was the alliance between central bureaucracies and provinces that mattered the most.

During phase 3 (2008–2012), China had different internal and external economics. The massive stimulus plan announced by Hu paradoxically reduced the importance of central state actors. Easy credit bolstered state banks and SOEs that worked with local governments in western China. This alliance in block 3 ratcheted into credit-based infrastructure, resources, and urban transformation in the western region. In short, after 2008, the state and state capital in the tri-block system started to crack; state capital often operated without effective regulation from the central state.

President Xi Jinping came to power in 2012, and the following period was characterized by a new round of fiscal crisis and economic downturn.

Initially, the fate of the WDP seemed uncertain, and many of the region's previously approved projects stalled. Following the downfall of party secretary Bo Xilai, Chongqing in particular saw programs and projects put on hold.[42] President Xi did not terminate the WDP. Rather, by announcing the Silk Road Economic Belt that overlapped with the WDP's geographic coverage inside China, he provided political safety for continuing projects from the previous strategy. Furthermore, the WDP's central agency was put in charge of coordinating implementation of the Belt and Road. With the new leader's BRI, "the WDP suddenly had a breath of new life."[43] In this period, active grassroot states surfaced. Most projects approved in this period were submitted by city governments, which worked with central agencies, state banks, and SOEs in planning various special zones and e-commerce projects.[44]

As examples of local initiatives, in Guizhou, eight cities started the "eight to eight" initiative to pair with eight cities in coastal China. In each pair of western–coastal cities, the western city solicits the coastal city for help in addressing its poverty issues and provides more favorable conditions for investors from this city in return. In Shaanxi province, local governments focused on expanding large industrial zones surrounding the capital city Xi'an, leveraging the city's human resources and industrial base. Like Shaanxi, Sichuan strived to expand its well-established capital city Chengdu in order to create major clusters of industrial zones for high-tech manufacturing and R&D. In Inner Mongolia, the Erlianhaote government submitted proposals for new development zones in order to exploit their border trade and natural resources.[45]

[42] Interview in Chongqing in 2015.

[43] Ibid.

[44] The city-level and functional special zone initiatives were frequent from 2012 to 2015. See, for example, State Council, "Guangxi haiyang gongneng quhua" [Guangxi Oceanic Economics Zones], State Council Circular #166, 2012; State Council, "Guanyu zhichi kashi huoerguosi jingji kaifaqu jianshe de ruogan yijian" [Opinions on Supporting the Construction of Kashgar and Horgos Open Area], State Council Circular #33, 2011; State Council, "Guanyu tongyi sheli guizhou gui'an xinqu de pifu" [Approval to Establish an Integrated Gui'an New Area in Guizhou], State Council Circular #3, 2014; State Council, "Guanyu tongyi sheli shaanxi xixian xinqu de pifu" [Approval to Establish Integrated Xixian New Area in Shaanxi], State Council Circular #2, 2014; State Council, "Guanyu lanzhoushi chengshi zongli guihua de pifu" [Approval to Comprehensively Plan Lanzhou Urbanization in Shaanxi], State Council Circular #109, 2015.

[45] State Council, "Guanyu tongyi sheli neimengu erlianhaote zhongdian kaifa shiyanqu de pifu" [Approval to Establish the Erlianhaote Special Zone as an Important Experiment in Inner Mongolia], State Council Circular #74, 2014.

Cities in Yunnan province also submitted requests for multiple experimental zones to leverage its ties with Southeast Asia.[46]

CRITICAL INFRASTRUCTURE CASES

The policy research above has focused on how state-mobilized globalization took place in the WDP from 1999 to 2012 and how the state interacted with market conditions in western China. To further understand how the WDP transformed the connection between western and coastal China and how market forces actively shaped state capacity, this section presents the three largest infrastructure projects. Infrastructure was a critical component in the WDP. These projects – the Qinghai-Tibet Railway (hereafter the Railway), the West to East National Grid (hereafter the Grid), and the West to East Gas Pipeline (hereafter the Pipeline) – were nationwide and absorbed most of central investment in the WDP strategy.

The analysis of the critical infrastructure is based on archival materials compiled by the government or reported in other sources. In each project, it shows the prior initiatives, how the WDP played *catalytic* roles, how it was implemented, and how it affected the state system. The narrative here entails process tracing and reveals that the WDP served as a catalyst to propel early initiatives into prominent status, that the state and market mechanisms were used extensively in implementation, and that the development outcomes strengthened both state and market in China.

In Table 3.4, the first project studied is the Qinghai-Tibet Railway connecting Qinghai's capital city Xining and Lhasa in Tibet Autonomous Region. The Railway took the Chinese government five years and $5 billion from the central budget to complete.[47] Outside China, the scheme was typically viewed as Beijing's penetration into an ethnic minority region, causing considerable damage to indigenous culture and ecology.[48] In China, however, it was popularly touted as "the iron dragon on the world's rooftop." Leaving the controversies

[46] The local initiatives are from Xu Shaoshi (ed.), *Guojia xibu kaifa baogao* [National Western Regional Development Report 2015]. Hangzhou: Zhejiang University Press, 2015.

[47] Anonymous, "China's Railway Marvel Heightens Tibetan Fears," *Sydney Morning Herald*, October 1, 2005, p. 17.

[48] See Zhu and Blachford, "Economic Expansion, Marketization, and Their Social Impact on China's Ethnic Minorities in Xinjiang and Tibet."

TABLE 3.4. *Critical infrastructures in the WDP*

Qinghai to Tibet Railway

Prior advocacy:
- 1982 Ministry of Railways (MOR) report to Deng; 1994 Tibet government appeal to Jiang; yet, finance and technology were not ready

WDP as a catalyst:
- MOR, China Construction Consulting Company, Tibet government; SPC. Justification: to showcase WDP; expand internal demand; stabilize border and ethnic politics

Implementation mechanism:
- State coordination: State Council, SPC, small leading group with functional agencies
- Market mobilization: new corporations, new technology, international publicity

Outcomes:
- Nationalist morale, technology breakthroughs, new SOEs, integration of Tibet

West to East National Grid

Prior advocacy:
- 1988 Ministry of Energy and National Energy Investment Company; 1991 China Southern Electricity Corporation; Guangdong, Guangxi, Yunnan, Guizhou Across-Provinces Electricity Sharing Conference

WDP as catalyst:
- Develop the western region by investing in resource exploration, supplying coastal electricity shortage, overcoming provincial fragmentation

Implementation mechanisms:
- Central–local politics: mobilization of western provinces and reining in of coastal provinces
- Market reform: separation of electricity production and transportation, adoption of market pricing, breakup of local fiefdom
- State capital: new power plant construction in the west; new SOEs; two national grid companies, five producers, and four auxiliary companies

Outcomes:
- Cheaper supply to the coast, growth in western energy suppliers; new energy-based industrial cities in western China, integrated electricity market

West to East Gas Pipeline

Prior advocacy:
- 1993 Jiang's energy planning; 1995 China National Petroleum Corporation (CNPC) and China National Offshore Oil Corporation (CNOOC) pipeline proposals; 1998 Zhou Yongkang proposal

WDP as a catalyst:
- SPC and CNPC elevated it into the WDP's flagship program

Implementation mechanism:
- Small leading group to coordinate governments, market expansion for gas use, foreign companies, marketization in the sector

Outcomes:
- New pipelines, new SOEs, profitable state capital, external extension to neighboring Asia

Source: Author, based on archival analysis.

aside, the Railway project had persistent support from powerful actors in the central government for some time prior to the initiation of the WDP.

The Railway into the Tibetan Plateau was first proposed by the Ministry of Railways (MOR) to Deng Xiaoping in 1982. Deng rejected the MOR proposal for fear of lacking the appropriate technology and other resources. The MOR, however, working with provinces near Tibet, continuously studied various possibilities for railway routes into Tibet. The Tibetan government, striving to achieve economic development, was also eager to have rail access to the rest of China. In 1994, the Tibetan government submitted a request to President Jiang, who agreed to give the project serious consideration once again. In the ensuing years, however, Jiang focused on other issues and tabled the proposal.

With the WDP's launch in 1999, MOR and the SPC seized the opportunity to push for the railway project. They sent multiple teams to the localities to review the feasibility of a Tibetan railway. During the 2000 National Party Congress convened in Beijing, Tibetan party secretary Yin Fatang made a strong appeal to President Jiang for railway access between Tibet and the rest of China. Within days, the MOR submitted to Jiang three detailed proposals for a Tibetan railway. Jiang then phoned WDP office director Zeng Peiyan to inquire about the MOR proposals. Zeng gave his support and explained, "While it was not ready for China to construct a Tibetan railway in 1982, the country now has enough technology and resources to take on this project."[49] Zeng further commented that among the three MOR proposals, "The Qinghai-Tibet Railway was the shortest, least expensive, and easiest to construct." Referring to Jiang's main concern at the time, Zeng argued that due to the AFC, China badly needed to expand internal demand and expedite western development. "We need big projects like the Railway," remarked Zeng.[50]

Following this, Jiang provided a three-page directive on the railway project to MOR, arguing that a Tibetan railway was important to China's politics, security, and economic development, and that it would help combat separatist movements in Tibet and enhance China's border

[49] Zeng, *Xibu dakaifa juece huigu*, pp. 218–219.
[50] Ibid.

security. With Jiang's strong endorsement, construction of the Railway began in earnest, with the SPC, MOR, and China International Project Consulting Company leading the process. Foreign companies with more advanced technologies were also brought in. The Canadian aerospace and rail company Bombardier, for example, was contracted to build special pressurized carriages.[51]

In early 2001, the Railway Small Leading Group was established, with WDP director Zeng Peiyan serving as group leader. Expecting low rates of return, the central government shouldered all of the Railway's costs. Of this funding, 75 percent came through national loans and 25 percent from the railway construction fund. In terms of outcomes, the Railway did not make an immediate profit, but it did boost nationalist morale, improve China's railway technology, establish links with international companies, and help the Chinese railways industry in general. Put simply, it strengthened industry and state capital in China.

As can be seen in Table 3.4, the West to East National Grid was the second major project, and it sought to transmit surplus power in western China to energy-scarce eastern provinces. This project eventually became the most expensive in the WDP, extending from 2001 to 2010 with a price tag of RMB ¥520 billion (around US $65 billion). Structural imbalances between resource concentration in China's interior and energy consumption in the coastal region have long existed and became even more severe during the rapid industrialization in coastal China in the 1980s and 1990s. The central government had few countermeasures, as the power sector was deeply fragmented. Different provinces used different types of electricity and transportation systems; every province preferred to use electricity generated by local companies.

In 1988, the new Ministry of Energy (MOE) was established and sought to integrate the power sector and construct new power plants in resource-rich western China. There were many power-generating plants in western China in the 1990s, but these could not overcome cross-provincial fragmentation. In 1991, the MOE managed to rally the southern provinces of Guizhou, Yunnan, Guangxi, and Guangdong to start the first interprovincial conference on transmitting electricity from the three western provinces to Guangdong. After the conference, MOE and the four provinces established a joint SOE, China Southern Electricity Company.

[51] Anonymous, "China's Railway Marvel Heightens Tibetan Fears."

By 1993, a project transmitting electricity from Guizhou to Guangzhou and the Southern Electricity Grid was in operation.[52] These early efforts enabled conditions for the initiation of a nationwide electricity grid under the WDP.

The central–local dynamic was clear in late 1999, when Guangdong suffered an unprecedented power shortage and proposed the establishment of several coal plants in the province. Concerned about transporting raw materials over a long distance and environmental pressures from coal plants, the central government was reluctant to approve Guangdong's proposal. As the West-East National Grid was elevated as a project under the WDP in June 2000, the central government ultimately rejected Guangdong's request. In order to address Guangdong's power shortage, Premier Zhu and the MOE pledged to expedite construction of the national grid. Planning for the project took place quickly among the SPC, MOE, energy companies, and local provinces. Similarly, in August 2001, when the coastal city Shenzhen proposed the establishment of a new power plant, Premier Zhu Rongji dictated, "Guizhou (in western China) can establish a power plant as its WDP project and send electricity to Shenzhen. Shenzhen can use this as a way to help Guizhou's development."[53] In short, the WDP enhanced central power over local interests in coastal China and, in the meantime, helped the central state mobilize western provinces to participate in development.

After freezing Guangdong's new power plant proposals, the central government asked power-generating western provinces to do their best in producing and transporting electricity to satisfy the need in Guangdong. In late 2000, WDP director Zeng Peiyan spoke at a mobilization conference in Yunnan:

> This year, Guangdong had energy shortages, and its Tenth FYP proposed new coal and nuclear power plants. Yet the central government has decided to invest energy production in the western region, as a means to implement the WDP and asked Guangdong not to construct power plants. Guangdong is not happy and believes that its tax revenues are being spent in other provinces.... Your province must not miss this opportunity. You must prioritize hydropower projects. We [at the SPC] will speed up the approval. I hope you do not miss the opportunity and will work with Guangdong.[54]

52 Zhou Xiaoqian, "Xidian dongsong, quanguo daju" [Western Electricity to the East Is a National Necessity], *zhongguo nengyuan bao* [China Energy Newspaper], November 6, 2016.

53 Zeng, *Xibu dakaifa juece huigu*, p. 263.

54 Zeng Peiyan's speech during his visit to Yunnan, September 6–10, 2000, quoted in Zhou, "Xidian dongsong quanguo daju."

In short, the power sector in China was deeply fragmented prior to the WDP, and energy resources and wages were highly uneven throughout the country. Drawing on an autocratic strategy, central agencies were able to rein in resistance in the sector and integrate the electricity sector under its wing.

In the third project, as seen in Table 3.4, the West to East Gas Pipeline connected the abundant gas reserves in Xinjiang with consumer markets in coastal China, covering the entire nation from west to east and requiring complex and onerous coordination across multiple agencies and provinces.[55] Anticipating that consumption of natural gas would increase rapidly in China in the near future, the central leadership conceived of this pipeline primarily as a commercial project in the 1990s. At this time, the market was not yet ready. The state, being one step ahead, sought to create a demand for gas. In 1993, at the Central Finance Small Leading Group meeting, President Jiang urged that China's natural gas policy should serve eastern China and at the same time help develop western China. In 1995, the Ninth FYP elaborated on Jiang's guideline and expedited the Natural Gas Exploration Planning committee, which concluded that China's natural gas reserves were concentrated in western China while the demand would be mainly in the eastern region. Sending western gas to the eastern region was therefore imperative and carried with it large market potential. The planning for the West to East Gas Pipeline was thus started in 1996 and involved key petroleum groups in Beijing.

In August 1998, when PetroChina's party boss Zhou Yongkang became the Minister of Land and Resources, he immediately submitted a proposal to the leadership to construct pipelines that would bring Xinjiang's natural gas to consumers in the richest coastal provinces of Jiangsu, Zhejiang, Shanghai, and Guangdong. With launch of the WDP, the SPC revisited PetroChina's plan for pipelines transmitting western gas to eastern China. As the political leadership was looking for major infrastructure projects that could be bracketed as WDP flagships, the SPC approved and elevated PetroChina's gas pipeline proposal and named it the West to East Gas Pipeline.[56]

[55] Huang Yanhua, "Xiqi dongshu guihua xijie" [Details on the West Gas to East Planning], *Nanfang nengyuan guancha* [Observation of Southern Energy], January 7, 2015, http://finance.sina.com.cn/chanjing/cyxw/20150107/080521241852.shtml.

[56] Li Yubao, *Qiguan changhong: xiqi dongshu gongcheng jianshe jishi* [Daring Act: The Real Record of the West to East Pipeline]. Beijing: Petroleum Industry Publisher, 2005.

Natural gas had the potential to achieve significant market value, yet a pipeline across China entailed multiagency coordination and cross-provincial support, which would be unthinkable for a commercial project. According to vice energy minister Zhang Guobao, many provinces had been resistant to the project from the beginning. The coastal provinces, for example, as main consumer markets, had planned to establish, manage, and profit from their own intraprovincial gas systems, with which they could import natural gas by sea. Under the WDP, the central government convinced party heads in Shanghai and Jiangsu to bring their provinces in line. However, Zhejiang province, one of the largest consumer markets, continued to reject this central pressure and opted to retain its own intraprovincial gas system. Zhejiang accepted the Pipeline only at its provincial border. Furthermore, most provinces involved with the Pipeline were just transit provinces and neither supplied nor consumed what the Pipeline carried. Nevertheless, they had to shoulder the burden of land appropriation and population relocation, earning Zhang's praise for their "political devotion" in playing their part in WDP implementation.[57] In short, while the Petroleum Group planned the Pipeline, the WDP gave them the political clout to overcome local and agency opposition.

As a commercial project, the Pipeline involved foreign capital and international technology from the beginning. The stakeholders – the energy ministry and major petroleum SOEs – had pledged to follow market principles.[58] This was perhaps because gas as a power source was new in China, and therefore few had vested interests in protecting the sector, intraindustry variations notwithstanding. In 2000, the SPC and PetroChina held a news conference to invite the participation of foreign companies. They also published an invitation to bid on the Pipeline in *Renmin ribao* (the overseas edition). Some 90 international companies showed interest, of which 19 submitted official bids. In May 2001, Exxon Mobile, Hong Kong–based Sinopower, Royal Dutch's Shell, British Petroleum (BP), and the Russian Natural Gas Company were selected as joint venture (JV) partners.[59] After four years of negotiations, however, no conclusive agreements were reached on revenue sharing. In 2004, the JV partners agreed to terminate their cooperation. Shell eventually participated in downstream operations with PetroChina;

57 Huang, "Xiqi dongshu guihua xijie."

58 For an introduction the stakeholders in China's energy game, see Erica Downs, "The Chinese Energy Security Debate," *The China Quarterly*, 177, 2004, pp. 21–41.

59 For details on the deals, see Wang Yichao, "Tianranqi shidai kaiju" [The Natural Gas Era Opens], *Caijing*, No. 10, 2002, pp. 76–83.

in 2007, the collaboration finally took off. BP later invested in natural gas–related business and formed a joint venture with China National Gas Company. Russian Natural Gas and Exxon Mobile did not join in joint ventures but did transfer technology to China.[60]

In summarizing these major and controversial WDP projects, empirical findings are three-fold. First, all these projects had strong agency support that was proposed and practiced prior to the WDP. The WDP, as a politically ambitious strategy, elevated these projects and enabled them to overcome cross-agency divisions and local resistance. Second, while politically motivated, the projects' execution had strived to follow economic calculations. Considerable incentive-based persuasion, rather than political fiat as normally expected, was used as a mobilizing strategy. Whenever possible, foreign capital and international technology were highly sought after. Third, the short-term economic gains were unclear, as each of the projects lasted for decades. The long-term impact on the national economy, however, was profound. Beijing managed to bring the two largest and most complicated border provinces, Tibet and Xinjiang, into the center's fold, mobilizing western provinces and reigning in powerful coastal provinces. Infrastructure industries and some of the largest SOEs were born during these three projects: railway, power, and oil and gas industries and their state companies later became major players outside China.

CONCLUSION

China's reform and globalization have been remarkably successful; they were also uneven across economic regions and create challenges for the ruling Communist Party. In the late 1990s, such challenges reached their climax. On top of deeply divided regional economies, the country experienced the Asian financial crisis that severely reduced exports and incoming FDI; upon joining the WTO, the task of reforming state-owned enterprises in western China was extremely urgent and extremely difficult. It was in this context that the political leadership launched the ambitious and ambiguous WDP, hoping to use one strategy to solve myriads of policy problems and still help revive the high-growth economy.

This chapter analyzes national policy documents and countrywide infrastructure projects to pin down state-mobilized globalization in China's WDP from 1999 to 2012. It confirms, first, that the Chinese state is deeply fragmented in central bureaucracies, between central and local

[60] Zeng, *Xibu dakaifa juece huigu*, pp. 298–300.

governments, and across local governments in different regions. The most important value of the WDP was thus to coordinate diverse interests and make cohesive growth-stimulating policy possible. For example, industrial planning for western China and the cross-region infrastructure projects had existed before the WDP and yet could not gain cross-agency and cross-province agreements. With the WDP, such national coordination became feasible. Second, state intervention during the WDP was pro-market. Concrete policies included measures of market liberalization and preferential incentives to foreign investments; in the execution of major infrastructure projects, market calculation was widely observed; and foreign companies were constantly sought after as partners in the WDP projects.

More important, analysis of the WDP reveals that SMG is not just about enhancing the market, but also transforming the state itself. On the one hand, as shown in the phases of WDP implementation, the economic capacity of the state has kept moving down from the central government to provincial governments, and further to city governments. On the other hand, through the WDP, major state capital pertaining to power, resources, and railways was revitalized and expanded. The marriage of state capital and local governments has arguably weakened the central state's capacity to oversee development programs in China, both in the western region and elsewhere. As argued at the beginning of this book, deep globalization and decentralization, coupled with economic recessions, create a vacuum for autocratic intervention, although the actual effect on the ground is likely to be weak.

From a policy perspective, the WDP has been undoubtedly important to industrialization in western China, thereby making the Chinese high-growth economy more sustainable and expansive. Indeed, the ongoing Belt and Road Initiative is both an effort to replicate the WDP internally, by mobilizing local governments to reinvigorate economic growth, and an effort to *extend* the WDP overseas, by coordinating Chinese capital to achieve important commercial interests. Can the WDP's success portend BRI's success in the future, particularly outside China? The answer is uncertain and perhaps unlikely, because the WDP's domestic success was hinged upon the Chinese system of globalization, in which top-down mobilization was matched with proactive localized interpretation and implementation. Outside China, this system is not available.

Top-down mobilization, rooted in Chinese politics, is likely to face major opposition abroad. Localized implementation, on the other hand, is also difficult to emerge outside China. The mismatch between the Chinese system of globalization and external institutional contexts is clearly shown in the next chapter on China going global.

4

The Political Economy of China's Outbound Investment

> Now that we have joined the World Trade Organization, our struggles [douzheng, 斗争] will become more difficult.... We must remain clear-headed about this and recognize its true nature, so that we can be prepared, achieve our strategic objectives and promote our economic development.
>
> —President Jiang Zemin[1]

The Chinese leadership announced the China Goes Global strategy (CGG) in 2000, an announcement followed by extensive publicity and mobilization campaigns inside the country. At the time, however, foreign observers were preoccupied with China's pending admission to the World Trade Organization (WTO) and paid little attention to the CGG. It was only in the mid-2000s, when Chinese outbound investment rapidly increased, did the strategy begin to generate interest, debate, and serious discussion abroad. Scholarly research on China's outbound investment has since adopted three approaches: the economic statecraft framework that underscores the Chinese government using economic means to achieve diplomatic goals;[2] the state capitalism model that focuses on powerful SOEs shaping the country's foreign policy for their

[1] Jiang Zemin ([2002] 2013, 436, 437), Speaking to provincial and ministerial leaders of the Chinese Communist Party.

[2] Scott Kastner, *Political Conflict and Economic Interdependence across the Taiwan Strait and Beyond*. Stanford, CA: Stanford University Press, 2009; William Norris, *Chinese Economic Statecraft: Commercial Actors, Grand Strategy, and State Control*. Ithaca, NY: Cornell University Press, 2016.

own commercial interests;[3] and finally, a world development approach that asks whether Chinese outgoing capital helps or hinders industrialization in underdeveloped regions.[4]

Building on past studies, this chapter adopts a new focus on internal political dynamics that have shaped the CGG and China's outbound behavior. Indeed, while Chinese outbound investment has traces of effects in line with economic statecraft, state capitalism, and world development, respectively, the main driver, dynamics, and outcomes are internal to the country, with external expansion as a secondary trajectory. In this internal dynamic, by mobilizing subnational actors to conduct *de facto* liberalization and helping commercial actors revive growth inside the country, the CGG here is similar to the WDP and BRI. However, because of its deep roots in state capital and extensive involvement of political mobilization, the CGG has faced Persistent suspicion and resistance abroad. Unless China's outbound behaviors fundamentally change under the BRI, its capital globalization [*ziben quanqiuhua*] is likely to face tremendous constraints in the foreseeable future.[5]

THE DISCURSIVE ENVIRONMENT

China's reform and openness were economically successful; they were politically contested, however. Dissatisfaction and discontent were prevalent in the late 1990s, just as the country was stepping up efforts to engage globalization more deeply. President Jiang Zemin personally argued that the imbalance between inbound and outbound FDI was not beneficial to China. Facing competition from foreign producers, lost-out SOEs and laid-off workers were unhappy; they complained about the influx of foreign goods in China.[6] At the time of China's WTO negotiation and accession, there were many writings in China that blamed globalization

[3] Erica Downs, "The Dragon Steps Out: What Became of China, Inc.?" www.brookings.edu/wp-content/uploads/2016/06/china-inc-erica-downs.pdf, accessed on March 20, 2019.

[4] Deborah Brautigam, *The Dragon's Gift: The Real Story of China in Africa*. New York: Oxford University Press, 2009; Kevin Gallagher, *The China Triangle: Latin America's China Boom and the Fate of Washington Consensus*. New York: Oxford University Press, 2016.

[5] David Shambaugh, *China Goes Global: The Partial Power*. New York: Oxford University Press, 2013.

[6] For an analysis of Chinese debates on FDI, see Ye, *Diasporas and Foreign Direct Investment in China and India*, pp. 111–112.

and argued that globalization exemplified, privileged, and expanded political–economic values from the advanced capitalist societies.[7] Hence, the argument went, China's political autonomy and economic interests were likely to be challenged by deepening globalization.

There were pro-globalization technocrats. But against such contentious politics of globalization, the supporters stepped carefully. In 1999, near the end of negotiations with the United States on China's accession into the WTO, Trade Minister Long Yongtu gave a lengthy interview with leading economics journal *Caijing*. He carefully argued that globalization had benefits and costs and that China's purposes in joining the WTO were to extract economic gains from globalization and to increase China's political influence in the world.[8] A year later, Long, in an interview with the same magazine, commented carefully on the WTO's potential impact in China; "The day after China's WTO membership will be a calm day," Long observed, "yet in retrospect of a year, two years, five years, and ten years, China will show profound transformation."[9] In the interview, Long highlighted the long-term gains from engagement in globalization while downplaying the short-term gains of WTO membership.

Long's careful remarks reflected both contentious politics and economic troubles in China at the time. At the turn of the century, China experienced industrial overcapacities, sluggish exports, and slow FDI inflows.[10] The gravest concerns were the large-scale unemployment and potential social instability during the economic downturn.[11] It was in this anxious climate that the Chinese leadership launched the CGG and framed this policy – not the WTO membership – as being "critical to China's long-term development and future destiny."[12]

[7] For Chinese debates on the WTO, see Lin Qiping, "Zhongguo rushi hou de 'sange bu zhenglun' he 'sange guanjian'" [On Three No Debates and Three Keys after China's Entry into the WTO], *Guoji maoyi wenti* [Issues in International Trade], No. 12, 2002, pp. 1–4.

[8] Interviews with the *Caijing* magazine after the 1999 WTO Ministerial Meeting in Seattle, published in Anonymous, "Long yongtu shentan rushi" [Minister Long Deep Talk on China's WTO Entry], *Caijing*, No. 12, 1999.

[9] Ibid.

[10] Lardy, "China and the Asian Contagion."

[11] Such worries were clear in Zhu Rongji, "Shiying xinqingkuang xinrenwu, nuli ba liyong waizi gongzuo tigaodao xinshuiping" [To Adapt to the New Circumstances, To Improve the Level of Promotion to FDI], *15da yilai zhongyao wenxian xuanbian* [Important Documents since the 15th Party Congress], 2001, http://cpc.people.com.cn/GB/64184/64186/66690/4494593.html.

[12] See the Tenth Five Year Plan passed at the 5th Plenum of the 15th National Party Congress, October 2000.

Chinese discourse at the time viewed WTO membership – binding China to open more sectors for global competition – with considerable apprehension; by contrast, the CGG was framed as "an independent and proactive globalization strategy."[13] Local governments and Chinese companies in particular viewed the CGG as a promise of political support and assurance of government assistance with their participation in global competition.

Whereas Chinese subnational and commercial actors were mobilized to conduct the CGG as an adaptation to challenges from globalization, foreign observers paid little attention to the strategy until the mid-2000s. Then they focused on asking whether Chinese outbound capital challenged US strategic interests and whether Chinese behaviors amounted to a new model in the world.[14] The views were split. Washington-based scholar David Shambaugh argued that China's outbound capital did not amount to a model for others to emulate and that a common denominator of Chinese outbound investment was the country's mercantilist interests.[15] Boston-based scholar Edward Steinfeld countered and argued that China had been "playing our game"; consequently, the rise of China would not threaten the West.[16]

Other specialists investigated China's outbound behavior and focused on policy dynamics and/or interest group coalitions. Among them, security specialist Scott Kastner formulated the theory of economic statecraft and examined how China's growing economic power had facilitated its foreign policy agenda.[17] Following a similar logic, William Norris – another security specialist – investigated whether economic instruments served Chinese foreign strategic goals and what domestic conditions had made "economic statecraft" more or less effective.[18] Furthermore, in an edited volume, Joshua Eisenman and Eric Heginbotham comprehensively examined the strategic interests, tactics, and effectiveness of China's

[13] Yu, *Globalization and Changes in China's Governance*, p. 28.

[14] Harry Harding, Ian Bremmer, Thomas Stewart, et al., "China Goes Global: Implications for the United States," *National Interest*, September/October 2006, https://nationalinterest.org/article/the-gramercy-round-china-goes-global-implications-for-the-united-states-1046.

[15] Shambaugh, *China Goes Global.*

[16] Edward Steinfeld, *Playing Our Game: Why China's Economic Rise Doesn't Threaten the West.* New York: Oxford University Press, 2010.

[17] Kastner, *Political Conflict and Economic Interdependence across the Taiwan Strait and Beyond*; Scott Kastner, "Buying Influence? Assessing the Political Effects of China's International Trade," *Journal of Conflict Resolution*, 60(6), 2016, pp. 980–1007.

[18] Norris, *Chinese Economic Statecraft.*

outbound investment and infrastructure in the developing world.[19] It is fair to say that economic statecraft has become the dominant approach among Western scholars to study China's outgoing investment.

Focusing on late industrialization, development specialist Deborah Brautigam examined patterns of Chinese engagement in Africa, focusing on the aid programs and infrastructure projects and refuting the popular charge of China as "a new colonial power."[20] Brautigam's China-Africa Research Institute at School of Advanced International Studies of John Hopkins University (SAIS) has produced many empirical studies of Chinese investment in Africa, which can be quite useful to scholars who follow this industrialization and development approach. Similarly, with regard to China's activities in Latin America (LA), Kevin Gallagher had initially been concerned about the "crowding out" of manufacturing in LA by Chinese imports.[21] Gallagher's later publication, using the concept of the "China triangle," studied China's development finance in the region and yielded more positive findings on the "China Boom" in LA.[22]

The third approach to China's outbound behavior focuses on the Chinese economic system. Erica Downs, for example, following the state capitalism literature, evaluated domestic stakeholders and debates among Chinese industries and underscored that the "fragmented" decision making had driven China's energy policies abroad.[23] Bo Kong and Kevin Gallagher in turn examined the connections between Chinese policy banks (the main financiers for China's outbound investment) and SOEs (China's main external investors) and how these two sets of actors shaped China's external energy acquisitions.[24] Still, contradictory phenomena are on display as to how Chinese domestic economy shapes its external behavior. Extant empirical research is too limited to make a cogent story that applies to China overall. Furthermore, granted that domestic capitalism has a strong impact on China's foreign policy, the causal channels and directions of influence have not been established in the past works.[25]

19 Joshua Eisenman and Eric Heginbotham (eds.), *China Steps Out: Beijing's Major Power Engagement with the Developing World*. New York: Routledge, 2018.

20 Brautigam, *The Dragon's Gift*.

21 Kevin Gallagher, *Dragon in the Room: China and the Future of Latin American Industrialization*. Stanford, CA: Stanford University Press, 2007.

22 Gallagher, *The China Triangle*.

23 Downs, "The Chinese Energy Security Debate."

24 Bo Kong and Kevin Gallagher, "Globalizing Chinese Energy Finance: The Role of Policy Banks," *Journal of Contemporary China*, 26(108), 2017, pp. 834–851.

25 Business cases are abundant showing that globalization was more a corporate initiative. See Wang Huiyao, *China Goes Global: How China's Overseas Investment Is Transforming Its Business Enterprises*. New York: Palgrave Macmillan, 2016.

To summarize, China's internal debates and politics surrounding globalization were central to the passage of the CGG at the turn of the century. Yet foreign observers' analysis of the CGG came only after China's outbound capital caught their attention. Speaking to different audiences and interests, foreign observers produced quite different evaluations of China's outbound investment and the CGG policy. While development scholars provided more positive writings on China's outward investment, security specialists and political economists were generally quite concerned about China's external expansion and the way it was dominated by state capital.

These diverse assessments of China's outbound investment have some validity; empirical investigation in this chapter confirms some of their concerns. The focus here, however, is China's internal political dynamic and how it has shaped the country's adaptation to globalization pressure. As a whole, the research sheds important light on how Chinese state and market interact and are mutually transformed during the globalization process.

PROCESS TRACING

Globalization and Its Discontent

The People's Republic of China (PRC) was a successful case of economic globalization, attracting FDI that helped the country's industrialization and market reform after 1979. The success, however, was based on the government providing preferential policies to foreign investors that were not available to domestic firms, generating charges against the Chinese state of "selling China."[26]

At the corporate level, incoming FDI mounted challenges and pressures on domestic market in the 1990s. SOEs had suffered long losses and were on the verge of massive bankruptcy. Infant private entrepreneurs also saw their market shares being encroached upon by more competitive foreign products. As China was preparing for more opening after WTO membership, anxiety over foreign capital was profound, and the need to reform the state sector was particularly acute.

Facing intense competition and pressure to self-reform, policy communities in Beijing were fraught with concerns about China's place in globalization. People associated with SOEs, central agencies, and

[26] Yasheng Huang, *Selling China: Foreign Direct Investment during the Reform Era*. New York: Cambridge University Press, 2002.

research institutions were particularly critical of the status quo globalization. They argued that China's openness to FDI – originally justified as "using market in exchange for technology" [*yi shichang huan jishu*] – had failed because Chinese markets were yielded but indigenous technology did not catch up with advanced industrial countries in key sectors. This failing was clear in the near wipeout of indigenous brands and companies in China and the growing dominance of foreign brands and products in the Chinese market, ranging from automobiles to household detergent.[27]

The critics were also dissatisfied with the structure of manufacturing and exports in China, in which global production had placed China at the bottom of the value chain, supplying cheap labor and resources to serve foreign-invested firms in China. To them, globalization forced China "to accept [this unwelcome] division of labor" [*bei fenggong*]. In the Chinese media, two products galvanized particularly strong discontent with the global trade structure. The first was the now defunct video cassette recorder (VCR), which foreign companies had assembled in China and exported around the world. A typical VCR would cost about $90 in US retail, yet the import price for a VCR in China was only $20. Of this amount, Chinese workers earned just a small fraction, with the rest going to materials, transportation, and technology licensing fees. Another widely cited product was the American Barbie doll, made at foreign-invested firms in China and then exported. A typical Barbie cost $10 in US retail; at customs, a doll imported from China was priced at $2, of which Chinese workers earned only $0.35.[28] Confronted with such a structure of production and trade, it was common for Chinese critics to argue that inbound FDI had *entrapped* China at the low end of global production chains and to advocate for measures to restrict preferential policies to foreign capital.[29]

In spite of the above populist arguments and movements, however, the reformist leadership, as shown in remarks by President Jiang Zemin, Premier Zhu Rongji, Minister Long Yongtu, and many others, shared a general consensus that the tide of globalization could not be reversed. Instead of caving in to antiglobalization discourses, or ignoring the

[27] Ye, *Diasporas and Foreign Direct Investment*, pp. 110–116.

[28] The case is cited in Yao Wang, "Zhongguo 'zouchuqu' zhanlue huanjing yanjiu" [The Study of Strategic Environment of China Goes Global Based on SWOT-PEST Modeling], *Jingji luntan* [Economics Forum], 22, 2006, pp. 54–57.

[29] Zhang Yansheng, "Cong yinjinlai dao zouchuqu de kuayue," *Liaowang* [The Outlook], August 22, 2012, pp. 35–37.

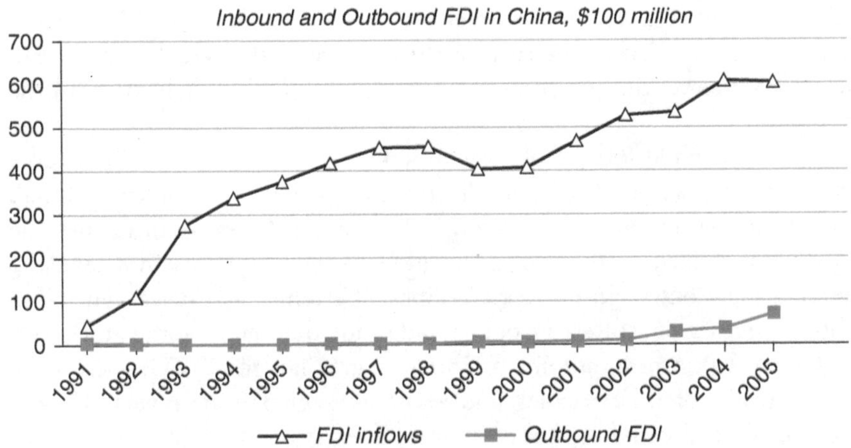

FIGURE 4.1. China's large gaps between inbound and outbound FDI. *Source:* Inbound FDI data from National Bureau of Statistics of China, *China Statistical Yearbook*, annual editions, available www.stat.gov.cn; outbound FDI from Ministry of Commerce (MOFCOM), *Outbound Direct Investment Statistical Bulletin*, 2004, plus online statistics for 2004 and 2005, available www.mofcom.gov.cn.

critics, the leadership channeled antiglobalization discourses toward more active, proactive, and better globalization. The above mentioned "failings" on inbound FDI and exports became grounds for China to pursue better globalization that would enhance national interests, not to pull back from the trend of globalization. In this tug of war, the CGG was launched, through which the government sought to mobilize SOEs and local governments to *deepen* globalization, with the "promise" of political support from the top leadership.

Statistics show that China's outbound and inbound investment flows were highly uneven. In Figure 4.1, for example, outbound investment from China is much smaller than inbound FDI. From 1991 to 1998, inbound FDI rose from $3.4 to $45.5 billion. Outbound investment, by contrast, was almost negligible. Given that foreign brands had dominated the Chinese consumer market and rendered China in the low-value-added export structure, the enormous gaps in inbound and outbound FDI became justifications for launching the CGG to correct the lopsided investment structure.

Furthermore, during the 1990s, China began to feel the squeeze in terms of natural resources and was becoming a major importer of raw materials and energy. Beijing increasingly viewed that the pressure on

Chinese resources and environment had reached unsustainable levels.[30] The economic crisis at the turn of the century further enhanced the call for state intervention in domestic development and globalization in the country.

In short, while foreign observers highlight the CGG's ambition for a global power contest and/or implications for world development, China's own thinking on – and motivation for – going global were different. The CGG was rooted in the process of globalization and was motivated by extensive discontent in domestic politics. Prevailing industries and indigenous interests had suffered from a rapid influx of foreign capital and goods in China. Upon negotiation for China's entry into the WTO, there were widespread economic troubles, and resistance to globalization was strong in Beijing. To deal with both the economic necessity of and political resistance to globalization, the CGG was launched to mobilize SOEs and subnational governments to make changes that would facilitate globalization, both inbound and outbound. At this critical juncture, the political leadership was critical to China's successful adaptation to globalization. The CGG's implementation then shows that subnational and commercial actors inside China played important roles in reinforcing market mechanisms in the country.

The Political Leadership

President Jiang was the first Communist leader in China who did not have revolutionary war experience. In 1989, as a retiring career bureaucrat, Jiang was helicoptered from Shanghai to become the general secretary of the ruling party, a compromise choice by elderly leaders following the June 1989 Tiananmen Square crisis. Jiang turned out to demonstrate more staying power than many anticipated. Building power in the shadows of two elder political giants, Deng Xiaoping and Chen Yun, Jiang had been careful not to reveal his true policy preferences. He consolidated power in 1995 and formally stepped down in 2004, with informal power lasting until 2012. While President Jiang was often called a transactional leader, less powerful than "transformative leaders" such as Deng Xiaoping and Mao Zedong,[31] it was under Jiang that globalization in China greatly deepened and that state institutions and bureaucracies as we know them today were constructed. In Chapter 3,

[30] Yao, *The Study of China Goes Global Strategy.*

[31] David Lampton, *Following the Leaders: Ruling China, from Deng Xiaoping to Xi Jinping.* Berkley: University of California Press, 2014.

we saw how Jiang played an important part in launching the WDP; in the case of the CGG, Jiang's influence was even greater. Indeed, the CGG and its related outbound globalization ideas most strongly represented Jiang's policy visions.

In the early 1990s, in the aftermath of the Tiananmen crackdown, Jiang repeatedly made speeches that advocated for continual globalization and for Chinese companies going global. At the 14th National Party Congress in 1992, Jiang argued, "[China] should actively expand outbound investment and overseas operations."[32] In 1993, facing pressure from US and European economies that imposed economic sanctions against China, Jiang urged diversification of international markets beyond these advanced capitalist countries and espoused the notion that China should "fully utilize international and domestic markets and resources."[33] He continued, "as long as we firmly grasp economic development, [our] economy keeps growing, and our nation keeps strengthening, we can handle any challenges in the world."[34] During a period in which the Tiananmen crisis presented severe political uncertainties inside China, as well as challenges in diplomatic relations between China and the West, Jiang's consistent messages on globalization and economic development were reassuring to commercial actors in the country.

In the mid-1990s, when China's diplomatic predicament was alleviated, grave economic problems surfaced: Industrial overcapacity was rising, nonperforming loans at the state banks accumulated, SOE losses became apparent, and the task of SOE reforms loomed large.[35] Against this backdrop, Jiang concentrated his economic policy on mobilizing Chinese SOEs to go global and find alternative financing and markets. In July 1996, after his return from Africa, he went to Tangshan in Hebei province, where SOEs had dominated the local economy and the issue of SOE reform was extremely pressing. There, Jiang explained how SOEs should be restructured to go global and utilize international markets and other foreign resources. He further explained that countries in Africa and Latin America could provide markets for Chinese goods and investments.[36]

[32] Jiang Zemin, *Jiang Zemin Selected Works*, Volume 1. Beijing: People's Publisher, 2006, pp. 230–231.
[33] Ibid., p. 312.
[34] Ibid.
[35] Lardy, "China and the Asian Contagion."
[36] Chen Yangyong, "Jiang zemin zouchuqu zhanlue de xincheng jiqi zhongyao yiyi" [Jiang Zemin's "Go Out" Strategy's Formation and Its Significance], *Party Archives*, No. 1, 2009, www.wxyjs.org.cn/wxzj_1/dbzb/201305/t20130531_140005.htm.

The CGG was launched in a set of speeches by the political leader. In the late 1990s, as the AFC erupted, Jiang pushed hard for the CGG. He remarked at the 15th National Party Congress work meeting in January 1997, "In order to better utilize internal and international markets and the two kinds of resources, [we] need to actively participate in regional and global multilateral regimes and encourage outbound investment that reflects our comparative advantages."[37] In the same year, at the National Foreign Investment Work Conference, Jiang said, "We not only [should] attract foreign companies to set up factories in China but also actively guide and organize competitive Chinese companies to go global, establish factories abroad, and utilize external markets and resources. Attracting inward investment and going global are two closely connected and mutually reinforcing aspects of China's openness policy. One cannot go without the other."[38]

Continuing in May 1998, in order to withstand regional and global financial crises, Jiang urged, "[We] need to further study and expedite [the] 'going global' strategy. In Africa, Middle East, Central Asia, South America, where market potential and resources are significant, [we] need [to] organize a group of state-owned companies to invest in and establish factories."[39]

As China was preparing to enter the WTO and pressures from an influx of foreign capital rose rapidly, Jiang elevated the CGG as a national strategy [*guoce*] in 2000 and argued that it would be "critical to China's overall development and future destiny."[40] He promulgated the strategy to all members of the National Party Congress (NPC). In drafting the 10th Five Year Plan (FYP) in 2001, Jiang ensured that the FYP included the CGG strategy and asked the state agencies involved with finance, insurance, foreign exchange, taxation, human talent, law, information, and customs to support companies making outward investments. However, Jiang's pledges and commands were framed in rather nebulous terms and allowed different state agencies to reinterpret the CGG. Agencies such as MOFCOM and SAFE signaled new provisions to support the CGG.[41] Other agencies did not follow through.

[37] Jiang, *Jiang Zemin Selected Works*, Volume 1, p. 613.
[38] Jiang, *Jiang Zemin Selected Works*, Volume 2, p. 92.
[39] Ibid., p. 105.
[40] Ibid., p. 569.
[41] Anonymous, "Shishi zouchuqu zhanlue cujian chengxiao" [Early Effects of Implementing the China Goes Global Strategy], *Liaowang* [The Outlook], No. 19, May 6, 2002, p. 12.

In addition to national bureaucracies, Jiang mobilized local governments to embrace and implement the CGG as well. Meeting a Shanghai delegation in early 2000, he emphasized that "in order [for China] to win international competition, China must implement [the] 'going global' strategy right away."[42] Speaking to business and government representatives in Guangdong province in 2000, he warned that America and other advanced economies had stepped up control over their resources via economic and political means and insisted that Chinese companies should do the same. Addressing all provincial leaders at the CCP Party School in late 2001, Jiang spoke:

> With our economic development, we must expedite the implementation of [the] China goes global strategy. Like the western development program, [the strategy] relates to our national modernization in the future. Going global and attracting inward investment are two aspects of our openness policy. One cannot be without the other. It is different from 20 years ago. We are ready to go global. Once we join the World Trade Organization, there will be more opportunities to go global. Our companies need to go on the international stage to test their ability.[43]

Jiang's rhetoric on the CGG embodied nationalist ambition, as in the cases of the WDP and BRI. On separate occasions, for example, Jiang repeated that "global competition in the new century is about competition among large companies in different countries." Unfortunately, at this stage, there were almost no Chinese multinational companies operating at a global scale. In the long term, Jiang said, "we have to participate in international competition and create a set of globally competitive firms and MNCs." Large MNCs, in Jiang's words, are "economic aircraft carriers" that would help China withstand competition through deep globalization. "We should, after joining WTO, seize all opportunities, via overseas factories and technology competition, start developing a set of Chinese MNCs. This is our urgent need for further openness, to improve global competitiveness, withstand challenges and pressures from globalization, and truly become a strong economic nation."[44]

Jiang's speeches on the CGG and occasions on which he made those speeches indicate that the leadership had launched the strategy to mobilize commercial and subnational actors to address economic problems associated with globalization. While the strategy targeted specific

[42] See Jiang's Speech to Shanghai's delegation, reported in *Renmin ribao*, March 8, 2000.

[43] Jiang, *Jiang Zemin Selected Works*, Volume 3, pp. 456–457.

[44] Ibid., p. 453.

economic problems, such as industrial overcapacity, SOE losses, and declining exports, the mobilization campaign of the CGG primarily employed nationalist rhetoric to rally diverse state actors – local governments, companies, and externally oriented technocrats. The rhetoric was also ambiguous and enabled different actors to interpret the CGG differently. For example, the liberal technocrats were able to carry out *de facto* liberalization in the localities, but the more conservative bureaucracies managed to prevent change in overall control over outward FDI. Only when the domestic economy changed considerably during the second phase (2004–2008) were the controls moderately loosened.

To be specific, while the political leadership was promoting the CGG campaign, bureaucracies remained divided. There was a liberal wing, led by MOFCOM and SAFE, whose resources and power had grown during globalization in the 1990s. There was also a conservative wing of industries and sectors, which were more traditional and saw their influence decline during the same period. In the early 2000s, during the author's field research at different agencies in Beijing, it was striking how externally oriented agencies were obsessed with attracting FDI, while domestic-industry agencies displayed heartfelt concerns about indigenous industry and technology. Both sets of bureaucrats were patriotic and deeply convinced that their visions and policy ideas were in the best interests of the country.

In such a divided state, a cohesive policy platform for the nation state would be extremely difficult to devise. Against such ideological and institutional divisions, the CGG, *ambitiously* supporting Chinese companies to go global and *ambiguously* allowing different actors to pursue their own projects and programs, provided a "cohesive" platform for political mobilization, thus easing economic and political divisions.

The CGG did not resolve state fragmentation, however. Even when different factions rallied behind the CGG, actors had implemented the strategy in very different ways. They were versatile in utilizing the nationalist strategy to facilitate their own policy agendas. Internally, the CGG strengthened Chinese companies' and local governments' programs that helped domestic development. Externally, however, problems were abundant. The CGG, nominally to expand China's economic footprint abroad, had only mixed records overseas. In the advanced capitalist markets, the CGG encountered suspicion and resistance; in the less developed countries, it faced charges of exploitation, neocolonialism, and environmental and social damage in the receiving nations. Political mobilization and ambitious rhetoric, so central to the domestic success of the CGG, turned out to be rather vulnerable outside China.

Fragmented Implementation

A popular Chinese proverb goes, "Eight immortals cross the sea, each with a unique supernatural power" [*baxian guohai, gexian shentong*], which describes how different individuals and agencies rely on their own skills to achieve their goals. Ambitious and ambiguous strategies launched by the political leadership are good occasions to observe the "skills" and "goals" of different actors and groups in China. The CGG was launched to all actors inside China; different groups interpreted and improvised the strategy to facilitate their own agendas. For example, local governments in the coastal region managed to convince the central agency (SAFE) to designate selected cities as experiment sites for freer use of foreign exchange. Drawing on the CGG, private companies in the coastal region benefited and experienced a freer environment for investing abroad. SOEs (the main target of the CGG) experienced self-restructuring to streamline their operations.

This section analyzes the documents from different state agencies to tease out how they have devised fragmented and complex policy changes regarding China's outbound investment in the context of CGG. There are three patterns: First, pertaining to the general regulation of outbound capital, the formal policy change came quite late and lagged behind actual economic conditions. Second, despite the lack of formal "liberalization," liberal-leaning state agencies implemented agency-specific and sector-specific loosening in fragmented fashions. Finally, economic planners, the State Council overall and the NDRC in particular, rallied multiple agencies to use outbound investment to facilitate domestic industrial priorities.

To elaborate, in the first pattern, as shown in Table 4.1, the CGG's launch resulted in little to limited change in the general framework governing Chinese capital going global. For example, from 2000 to 2004, the national guidelines on outbound FDI continued to be two provisions – the 1989 SAFE regulation and the 1991 SPC decision – both of which sought to control and *restrict* outbound investment. Only in 2004 and 2005, when the Chinese economy greatly stabilized and the capital account was in significant surplus, was a new round of outbound FDI policy being made: The first was the temporary regulation passed by NDRC in 2004, and the other was a new procedure passed by MOFCOM in 2005.

Furthermore, the text of the NDRC document shows that the agency sought to *regulate* outbound FDI because it clearly emphasized domestic development priorities, without mentioning the commercial interests

TABLE 4.1. *Comprehensive regulation of outbound investment*

1989, SAFE: Restriction
"Regulating Foreign Exchange in Overseas Investment": To ensure balance of account. Includes multistep review, prior business agreement, foreign exchange deposit, mandatory repatriation.

1991, SPC: Restriction
"Opinion on Enhancing the Management of Overseas Investment Projects": To control and limit outbound projects. Includes outbound investment needs to serve Chinese market and prioritizes South–South cooperation, spells out multistep approval and extra regulation over state assets in outbound projects.

2004, NDRC: Regulation
"Temporary Regulation on Overseas Investment Projects": To regulate and reign in overseas investment projects. Includes power and approval procedure for investments, concentration in NDRC and provincial branches, foreign investment to serve domestic strategic and industrial needs.

2005, MOFCOM: Liberalization
"Procedures on Overseas Investment and Cooperation": To enhance overseas investment by spelling out conditions for overseas investment reviews; avoid dual tax.

2012, Multiple agencies: Regulation
"Guideline on Enhancing Chinese Comparative Advantages through International Cooperation and Competition": To enhance China's position in international cooperation and competitive advantage with measures such as upgrading industries, gaining more control over foreign trade, developing services trade, attracting foreign capital and talent, expediting China goes global.

Notes: First, "restriction" refers to the state's intention, as indicated in the documentary content, to limit outbound capital. Second, "regulation" refers to the deduced intention to channel outbound capital to serve priorities in the national industry. Finally, "liberalization" is concluded because the state agency (MOFCOM) provides supporting rules for outbound Chinese investors.

Source: For the complete Chinese documents, see the sources in Appendix III.

of companies. By contrast, the MOFCOM document laid out procedures on overseas investment and cooperation and *facilitated* outbound investors, thus leading to liberalization categorization. The MOFCOM document also set up provisions for companies to avoid dual tax collection on their outbound investment.

The 2004 NDRC and 2005 MOFCOM regulations continued until 2012, when multiple agencies, led by NDRC, passed comprehensive guidelines on international cooperation and competition. This guideline suggests that the national government aimed to adopt a cohesive policy to rein in disparate outbound behaviors by Chinese companies.

The 2012 guidelines were signed by NDRC, MOFCOM, Ministry of Foreign Affairs (MFA), Ministry of Science and Technology (MOST), Ministry of Industry and Information Technology (MIIT), Ministry of Finance (MOF), People's Bank of China (PBOC), and the Customs Bureau. While stressing the need to expedite China going global, the text included a wide range of industrial policies such as upgrading manufacturing, gaining more control over trade, developing services trade, and attracting more advanced foreign and human capital to help Chinese industrial upgrades.[45] Comparing the policy frameworks from 2000 to 2012, the liberalization trend grew in a *nonlinear* fashion: Limited liberalization was provided by MOFCOM in 2005, but it was re-regulated through multiagency guidelines in 2012.

In the second pattern, which pertains to agency-specific provisions, liberalization was evident and, in many aspects, helped investors overcome restrictive national regulations. This phenomenon suggests that the Chinese state was further fragmented during globalization, as effective regulation of commercial interests has become extremely difficult. As can be seen in Table 4.2, in 1999, for example, the liberal-leaning agencies MOFTEC (MOFCOM's predecessor) and MOF disregarded the 1989 SAFE rule and the 1991 SPC restriction and jointly passed "measures to encourage overseas assembly manufacturing projects using foreign aid." They spelled out corporate business reviews, conditions for China Ex-Im Bank (CEIB) lending and approval procedures. The case-by-case liberalization by MOFTEC and MOF was not alone; SAFE and SASAC had both participated in *de facto* liberalization of outbound investment.

Fragmented liberalization took place primarily by externally oriented agencies. In Table 4.2, MOF, rapidly accumulating capital surplus, worked with trade, commerce, and foreign affairs, as well as SASAC and other bodies, to pass case-by-case funds and support measures. These included a 2001 temporary measure to manage a risk insurance fund for overseas contractual projects, a 2002 measure to approve a SME overseas exploration fund, 2003 SAFE foreign exchange experimental reform, a 2004 notice to finance the early cost in resources of companies' overseas project, a 2005 opinion to ensure personnel safety at

[45] For tech-industrial policy, see Ling Chen and Barry Naughton, "An Institutionalized Policy-Making Mechanism: China's Return to Techno-Industrial Policy," *Research Policy*, 45(10), 2016, pp. 2138–2152.

TABLE 4.2. *Fragmentation that facilitates outbound investment*

1999, MOFTEC and MOF, "Measures to Encourage Overseas Assembly Manufacturing Projects Using Foreign Aid": MOFTEC and Ex-Im Bank lending
2001, MOF and MOFTEC, "Temporary Measures to Manage the Overseas Contractual Projects Risk Insurance Fund": To provide overseas project insurance fund with central budget
2002, MOFTEC and MOF, "Measures on Regulating the small- and medium-sized enterprises (SME) Overseas Exploration Fund": To set up international market exploration fund for SMEs with central budget and supplementary local budget
2003, SAFE, "Further Reform Foreign Exchange Regulation in Overseas Investment": To set up local experimental sites for foreign exchange use under US $3 million
2004, MOF and MOFCOM, "Notice on Financing the Early Cost in Resources Companies' Overseas Projects": To provide the budget to cover preinvestment costs
2005, MOFCOM, MFA, and SASAC, "Opinion on Ensuring Personnel Safety in Overseas Investing Companies and Institutions": To protect Chinese personnel abroad and promote the CGG
2007, Bureau of Stocks and Bonds, "Measures on Authorizing Eligible Domestic Institutions to Invest in Overseas Bonds": To authorize overseas investment in bonds and stocks
2009, MOFCOM, "Measures to Service Overseas Investment": Commitment to speedy review and to provide risks assessment of overseas investment
2011, SASAC, "Temporary Measures to Monitor and Manage Central SOEs' Overseas State Assets": To protect state assets, establish overseas state asset monitoring system, ensure accountability and value of state assets, serve industrial planning, control budget and expenses of SOEs abroad
2012, SASAC, "Temporary Measures to Monitor and Regulate Central SOEs' Overseas Investment": To limit central SOEs' overseas expansion to core corporate strategies, national industrial planning, asset safety and returns

Note: Shaded rows indicate restriction and regulation of overseas investment. Liberalization, in fact, has been nonlinear in China in the past decade.
Source: For complete Chinese documents, see Appendix III.

overseas companies, a 2007 authorization to invest in overseas bonds, and a 2009 measure to service overseas investment.

In short, during the period 2000–2010, the CGG, which was intended to mobilize cohesive adaptation to globalization, helped different agencies interpret the policy differently and enabled local governments and private capital to go around restrictive policies in pursuing their economic interests. Flexible *self-interpretation* and *reinterpretation* of the CGG thus allowed policy change to occur rapidly in specific sectors in keeping with new sectoral realities, without abolishing restrictive regulations in general.

Going in the other direction, fragmented reinterpretation also helped regulators change course easily without having to change the earlier regulations. In 2011, for example, as the state sector incurred financial losses, the SASAC passed measures to limit SOEs' outbound investment; in 2012, the SASAC passed another guideline that mandated SOEs' outbound investment only to serve "core corporate strategy, national industrial policy, and safety and return of assets." Such flexible "layering" of contradictory policies makes the Chinese regulatory system cumbersome and perplexing to outsiders.

Finally, just as functional agencies took advantage of the CGG to pursue sector-specific support for outgoing capital, economic planners in the State Council also used the CGG to pass measures and promoted their preferred industrial policies. As seen in Table 4.3, in 2001, as the central planners decided that the priority for Chinese domestic development was to promote exports of electronics and machinery, thus upgrading the structure of manufacturing and exports in China, the SPC (reorganized as the NDRC in 2003) rallied all functional bureaucracies to expand electronics exports by encouraging overseas investment in research and development as well as other supporting provisions. The wording of the policy was framed in the spirit of China going global, leveraging the nationalist strategy. In the coastal localities, CGG implementation to the construction of various economic and development zones that focused on electronics processing and exports.

In the same spirit of facilitating the CGG, in 2006, the NDRC rallied multiple agencies to pass a notice to expedite the export of electronics and machinery in particular by helping *indigenous brands and indigenous companies*. Synthesized in Table 4.3, the policy explicitly encouraged financing for Chinese companies to upgrade technology and conduct overseas mergers & acquisitions (M&A). Then, in 2012, the NDRC led the multiagency effort to urge Chinese companies to participate in global cooperation and competition that would enhance China's position in the global system. As services were deemed the new priority in industrial planning, the State Council approved the motion to promote the services outsourcing industry in China by developing new technology, connecting the CGG with the BRI, as well as enhancing economic integration within China.

TABLE 4.3. *The CGG as industrial policy*

2001, Multiple agencies, "Opinion on Promoting Electronics and Machinery Exports during the 10th FYP": To expand electronics exports by encouraging overseas investment in R&D, encouraging overseas manufacturing and assembly, encouraging foreign aid programs to facilitate exports, encouraging localization and sales investment, providing export insurance, simplifying exporting companies' international travel regulations, deregulating exporting industries.

2006, Multiple agencies, "Notice on Expediting Electronics and Machinery Exports during the 11th FYP": To expand electronics exports and increase indigenous brands by helping develop indigenous electronics brands' exports, guiding electronics companies in mergers, consolidations, and overseas expansion, encouraging overseas R&D investment; expanding exports in newly emerging markets, using foreign aid programs to enhance exports, helping SMEs.

2012, Multiple agencies, "Guidelines on Enhancing Chinese Comparative Advantages through International Cooperation and Competition": To enhance China's position in international cooperation and competitive advantage by strengthening industrial upgrades, gaining more control over foreign trade, developing services trade, attracting more advanced foreign capital and talent, expediting China goes global.

2014, The State Council, "Opinion on Promoting Services Outsourcing": To promote China's services abroad by developing software, medical, insurance, energy, etc.; One Belt and One Road; optimize domestic regions; combine the CGG with loans and overseas lending to promote overseas services; establish services outsourcing experimental cities.

Note: Industrial policy refers to state measures to shape economic performance and directions. Here, multiple agencies in the State Council were typically led by the SPC prior to 2003 and by the NDRC hereafter.
Source: For complete Chinese documents, see Appendix III.

It needs to be clearly stated that the Chinese industrial policy encapsulated in the CGG documents is *not obligatory but directional.* All the above-mentioned measures were about encouraging, supporting, and helping certain industries; they did not provide concrete and mandatory financial support for Chinese companies. Other than mentioning the combination of the CGG and loans and overseas lending, as well as establishing services outsourcing experimental sites, the 2014 State Council's views on promoting services outsourcing, for example, made no reference to concrete measures or support mechanisms. Even in terms of loans and experimental cities, there were no detailed guidelines or information. Such directional but nonobligatory industrial policy is consistent with what we find in the policy framework on the WDP, which enabled subnational and commercial actors to improvise their own projects that conformed to market calculations.

In summary, the policy fragmentation and evolution from 2000 to 2014 demonstrate how ambitious and ambiguous strategies announced in the background of major crises proved to have a lasting impact. The CGG, with its autocratic mobilization, allowed commercial actors to more freely interpret the strategy to facilitate their market-based behavior. It also allowed the national government *not* to enact actual liberalization, for fear of capital flight and losing control too quickly. And that was not all. The CGG allowed other functional bureaucracies to pass their own provisions to support sector-specific actors as they drew on state subsidies and facilitation. When economic conditions changed, the agencies could freely pass different and more restrictive policies to reign in their sectoral actors without going through major reshuffling of the national policy environment. Even the regulators and economic planners could tie their industrial policy more effectively with the CGG's mobilization. With central agencies going different directions and an autocratic program that could be self-interpreted, commercial and local governments could exploit markets freely and effectively.

There were clear costs to this model, however, because it ultimately enabled interests and industries to continuously fragment the state system, with national regulators having to play catch-up. Furthermore, fragmentation, not liberalization, has created uneven playing fields in China, for companies with government connections and those without. Because of the importance of government connections, both private and state companies in China have intensified their dependence on the state. The experiences of local governments and different companies (see Chapters 6 and 7) demonstrate such structural vulnerability in this state-mobilized globalization.

POLICY OUTCOMES

General Trends

The statistical trend in China's outbound and inbound FDI flows supports several observations that are in line with the state-mobilized globalization framework. First, state mobilization of investment *follows*, not precedes, changes in the market condition. This was the case in the WDP; it was the case in the CGG. Second, state mobilization has a faster development effect within the domestic arena than outside. This was clear in the WDP; it was clear in the CGG, too. The CGG suggests, in particular, although the nationalist strategy claimed to promote external expansion domestic development was the primary driver and the pace of implementations was largely determined by market forces.

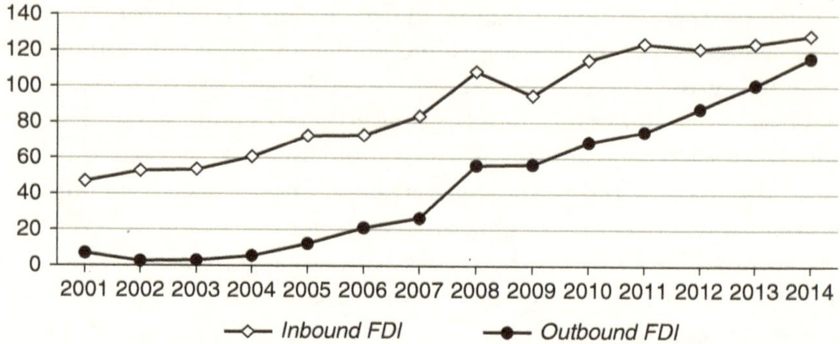

FIGURE 4.2. China's capital flows under CGG, unit = US $ billions. *Source:* Author, based on raw data from China Ministry of Commerce, *Direct Outbound Investment Statistical Bulletin*, various annual editions, available at: www.fdi.gov.cn.

Figure 4.2 presents the statistical indicators of inbound and outbound investment following the strategy's launch. In the first period (2001–2003), outbound FDI actually decreased. Only when domestic market conditions changed significantly, with increasing capital reserves and demands for the import of raw materials, did outbound FDI start to grow visibly in the mid-2000s. Furthermore, because much of the *de facto* liberalization took place in the localities to attract inbound FDI, the CGG strategy contributed to the rapid rise in FDI inflows in China. Starting in 2008, due to the massive stimulus plan, China's outbound capital increased rapidly, and the gaps between inbound and outbound FDI narrowed. As a whole, the statistical pattern in China's outbound investment is in line with the market conditions and priorities in Chinese economy.

To elaborate, in the early 2000s, the Chinese economy was in distress, with the SOEs in particular experiencing major losses. Thus, despite the launch of the CGG that sought to mobilize SOEs to go global, outbound FDI did not rise. Internally, the CGG sparked local liberalization and attracted more FDI into China. The CGG hence helped the revival of Chinese economy and in turn contributed to considerable capital surplus in the country. Driven to find better returns for the surplus capital, the Chinese state then made clear policy to precipitate outbound investment.

For example, in 2004, China's foreign exchange reserve reached $189 billion, 80 percent of which was in dollar assets. Concerned about dollar depreciation, the MOF and SAFE were eager to diversify these dollar assets to different forms. Furthermore, rapid industrialization in China led to a surge in infrastructure construction and demand for resources, resulting in rapid increases in global commodity prices. In Beijing, strong arguments emerged among central bureaucrats for "using resources to replace dollars" [Yi Ziyuan huan meiYuan].[46] In other words, the increase in and patterns of China's outbound investment in the mid-2000s were in line with major changes in Chinese domestic market and industry.

The policy shift was also engineered by leading financial regulators in banks and foreign exchange.[47] New moves by SAFE, PBOC, and MOF at that critical juncture incentivized other agencies and SOEs to more actively explore overseas opportunities. In 2005, Hu Xiaolian, who had a long experience in PBOC and SAFE, became the new head of SAFE. She immediately made it clear that SAFE would "continue to diversify foreign exchange investment areas ... and to align foreign exchange use with the [CGG] national strategy, to ensure safety and increase returns on foreign exchange reserves."[48] In April 2006, the PBOC document #5 passed three new measures, which, Hu explained, were not due to RMB appreciation pressure, but a key step in the long-term plan for reforming the exchange regime.[49]

In the same year, SAFE published new rules that had a threefold impact: authorizing eligible Chinese institutions and investors to purchase foreign exchange to invest abroad, allowing eligible fund management companies to rally Chinese institutional and individual foreign exchange to invest abroad, and permitting eligible insurance institutions to hold and self-manage earnings from overseas investment.[50] Furthermore, as the state commercial banks also had abundant capital resources, they welcomed and financed Chinese investors in investing and expanding outward.

In this period, because the MOF and SAFE had been key drivers behind Chinese capital going global, and because state banks had been

[46] Xu Sitao, "Shentan waihui chubei touzi zhanlue" [Be Careful with Strategic Investment of Foreign Exchange], *Caijing*, No. 3, 2006.

[47] Anonymous, "Woguo jue waihui chubei ruhe yong" [How to Use the Massive Foreign Exchange Reserve in China], January 2016, 2006, http://news.QQ.com, accessed on November 22, 2018.

[48] Hu Xiaolian speech, quoted in Anonymous, "Woguo jue waihui chubei ruhe yong."

[49] Anonymous, "Interview of SAFE Director Hu Xiaolian," *Caijing*, No. 9, 2006.

[50] Anonymous, "Zhongguo qian chuhai" [Chinese Money Goes Global], *Caijing*, No. 9, 2006.

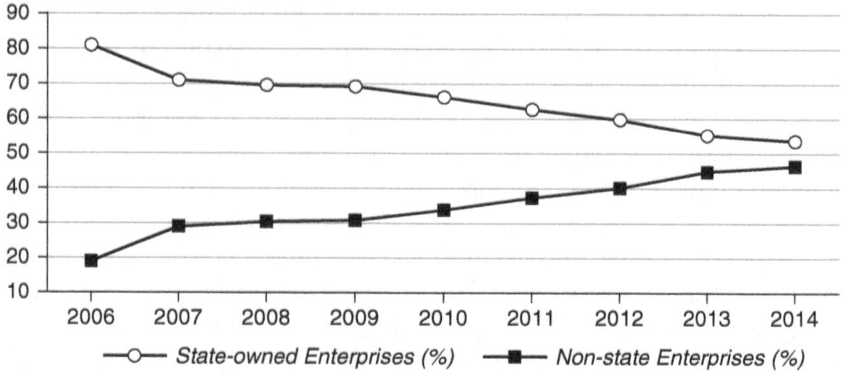

FIGURE 4.3. State dominance in China's outbound FDI. *Source:* Author, based on raw data from MOFCOM, *China Outbound Direct Investment Statistical Bulletin*, 2006–2016 annual editions, available at: www.fdi.gov.cn.

the main financiers for China's outbound investment, China's outbound FDI was dominated by state capital, that is, state-owned companies and state-affiliated institutions. Comparing the shares between state and nonstate outbound investment from China, Figure 4.3 shows that in 2006, state capital accounted for 81 percent of China's total outbound investment. Nonstate capital rose rapidly; in 2010, SOEs still accounted for 66 percent of total outbound FDI from China. In recent years, as SOEs experienced significant financial distress as economic recession hit China, the SOEs' shares have declined, with private investors' shares increasing. However, because of state dominance in major companies and banks, the SOEs' central role in China's outbound investment is likely to continue into the foreseeable future.

State roles in China's outbound capital, both in terms of statistical trends and political mobilization, has given rise to suspicion about and resistance to China's outbound investment abroad. On the one hand, foreign observers tend to observe that China's outbound investment primarily serves the state's political purposes, which is the economic statecraft perspective. On the other hand, domestic observers are deeply concerned about "state capture" by SOEs, in which state serves the commercial interests of companies.[51] Both perspectives – economic statecraft and state capture – are quite logical in their own right and have cases to support them, both in China and elsewhere. However, they have failed to account for the fragmentation between the state and state capital in

[51] Anonymous, "Zhongguo haiwai binggou bixiuke" [The Must Take Lesson of China's Overseas Acquisition], *Caijing*, No. 9, 2012.

China's outbound investment. Indeed, outside China, the fragmentation has undermined both the state's political agendas and state capital's commercial interests. It is this pattern that the case studies here focus on.

Failed Outward Investment Cases

The cases examined here are high-profile overseas acquisitions by Chinese SOEs. They have been compiled from the Chinese economics magazine *Caijing* from 1996 to 2012; in each case, I analyze the relative roles of the state and market mechanisms. First, the materials demonstrate that despite state ownership and the privileged political status of SOEs, the companies' main mandate in going global was to ensure returns on their investment.[52] Their decisions on whether to invest were determined by whether such investments made commercial sense and whether they were indeed feasible. In short, the cases here do not support economic statecraft as an overriding explanation.

Second, the cases do not support a consistent pattern of "state capture." The national bureaucracies were clumsy in regulating SOEs' overseas acquisition and were mistrustful of SOEs' profit motivation. Instead of state capture, overseas acquisition by SOEs was subject to fragmented and often contradictory regulatory hurdles. The cases help demonstrate how the CGG did *not* work smoothly abroad while domestic mobilization had proceeded expeditiously.

In 2006, China Mobile – a national SOE that has monopoly over China's cellular services – tendered $5.6 billion for the acquisition of Luxemburg telecom operator Milicom, the largest acquisition deal in China at the time. After months of waiting and speculating, China Mobile walked away from the deal at the last minute, causing a sharp decline in Milicom's stock performance. China Mobile's action caused uproar in advanced capitalist markets. The suspicion was that the Chinese state had interfered in the deal. The real story was not that simple. Nor was political motivation the driver. First, China Mobile, as a state company, was under a mixture of mandates in going global, to "target at newly emerging market, expand overseas business, and make *profit*."[53] The Milicom deal was China Mobile's largest move ever in

[52] Arthur Kroeber, *The Chinese Economy: What Everyone Needs to Know*. New York: Oxford University Press, 2016.

[53] Anonymous, "Zhongguo yidong, fangqi de yiyi" [China Mobile: Significance of Giving Up], *Caijing*, No. 15, 2006.

terms of outbound investment. Because of the large price tag and concerns about the safety of state assets, China Mobile's management team had to wrestle with some complicated issues.

In an investigative report in *Caijing*, the China Mobile–Milicom deal was presented as having been full of miscommunication and management conflict between a Chinese state company and a Western private one. It turns out that the much-discussed $5.6 billion price tag was not China Mobile's offer but rather the asking price from Milicom. However, instead of clarifying this issue, China Mobile was independently conducting a lengthy and extensive evaluation of Milicom's multicountry business, thereby leaving market observers to conclude that the $5.6 billion price had been agreed upon. In the meantime, China Mobile hired China International Capital Corporation (CICC), Merrill Lynch, and KPMG Accounting to conduct financial and accounting research on the deal and eventually determined that the price was too high. Instead of going back to renegotiate the deal with Milicom, China Mobile's CEO decided to walk away altogether.

In any event, the site evaluation carried out by China Mobile suggests that the company was not ready to take on a multicountry telecom business. Milicom's business covered 16 developing countries in Africa, Asia, and Latin America. Five of these countries had no diplomatic relations with China, which presented huge headaches for China Mobile's on-site evaluation. The evaluation teams reported discomfort and obstacles in managing a business in countries where China had no normal ties. Irrespective of what kind of business opportunities Milicom did present, China Mobile's management decided that pursuing their interest was ultimately not worthwhile.

Furthermore, inside China, China Mobile shared a monopoly with another state carrier, and domestic business was growing rapidly. To China Mobile's leadership, the efforts spent overseas were not as efficient as those in the domestic market. The company's decision to withdraw from the Milicom deal was supported by the market. When the acquisition was aborted, China Mobile's stock price went up quickly, while Milicom's stocks plummeted. To the watching global investment professionals, China Mobile's behavior in making a last-minute decision without alerting and preparing the market and the management team of Milicom was unprofessional and unethical.[54]

[54] Ibid.

The China Mobile case revealed key obstacles in China's outbound investment rooted in the institutional environment of Chinese SOEs. First, corporate leaders operate under the mandate of commercial interests but also act as politicians that care deeply about the political risk of outbound projects. Second, the domestic market monopoly that the companies enjoy at home makes going global less attractive to SOE managers. And finally, in order to secure state assets, the regulatory process is more rigid and lengthy. In the China Mobile–Milicom deal, China Mobile's own management teams had to complete all site evaluations before it could submit the deal for approval at the SASAC. In the next case, a business deal that made significant commercial sense and indeed had already secured financing had to be aborted because of regulatory disapproval.

In 2004, China Minmetals – a national SOE operating in resources and raw materials – tendered a proposal to acquire Canadian Noranda. At the time, this was seen as a great business move: China had been the world's largest consumer of iron ore in the early 2000s, yet it did not have any relationship with upper-stream suppliers, making the industry dependent on global suppliers. Then, in early 2004, the opportunity to acquire Noranda arose. China Minmetals tendered a bid of $4.5 billion, even though its net assets at the time were only $4 billion and the company had no experience with overseas acquisitions.[55] In fact, China Minmetals' offer was not even the highest, but it was an all-cash offer and the company agreed to retain Noranda's managerial team. When Noranda accepted the offer, the deal had to gain approval at NDRC, in addition to the State Council, MOFCOM, SAFE, SASAC, and MFA.

The NDRC approval was a key step in the process. Despite the fact that Minmetal had secured financial backing from CEIB and CDB, the NDRC did not approve the deal; as a consequence, the banks could not clear the financing arrangement in time. Ultimately, China Minmetal had to walk away from Noranda's acquisition. Within a year, Xstrata acquired Noranda for $19.2 billion! The lost profit opportunity was obviously huge. This case demonstrates that while the financial group in the central government had stepped up support for SOEs' overseas investment in approximately 2004, the formal regulatory environment did not change much. As a super ministry with a priority on domestic economic development, the NDRC was generally risk averse regarding outbound investment and prioritized domestic investments over external

[55] Anonymous, "Chongkao haiwai tankuanglu" [Retake the Test of Finding Overseas Ore], *Caijing*, No. 24, 2007.

expansion. SOEs, reliant on government financing, were subject to stringent regulatory oversight, as evidenced in the multistep, multiagency approvals.

In summary, Chinese SOEs, having better access to credit and monopolistic power over the energy and raw materials sectors, had led China's growth in outbound FDI since 2005. Nevertheless, state companies are nominally the holders of government assets; SOE managers are also politicians who are risk averse when it comes to exploring new markets abroad. These institutional limitations make it difficult for SOEs to compete globally, as we have seen in the above cases. Over time, the emergence of private investors has gradually eroded the SOEs' advantage, with the relative shares in China's outbound FDI changing in favor of private capital. Under the current BRI strategy, private companies have intensified their investment abroad. Yet private investment has taken place more in advanced economies that offer safe returns, than destinations highlighted in the BRI's strategic statements.

Statistical Complexities

The statistical trends further establish that a fragmented regulatory environment has shaped the perplexing destination patterns of China's outbound investment. The state's onerous conditions for approving outbound investment and the unpredictable and often irregular approval process have created considerable pressure for Chinese commercial actors to hide or park their investible assets in offshore accounts. In Figure 4.4, the graphic to the left is based on Chinese MOFCOM data; the top three destinations for its outbound capital were Hong Kong, the British Virgin Islands, and the Cayman Islands. The graphic to the right is based on China Investment Tracker (CIT) by the Heritage Foundation in Washington, DC. The CIT database was compiled from reports in the destination countries and back trace to its home origin in China. In the CIT database, the three tax havens – Hong Kong, Virgin Islands, and Cayman Islands – were not even in the top ten; by contrast, in the MOFCOM database they accounted for almost 70 percent of China's total outbound FDI.

In 2015, as reported in the MOFCOM database, Hong Kong ranked as the dominant number 1 destination for Chinese investment and accounted for 58 percent of this investment. In the earlier period (2006–2010), Hong Kong's share were even higher: In 2008, for example, Hong Kong alone accounted for 76 percent of total outbound

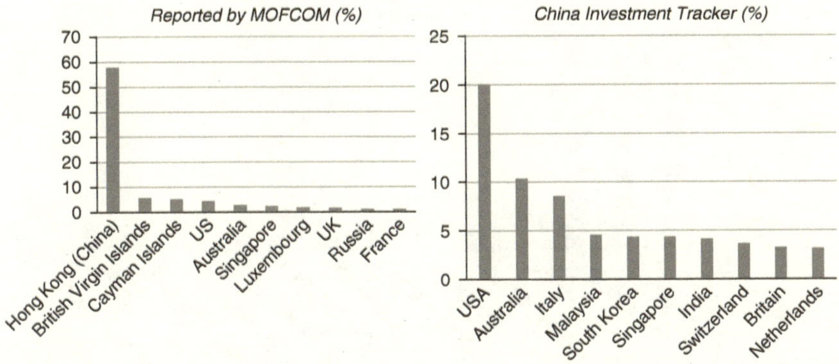

FIGURE 4.4. China's top destinations for outward FDI: Discrepancies. *Source:* Author, based on statistical reporting by MOFCOM and China Investment Tracker.

investment from China. Hong Kong's heavy concentration of China's outbound FDI is likely due to commercial actors using Hong Kong's liberal financial market to circumvent the restrictive and irregular policy environment in mainland China. As a result, China's government statistical reporting – conducted by MOFCOM – did not tell where this "transit capital" went after it was parked in Hong Kong, or in the Cayman and Virgin Islands.

Based on the CIT database, the top destinations for China's outbound FDI were entirely different: United States (20%), Australia (10.3%), Italy (8.5%), Malaysia (4.5%), South Korea (4.3%), Singapore (4.3%), and so on. It is clear that once the capital went abroad, Beijing lost much oversight regarding what exactly happened next. It is hard to imagine how economic statecraft or "state capture" is possible under this fragmented system.

In terms of sectors where China's outbound capital concentrates, the pattern demonstrates a disconnect between the CGG strategy and actual investment behaviors; nonetheless, it is in line with China's market conditions. As reported in the MOFCOM data in Figure 4.5, the largest sector attracting Chinese outbound investment in 2015 was leasing and business services (36%), followed by financing in a distant second place (15.6%) and mining in third (14%). This pattern reflects China's status as a major global exporting economy, which requires appropriate logistics support in different global markets.

Remember that the CGG was announced to help companies acquire resources and access advanced technology, but such goals did not show salience in the sectoral distribution of China's outward FDI in Figure 4.5.

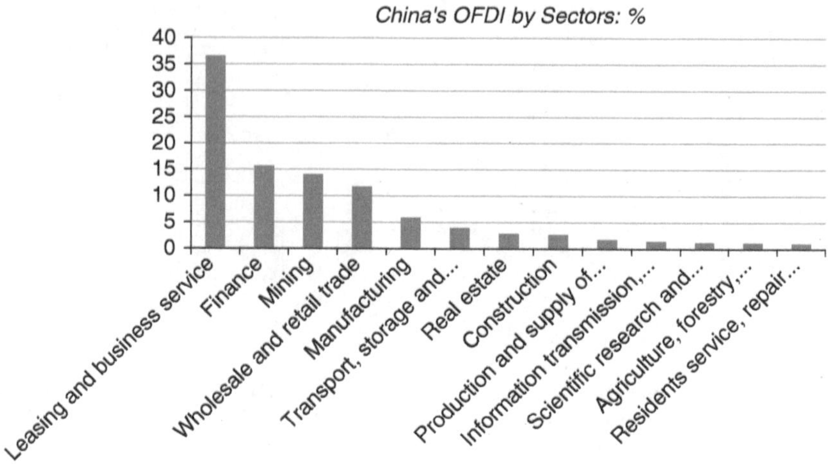

FIGURE 4.5. China's outbound investment by sectors. *Source:* Author, based on MOFCOM, *Direct Foreign Investment Statistical Bulletin*, 2015, available at: www.fdi.gov.cn.

As China's market condition changes overtime, such sectoral concentration is likely to change too. One thing is for sure: However China's outbound investment serves more the companies' own business needs than the country's global ambition.

Returning to our concern with the BRI and how China's outbound globalization has gone to different regions from 2005 to 2015, the BRI's emphasized regions are Central, South, and Southeast Asia, where most of its bilateral memorandums of understanding (MOUs) were signed. In Table 4.4, we compare these regions' representation in China's outbound investment over a decade. In 2005, North America accounted for a quarter of China's outbound investment; five years later, it had a slightly smaller share at 23.8 percent, which dropped further to 21.8 percent in 2015. Central Asia's share was a staggering 41 percent in 2005, reduced to almost none in 2010, and revived to a modest 0.65 percent in 2015. South Asia had no presence in 2005, but increased to 6.7 percent in 2015, a large gain under the BRI. Southeast Asia also gained strongly over the decade. Overall, however, regional trends in 2010 and 2015 were highly comparable and suggest that the BRI has limited short-term effects on changing outbound capital from China, with the exception of South Asia.[56]

[56] Liu, Tian, Ou, *Yidaiyilu zhanlue yanjiu*.

TABLE 4.4. *Regional trends in China's outbound investment (%)*

	2005	2010	2015
North America	24.3	23.8	21.8
Central Asia	41	0.2	0.65
South Asia	0	0	6.7
Southeast Asia	0	6.45	10.1
Others	34.7	69.5	60.7

Source: Author, based on China Investment Tracker 2005, 2010, and 2015, available at: www.aei.org/china-global-investment-tracker/.

What do the statistical trends tell us about the nationalist strategies and China's outward investment? First, policies have a lagging effect on actual capital flows. When the CGG was launched in 2000, there was no noticeable rise in outbound investment. A significant increase occurred mostly after 2004; only in 2008, though, did outward FDI increase dramatically. Similarly, when the BRI was launched in 2013, outward FDI did not increase visibly. The outward flows rose rapidly in 2016, and yet they declined sharply in 2017, going back to the 2015 level. Second, in shaping the flows of China's outward FDI, market conditions have been more influential than top-down political mobilization. Despite the political leadership's push for the CGG and BRI, outbound FDI flows increased when the Chinese national market stabilized and more capital was available to invest. Similarly, where outbound FDI went and into which sectors also conformed more to corporate business needs than strategic priorities set in the policies. Finally, as the process analysis of CGG demonstrates, the real value of nationalist strategies lies not in driving actual capital flows abroad, but rather in their ability to mobilize domestic companies and local governments to pursue growth-generating programs.

CONCLUSION

State-mobilized globalization is most evident during moments of crisis and uncertainty. Rather than being incapacitated by global challenges and bureaucratic fragmentation, the Chinese leadership launched politically ambitious programs that speak to nationalism and growth consensus in the country. In the meantime, the policy content was ambiguous, was devoid of specific measures, and consequently provided maximum flexibility to different actors to implement strategies in their own ways.

Some actors – such as national agencies – have responded by doing nothing. Others – such as competitive companies – expedited their investment plans and expanded business. As a whole, these programs did not result in systematic liberalization or institution building in the economic system, with preexisting fragmentations largely staying intact. Nonetheless, under the CGG, localized market behavior and entrepreneurial freedom were greatly enhanced.

Furthermore, while the CGG had been effective in rallying pro-growth momentum against fragmentation inside China, it was far less productive when it came to directing Chinese capital abroad. The strategy was nominally launched to promote outgoing Chinese capital; in reality, it could not stimulate outward FDI in the early 2000s. After the mid-2000s, as the Chinese economy was in large surplus, the financial and banking regulators, leveraging the CGG, passed new measures to use outbound investment to help with domestic economic priorities and to ensure safety and return return of state assets.

Unfortunately, the nationalist rhetoric and political mobilization embodied in the strategy created suspicion and resistance to Chinese capital in the recipient regions. On the other hand, deep-seated fragmentation in the state allowed commercial actors to bypass various policy guidelines from the center. The analysis of the CGG and China's outbound investment demonstrates that China still has some way to go before it becomes a truly global player in the world economy.

In June 2017, former SAFE director Hu Xiaolian, who helped stimulate outward investment and a lending spurt from China in the mid-2000s, was appointed the chair and party secretary of CEIB, the main financier of projects in the Belt and Road, a post that earned Madam Hu the title CFO of the BRI. Hu's chief lending principles were about tying CEIB's lending decisions closely to development and infrastructure in central China and along the Yangtze River. She underscores that investment in the BRI needs to be "rational" and of "a higher quality," and to help expand China's "industrial chain abroad."[57] The next chapter shows that seeking good investment abroad and linking up with domestic priorities have been consistent drivers behind the BRI strategy in the Chinese state system, but how to do it and how to do it without causing external backlash remain unclear.

[57] Anonymous, "China Set to Tackle Overseas Investment Risks," *Financial Times*, June 28, 2018.

5

The Belt and Road

> [We] must insist on companies as the main actors and market as the driving mechanism. [We] must follow international norms and commercial principles; the companies are responsible for their own decisions, their own returns, and the risks.
>
> —NDRC, 2015[1]

President Xi Jinping announced the Belt and Road in late 2013. By late 2018, dozens – if not hundreds – of related volumes were on sale in the Amazon marketplace, many of which were produced by long-term observers of China or global politics. Despite representing different disciplines and national interests, they invariably portray the BRI as the "centerpiece" of China's strategy to project power abroad. Robert Kaplan predicts that the new Silk Road will propel China's return to dominance.[2] Tom Miller also paints a picture of a future world in which global power shifts from Anglo-Saxon capitals to Beijing.[3] In Central, South, and Southeast Asia, strategic observers have been concerned about China's expansion at the expense of the existing order.[4] From a regional perspective, Nadege Rolland examines the BRI's political and strategic implications in

[1] NDRC, "Fagaiwei: woguo zhengzai zhiding guoji channeng hezuo sannian xingdong jihua" [NDRC: We Are Making International Capacity Cooperation Three-Year Action Plan], *Zhongguo jingji wang* [China Economics Network], December 25, 2015, http://politics.people.com.cn/n1/2015/1225/c70731-27978315.html.

[2] Kaplan, *The Return of Marco Polo's World.*

[3] Miller, *China's Asian Dream.*

[4] Bal Kishan Sharma and Nivedita Das Kundu (eds.), *China's One Belt One Road: Initiative, Challenges, and Prospects.* New Delhi: Vig Books India PVT, 2017;

Eurasia.[5] China specialist Elizabeth Economy describes the BRI as a "significant projection of power" in China's ongoing "Third Revolution."[6] Even China itself has been unusually outspoken in promoting the BRI as a global vision, as it never did with any preceding foreign policy.[7]

The focus on foreign policy and geostrategy is too limited and insufficient to understand the drivers and impacts of the Belt and Road, in China and on the global stage. Applying the SMG framework, the chapter establishes, first, that the BRI strategy was formed in the context of political–economic crises, as state agencies were deeply fragmented; well-reasoned and practiced policy proposals could not rally cross-agency support. Second, it details how the BRI announcements ushered in top-down political mobilization throughout the state system, providing "cohesive" messaging absent of policy directives. Finally, entering the implementation stage, state fragmentation resurges; subnational and corporate actors improvise projects and programs that serve their own economic interests and localized priorities. BRI policy formation and execution demonstrate a domestic political logic. The policy process is remarkably similar to that of the WDP and CGG, albeit with larger magnitude outside China and even greater fragmentation in the localities.

ORIGINS OF THE BRI

Undoubtedly, President Xi is a powerful politician in authoritarian China. In a short time span, he concentrated power to a level unseen in the past four decades. Xi's rapid ascent, however, masked the circumstances that had propelled him to power. That is, Chinese ruling elites had been struggling with major political–economic crises and the central state that was paralyzed by fragmentation. Xi's concentration of power at the top also disguised the fact that agents in the Chinese state have ample ways to interpret and improvise the BRI to suit their own functional priorities,

David P. Nicolas, *Chinese Infrastructure in South Asia: A Realist and Liberal Perspective*. Middletown, DE: Progressive Management, 2015; Will Doig, *High-Speed Empire: Chinese Expansion and the Future of Southeast Asia*. New York: Columbia Global Reports, 2018.

5 Nadege Rolland, *China's Eurasian Century? Political and Strategic Implications of the Belt and Road Initiative*. Washington, DC: National Bureau of Asian Research, 2017.

6 Economy, *The Third Revolution*.

7 L. C. Guo, *The Belt and Road: Official Documents*. Beijing & Washington, DC: ICP Intercultural Press, 2017; Liu, Tian, Ou, *Yidai yilu zhanlue*.

which may or may not conform to the autocrat's intent. In the SMG, state fragmentation works in both directions – strengthening the autocracy during the birthing of the strategy and weakening it as the state and commercial actors take charge of implementation.

President Xi's BRI was not conceived from a blank slate. Rather, it was an autocratic response to, and incorporation of, three separate efforts by different state agencies. These proposals drew on years of Chinese external engagement and sought to more effectively realize the country's external agenda. The first such effort, associated with diplomatic agencies, involved practices and proposals similar to the BRI, including infrastructure diplomacy and an earlier version of the AIIB. The second proposal, termed the Chinese Marshall Plan, was associated with the central economic agencies and argued for increased investment in overseas infrastructure as a way of relieving domestic overcapacity. Finally, the China Goes West proposal, put forth by security specialists and widely circulated in Beijing, recommended strategic rebalancing between maritime Asia and the Eurasia continent.

Diplomatic Motive: Mutual Connectivity [hulian hutong] in Asia

One of the BRI's signature proposals is "mutual connectivity," which aims to finance the construction of infrastructure connecting China with Southeast and Central Asia. This was not a novel idea or practice – the country had conducted this kind of "infrastructure diplomacy" since at least 2008. Prior to the BRI, Chinese diplomats proposed mutual connectivity projects within the Shanghai Cooperation Organisation (SCO) in Central Asia and ASEAN Plus Three (APT) in Southeast Asia. However, infrastructure proposals by Chinese diplomats did not go much further. Due to state fragmentation, Chinese diplomats did not have access to project reserves at Chinese banks. Nor did they have the power to orchestrate financing arrangements within the infrastructure proposals, as those functions belonged to the NDRC and state banks. Furthermore, China's complex relationships with its neighbors went beyond the purview of Chinese diplomats.

In 2010, domestic overcapacity began to intensify the efforts on infrastructure diplomacy. At the China-ASEAN Leaders' Summit in that year, former premier Wen Jiabao pledged that China would (1) increase trade with ASEAN to $500 billion by 2015 and establish a free trade agreement (FTA) with each member of ASEAN; (2) provide loans to establish a China–ASEAN Infrastructure Cooperation Fund; and (3) open up and integrate the financial markets of China and ASEAN countries.[8] Wen repeated the same message six months later while visiting Indonesia, where he announced that China would disburse $1 billion in concessionary loans and $8 billion in development financing. Indonesia's strategic importance was clearly on his mind.[9] Premier Wen espoused a similar message in November 2011 at the APT Summit, where he stated China's intention to speed up trade liberalization, improve regional financial cooperation, and increase investment in East Asia mutual connectivity.[10]

Former president Hu Jintao had also pursued infrastructure diplomacy. At the 2012 APEC Summit in Russia, Hu offered a concrete plan for infrastructure development in Eurasia in the speech "Deepening Mutual Connectivity and Realizing Sustainable Development." Hu's speech provided the justification for the subsequent BRI, as he remarked that "First, infrastructure provides the basis for economic development; second, connectivity is critical to trade integration; third, the present investment mechanisms need reform; [and] finally, Asian leaders need to promote communication and cooperation across borders."[11] President Hu proceeded to launch the China–ASEAN Mutual Connectivity Joint Committee, which held its first meeting in Indonesia in 2012. Member states agreed to hold regular meetings to coordinate infrastructure projects, create an overarching plan for mutual connectivity development, leverage diverse resources in the region, and set up institutions to promote coordination and cooperation.[12]

The Xi–Li administration continued infrastructure diplomacy. Premier Li affirmed the importance of infrastructure development in Asia and China's commitment to invest in it. In May 2013, while visiting Pakistan, Li announced that China would invest $14 billion in thirty-six projects covering energy, roads, and telecommunications in

[8] Wen Jiabao, speech at China–ASEAN Summit, *Renmin Ribao*, October 30, 2010, p. 1.

[9] Wen Jiabao, speech in Indonesia, *Renmin Ribao*, May 1, 2011, p. 2.

[10] Wen Jiabao, speech at ASEAN Plus Three Summit, *Renmin Ribao*, November 19, 2011, p. 2.

[11] Hu Jintao, speech at APEC Summit, *Zhongguo xinwen wanglue*, September 8, 2012.

[12] Hu Bing and Zheng Liansheng, "Yazhou hulian hutong: Zhongguo de zhanlue, zhengce, yu xingdong" [Asia's Mutual Connectivity, China's Strategy, Policy, and Action], *Xueshu qianyan* [Academic Frontiers] No. 23. 2015.

the country.[13] At the Boao Forum for Asia (BFA) in May 2013, BFA vice chairman Zeng Peiyan urged, "We must propose [an] Asia Infrastructure Cooperation Initiative (AICI) and work toward, one, coordinating infrastructure programs in the member countries, and two, establishing a specialized multilateral financial institution or an investment fund."[14] Zeng, former vice premier and a long-time minister of the State Planning Commission, was highly influential among China's economic technocrats. Prior to the BRI, Zeng published multiple articles promoting the idea of AICI and a special infrastructure fund.[15]

Infrastructure diplomacy had been robustly practiced before the BRI. In 2011, China provided $15 billion in concessionary loans to support fifty projects that included highways, railways, water, energy, telecommunications, and electricity linking China and ASEAN.[16] Cross-border rail and highway projects connected border cities such as Nanning and Kunming with Hanoi and Singapore, respectively. According to Zhu Caihua, professor at China Foreign Affairs University, when ASEAN members founded the ASEAN Infrastructure Fund (AIF) in 2012, Chinese diplomats attempted to expand the AIF into an East Asian Infrastructure Fund (EAIF), but they were not able to influence Chinese economic planners and financiers. Moreover, Japan and other "unfriendly" nations resisted their efforts to do so too.[17] Therefore, the EAIF proposal did not succeed in the context of APT. In Central Asia, Chinese diplomats encountered obstacles as well. Gao Jiangang, the Dean of Economics at Xinjiang University of Economics and Finance, concurred that Chinese political leadership should take charge and devise an "overarching" strategy to manage economic, political, and strategic relations in the region.[18]

[13] Li Keqiang, speech in Pakistan, *21st Century Economic Daily*, May 22, 2013, p. 8.

[14] Zeng Peiyan, "Yazhou jichu sheshi hulian hutong shizai bixing."

[15] Ibid.

[16] Zhu Caihu, "Dongya jichu jianshe hulian hutong rongzi" [Financing for East Asia Infrastructure Development Mutual Connectivity], *guoji jingji hezuo* [International Economic Cooperation], No. 10, 2013.

[17] Pan Feng, "Zhongguo yu 21 shiji yazhou jichu sheshi hulian hutong Jincheng" [China and the 21st Century Asia Infrastructure Mutual Connectivity], *Guoji yanjiu cankao* [International Studies Reference], No. 8, 2015, pp. 23–28.

[18] Gao Zhigang, "Sichou zhilu jingjidai kuangjiaxia zhongguo yu zhoubain guojia nengyuan yu waimao hulian hutong yanjiu gouxiang" [Silk Road Economic Belt and China's Energy and Trade Mutual Connectivity], *Fazhan yanjiu* [Development Studies], No. 1, 2014, pp. 46–51.

In summary, infrastructure diplomacy prior to the BRI had served to utilize China's excess capital and strengthen the country's commercial and diplomatic interests abroad. As pointed out in Chapter 4, this integration of commercial and diplomatic interests has also been pushed by financial agencies since 2006. But in the following years, overseas infrastructure projects were conducted in an uncoordinated fashion that was deemed ineffective to help Chinese diplomacy. Furthermore, the diplomats had limited power in overseeing infrastructure projects or making major foreign policy initiatives and could not come up with a forceful platform that would engage major actors in China and abroad. As a whole, infrastructure investment was rising fast overseas, but was seen as unsuccessful in achieving China's foreign policy agendas – China seemed to spend a lot of capital for very limited diplomatic gain. The diplomats thus asked for the leadership's support to push for stronger and more cohesive infrastructure diplomacy.

Economic Motive: The Chinese Marshall Plan

Now moving to the economic realm, the Chinese Marshall Plan proposal was in many ways a precursor to the BRI. The idea for the Chinese Marshall Plan was first laid out in a 2008 Shanghai government report. Authored by Professor Guo Shuyong of Shanghai Jiaotong University, the report evaluated three options for pursuing China's global economic and security interests: a grand comprehensive strategy; a security-oriented regime; and a Chinese Marshall plan.[19] Guo concluded that while the first two options were infeasible, the third option – which emphasizes economic over security cooperation – would be more acceptable to other countries and thus lead to greater stability in the region.

As China's growth pressure mounted, the Chinese Marshall Plan idea began to attract more attention from economic agencies. Zhang Monan, an economist at the Ministry of Industry and Information Technology (MIIT), argued that the 2008 financial crisis exacerbated China's industrial overcapacity and that a Chinese-style Marshall Plan could help address the problem by shifting industrial surplus abroad.[20] Former minister of state administration of taxation Xu Shanda refined the Chinese

[19] Guo, "Lun heping fazhan dazhanluexia de guoji jingji yu guoji anquan xietiao."

[20] Zhang Monan, "Jiji zhudong de chuangzao waixu shishi zhongguoshi maxieer jihua" [Actively and Proactively Create External Demand and Implement the Chinese Marshall Plan], *Zhongguo jingji daobao* [Chinese Economic Daily], June 27, 2009.

Marshall Plan and publicly supported it in a speech delivered on August 5, 2009. Xu argued that "China should learn from post-WWII America to implement a Chinese Marshall Plan" that would serve as a medium to long-term strategy to disburse foreign aid and foster international cooperation. Specifically, Xu proposed that China spend $500 billion in setting up a Harmonious World Plan and provide aid and loans to Asian, African, and Latin American countries, which would be conditional upon granting preference to Chinese companies in construction and equipment supply. The plan, according to Xu, would boost Chinese exports, reduce industrial overcapacity, accelerate renminbi internationalization, and advance China's global influence.[21]

Xu's proposition, however, was critiqued heavily within China. Media celebrity Qiu Lin, for instance, immediately attacked Xu's August 2009 speech, complaining that with China's interior regions hungry for state investment, "Why waste money abroad?"[22] He further cautioned that the Chinese Marshall Plan would increase tension with Japan and the United States, adding: "If our government has surplus funds, why not implement a Marshall Plan in underdeveloped regions within China, the western and other interior provinces?"[23] Pan Chengfu, a business professor based in Guangdong, echoed Qiu's critiques and raised vocal concerns in a business-oriented media outlet.[24]

As a result, the Chinese Marshall Plan was set aside, but as economic pressures continued to mount, the proposal reemerged in 2012. Former World Bank chief economist Justin Lin (or Lin Yifu as he is known in China) argued that a new Marshall Plan financing infrastructure development in poor countries would improve the growth potential there, thus helping to alleviate the global financial crisis. Lin argued that as the world's second largest economy, China had the potential to become a driver of global development.[25] Other government-affiliated economists

21 Chen Nan, "Zhuanfang yuan guojia shuiwu zongju fujuzhang xushanda: zhongguo maxieer jihua yu fazhanzhong guojia gongxiang fazhan" [Interview of Former State Administration of Taxation Vice Minister Xu Shanda: China's Marshall Plan and Joint Development in the World], *Shangwu zhoukan*, January 20, 2010.

22 Qiu Lin, "Maxieer jihua bu fuhe zhongguo guoqing" [Marshall Plan Does Not Work for China], *Zhonghua gongshang shibao* [Chinese Commerce Daily], August 17, 2009.

23 Ibid.

24 Pan Shifu, "Zhongguoban maxieer jihua xiaoguo chunyi" [China's Marshall Plan Is Doubtful], *Zhengquan shibao* [China Stocks], July 22, 2009, p. 3.

25 Lin, "Yong xinjegou jingjixue kan weilai quanqiu he zhongguo de jingji zengzhang."

echoed Lin's views.[26] The economic technocrats pushing the Chinese Marshall Plan asked the leadership to set up a special body that could (1) orchestrate overseas infrastructure investment and financing; (2) provide infrastructure loan insurance; (3) promote the expansion of the renminbi abroad; and (4) offer better intermediary services.[27]

However, the Chinese Marshall Plan proposal continued to face challenges. First, as reflected in the media outcry over Xu Shanda's proposal, the Chinese public remained divided, with many resenting the government's spending abroad. Second, with the MFA in charge of coordinating with foreign governments and MOFCOM controlling external economic treaties, the kind of cross-agency coordination needed for a successful Marshall Plan did not exist; neither the MFA nor MOFCOM was likely to subject itself to outside guidance from economic agencies. Finally, there was a general sense that China was not ready to compete with the United States on the world stage. As such, to some, the Chinese Marshall Plan appeared too assertive. To end the controversy, Zhou Xiaochuang, then governor of the People's Bank of China (PBOC), declared in 2015 that the Silk Road Fund "is not China's Marshall Plan."[28] The MOFCOM formally concurred: "China does not pursue a Marshall Plan" through the BRI.[29]

Strategic Motive: China Goes West

Since 2010, the US "pivot to Asia" policy has intensified China's contentious relations in maritime Asia. In the South China Sea, militarized tensions were on the rise. And on the multilateral front, the United States was excluding China and rallied allies to form the Trans-Pacific Partnership (TPP).[30] As Chinese strategists worried about America's geostrategic encirclement, renowned scholar Wang Jisi proposed "China Goes West" as a way to promote strategic rebalancing and prevent a US–China clash in maritime Asia.[31] This proposal became

[26] Jin, "Zhongguo de maxieer jihua tantao Zhongguo duiwai jichu jianshe touzi zhanlue."
[27] Ibid.
[28] "Silu jijin qibu yunzuo bushi zhongguoban faxieer jihua – zhuanfang zhongguo renmin yinhang hangzhang zhouxiaochuan" [Silk Road Fund Not China's Marshall Plan – Interview of PBOC Governor Zhou Xiaochuan," *Xin shangwu zhoukan*, No. 4, 2015.
[29] "Shangwubu fouren zhongguoban maxieer jihua" [MOFCOM Denies China's Marshall Plan], *Beijing shangbao* [Beijing Commerce], January 22, 2015, p. 2.
[30] Ye, "Competing Cooperation in Asia Pacific."
[31] Wang Jisi, "China's Search for a Grand Strategy: A Rising Great Power Finds Its Way," *Foreign Affairs*, 90(2), 2011, pp. 68–79.

popular among strategists in Beijing before the inception of the BRI. Similarities between Wang's proposal and the BRI – both moved the country toward Eurasian continental diplomacy – led many security scholars to claim that "China Goes West" was a forerunner of the BRI.

In the US magazine *Foreign Affairs*, Wang argued that China's grand strategy should be reoriented to place greater emphasis on the western part of Asia. "Today, East Asia is still of vital importance, but China should and will begin to pay more strategic attention to the west," wrote Wang. "This new western outlook may reshape China's geostrategic vision as well as the Eurasian landscape."[32] This westward rebalancing, however, faces two major difficulties. On the one hand, it is nearly impossible to achieve coordination across different Chinese government agencies; on the other, it is difficult to reconcile the vast diversity of views held both by China's political elite and the general public. In confronting these difficulties, Wang believed that a grand strategy spearheaded by strong leadership offered the best chance to coordinate across agencies and build coalitions.

Entering the scene in 2012, the US-led TPP was making major breakthroughs. With Japan's joining, the TPP imposed overwhelming pressure on Chinese economy and diplomacy. Government think tanks were busy researching TPP's negative impacts and how China should respond. Within strategic circles, however, the China Goes West proposal began to accumulate momentum. Between 2012 and 2013, Wang Jisi published articles explaining the China Goes West strategy in popular media – *Caijing Magazine* and the *Global Times*. In early 2013, influential strategists in Beijing convened fora to discuss the proposal and prepare to make policy suggestions to the central government.[33] Thus, when the BRI was launched, security specialists believed that Wang's proposal had been incorporated into the new strategy.

In summary, the BRI's origins reveal that the strategy's attractiveness to Chinese elites and its early popularity were not due only to autocratic power but also to preexisting practices and proposals at key state agencies. The BRI's birth supports the theory of state fragmentation, that is, despite each functional proposition making convincing argument on its own, none of them could survive opposition from other agencies and societal groups.

[32] Wang, "China's Search for a Grand Strategy," p. 78.
[33] Ye, "Competing Cooperation in Asia Pacific."

The BRI launched by the political leadership spoke to major imperatives in diplomacy, development, and security. When it was announced, the strategy thus rapidly galvanized support from top agencies and influential stakeholders in China. But with such sweeping support, combined with proclamations of external ambitions, it became confusing as to who truly was in charge of this initiative and where their priorities were.

"COHESIVE" MESSAGES OF MOBILIZATION

After President Xi made the two announcements on the BRI, within two years, the announcements became a nationalist strategy that mobilized virtually all agencies and think tanks in Beijing and many localities. In this process of mobilization, two mechanisms were salient. The first was the staging based on ambitious rhetoric, and the second was ambiguity that enabled different agencies to latch on the strategy for their own interests. The process demonstrates that despite "cohesive" messaging in formation of the BRI, concrete policy guidelines, if any, remain fragmented. Inside the state system, while the political leadership took advantage of state fragmentation to launch the nationalist strategy, state agencies took advantage of the strategy to pass their policy ideas and propositions. Analysis here draws on news reporting, industrial websites, and print media that focused on actors at the national level; the next two chapters investigate how top-down mobilization motivates local government and corporate behaviors.

Stages of Mobilization

In terms of staging, BRI mobilization began with consensus building at the apex of the party-state, followed by projecting the "consensus" across the state system. After returning from Indonesia in late 2013, Xi convened the Periphery Diplomacy Work Forum, which was attended by the entire standing committee of the Politburo, various organs of the Central Committee, state councilors, the Small Leading Group with the responsibility for foreign affairs, and Chinese ambassadors to neighboring countries. At the work forum, Xi focused on addressing the three policy agendas: enhance political good will, deepen economic integration, and improve regional security.[34] Following the forum, three national ministries – NDRC,

[34] Michael Swaine, "Chinese Views and Commentary on Periphery Diplomacy," *China Leadership Monitor*, 44, 2014, pp. 1–43.

MFA, and MOFCOM – issued statements to support and explain One Belt and One Road. The NDRC, in particular, called upon its affiliated industrial ministries and provincial governments to come up with ideas in line with the new strategy. The new strategy was later affirmed at the Third Plenum of the 18th National Party Congress and the annual Government Work Report, in December 2014 and January 2015.

The mobilization stage also involved international events and multilateral settings. Extensively reported in Chinese media, such "external" promotion was also targeted at internal readers and helped widen domestic acceptance of the BRI. At the 2014 BFA, China hosted a special session on Silk Road Rejuvenation, during which State Councilor Yang Jiechi evoked the ancient Silk Road to promote the new one, focusing on the revival of Central Asian economies and regional integration. At the sixth China–Arabic ministerial meeting in Beijing in June 2014, China promoted One Belt and One Road to journalists and officials from the Arabic countries. The resultant Beijing Declaration stated that China is at the critical juncture of "great-power rejuvenation" [*daguo jueqi*], and "look west" is the new diplomatic direction.[35] President Xi publicly and memorably spoke, "The Silk Road Economic Belt and Maritime Silk Road are the two wings of China, the Roc [中国大雕, a mythical bird]. Once they are constructed, China, the Roc can fly higher and farther."[36]

When the core messaging from the political leadership became clear, in Beijing, different agencies came out to support the BRI's strategic status, while *inserting* their own policy preferences. In summer 2014, Liu Jianchao, representing the MFA, explained that the BRI integrated China's own development with Asian regionalism through policy coordination, road connection, trade facilitation, currency exchange, and communication of public opinions.[37] MOFCOM minister Gao Hucheng, citing impressive growth in China's trade and investment in Central Asia (annually 19% and 54%, respectively, in the past ten years), observed that the strategy would "unleash the growth potential in the region."[38] NDRC publicized its action plan of the BRI construction,

35 Anonymous, "Yidaiyilu: Zhongguo waijiao xin siwei" [Yidai Yilu, China's New Diplomatic Perspective], *Guangming Ribao* [Englightenment Daily], June 7, 2014.

36 Anonymous, "Yidai yilu wei dapeng chashang xin chibang" [Yidai yilu, China the Roc's Two Wings], *Renmin Ribao*, May 7, 2014.

37 Liu Jianchao, "Yidai yilu jianshe shi yazhou guojia de gongtong shiye" [The Belt and Road Is the Common Project of Asian Nations], *Guangming Ribao*, May 28, 2014, p. 8.

38 NDRC, "Xin silu zhanlue de jingji zhidian" [The Economic Anchor of the New Silk Road], *Zhongguo jingji zhoukan* [China Economics Weekly], July 7, 2014.

in which investment, manufacturing, cross-border industrial parks, energy trade, and infrastructure were "the priority of the priorities."[39] The State Council think tank Development and Research Center (DRC) argued that the BRI would jointly develop coastal, central, and western China, while improving Asia's overall economic competitiveness in the world.[40]

Mobilization on behalf of the BRI heavily involved the state media. In July 2014, a Belt and Road media conference was held at the Great Hall of People, and representatives from provinces and state companies were invited. Representing interior interests, officials from inland China praised the BRI's potential to enhance investment, market liberalization, and infrastructure development in their localities.[41] Industrial hubs in western China – Kunming and Chengdu in particular – aimed to make their localities anchors of communication and transportation from coastal China to Central Asia. Cities in coastal Zhejiang and Jiangsu provinces also came up with ways to connect with the new initiative. At the conference, Chinese state companies, including China Tourism, China Tea, and CITIC, announced BRI-related projects.[42] Under such intense mobilization, the National Party's Congress and the National People's Congress of late 2014 passed resolutions that One Belt and One Road would serve as China's key policy over the next ten years [*weilai shinian de zhongda zhengce*].

Government-affiliated think-tank scholars were part of the mobilization, and they utilized the opportunities to disseminate their own policy ideas. Li Xiangyang, the dean of the Asia and Grand Strategy Institute at the Chinese Academy of Social Sciences (CASS), wrote in late 2014 that the BRI represented a new era of economic diplomacy in China.[43] Different from earlier practices that separated out economic and diplomatic interests, the BRI strategy, Li argued, integrates economic and diplomatic efforts and responds comprehensively to the strategic and economic environments that China faced. Under the BRI, Li advocated a series of

[39] Ibid.

[40] Ibid.

[41] "Yidai yilu fuxing chengshi rongguang". [One Belt and One Road Revives the Cities in Asia], *Renmin Wang*, July 4, 2014, www.gscn.cn/tourism/system/2014/07/04/01074915/shtml.

[42] Ibid.

[43] Li, "Lun haishang sichou zhilu de duoyuanhua hezuo jizhi" [On Multilateral Cooperation Mechanisms of the Maritime Silk Road].

geostrategic-conscious free trade areas (FTAs): China–Russia–Mongolia in northeast Asia, China–Hong Kong–Taiwan and China–ASEAN FTA in Southeast Asia, Bangalore–China–India–Myanmar economic corridor and China–Pakistan Economic Corridor in South Asia, and China and the Gulf countries in western Asia.[44] Chen Yao, chairman of regional economies and researcher at CASS, also underscored the BRI's strategic significance.[45] Chen tied the construction of the new Silk Road with the revival of China's former place in the world. In detail, he advocated for the BRI to connect land and maritime transport, deepen regional integration, and expand geostrategic space for China's rise.

Detecting Policy Messages

Political mobilization makes the investigation of BRI's policy directions difficult; yet it is important to understanding the real drivers and effects of the BRI. In this section, I draw on a database of top-level reports compiled by the DRC from 2013 to 2016 and systematically present the policy messages on the strategy available in Beijing. The DRC database only collects titles of the reports; I used Baidu search to locate and analyze the complete texts for policy inferences.

Based on who made those reports, I categorize the 139 top-level reports into two groups, those by Politburo standing members (PSM) and those by central agencies in the state. Among the Politburo statements, the focus was on President Xi and Premier Li, heads of the party and state, respectively, as well as Vice Premier Zhang Gaoli, head of the Belt and Road Leading Small Group (SLG). Among the agencies, I separated out statements by NDRC, MFA, and MOFCOM because they were designated as the central body of the BRI and jointly authored *The Belt and Road Vision and Action Plan* in March 2015.[46]

Figure 5.1 shows that political leaders, as represented by the Politburo standing members, include senior officials in charge of party organization, propaganda, politics and law, legislature, finance, security, and internal affairs. They made sixty-nine speeches on the BRI from 2013 to 2016, of which President Xi accounted for the majority at thirty-nine speeches (55%), while Premier Li made only nine speeches and Vice

44 Ibid.

45 Chen, "Yidai yilu zhanlue de hexin neihan yu tuijing silu" [The Core Meaning and Mechanism of China's One Belt and One Road Strategy].

46 This remains the most comprehensive document on the BRI. See Guo, *The Belt and Road.*

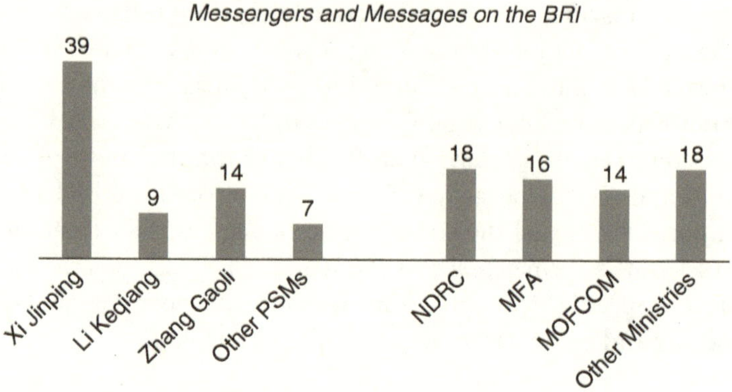

FIGURE 5.1. Top-level voices on the Belt and Road: 2013–2016. *Source:* Author, based on DRC, One Belt and One Road Strategic Support Platform, gaoceng shengyin [Voices from the Top]. Available at: http://ydyl.drcnet.com.cn/www/ydyl/Channel.aspx?uid=80091201.

Premier Zhang Gaoli made fourteen. President Xi not only delivered most of the remarks on the BRI but also defined the vision, ideas, and principles of the BRI. President Xi was directly involved in external promotion, signing major BRI contracts and projects abroad.

Recall the tri-block state structure in Chapter 2 (Figure 2.2). Inside block 1, party leadership, President Xi holds complete authority over the messaging of the BRI. This was as much to solidify the power of the leader as to present a "cohesive" voice from the party leadership. With a cohesive voice from the party, it is useful to observe the behaviors of the national agencies and subnational actors to detect the interactions across the three blocks.

BRI SLG chairman Zhang Gaoli's speeches were made mostly inside China and aimed to mobilize provincial actors to participate in the BRI. All four of the other PSMs made public speeches to support the strategy. Zhang Dejiang focused on Hong Kong's roles (three speeches), Liu Yunshang on party collaboration (two speeches), Liu Qibao on propaganda (one speech), and Yu Zhengsheng on policy research (one speech). Due to Xi Jinping and Zhang Gaoli's roles in the BRI, their activities and statements are analyzed below to capture top-level policy intent in the BRI. Premier Li Keqiang's speeches provide inklings of the relationships between the state and party heads: On the one hand, Li deferred to his new political superior, and in the few speeches he made, he clearly praised the BRI; on the other hand, he stresses industrial capacity going global and using economic means to achieve diplomatic gains – two consistent policy priorities in the State Council.[47]

Now moving to the national bureaucracies (block 2 in Figure 2.2), there were sixty-six speeches and statements. In Figure 5.1, it can be seen that the distribution between the NDRC, MFA, and MOFCOM was relatively equitable: NDRC had eighteen speeches; MFA made sixteen speeches; and MOFCOM made fourteen speeches. The rest of the central agencies, including transportation, taxation, customs, land and resources, and foreign exchange, together contributed eighteen speeches on the BRI. These functional agencies are a mixed and important group: Some of them merely parroted "official lines"; others provided real resources and mechanisms for implementation; still others were able to leverage the BRI and rolled out aggressive projects.

How different agencies play parts in the BRI is important not only to distinguish policy directions from nebulous "official lines" but also to identify the nature and shapers of the strategy in China and abroad. Were it to be truly a foreign policy strategy or a new global vision, as the political rhetoric stressed, we should see strong and concrete roles by the MFA (diplomacy) and MOFCOM (international negotiation). These two agencies had made a good number of statements and reports on the BRI, but judging by the content, neither the MFA nor MOFCOM was the policy driver or shaper of BRI implementation.

Most of the MFA statements were made by diplomats regarding President Xi's foreign trips; they rarely offered any new interpretations or propositions. The fourteen statements by MOFCOM also did not provide substantive policy messages, except for the proposals on free trade areas and e-commerce zones; yet the new BRI-related FTAs and e-commerce zones were inside China or have strong domestic connections.

The NDRC was evidently in the lead at the operational level and made new project proposals. The NDRC's statements are studied more closely below, along with Zhang Gaoli's and President Xi's remarks. In summary, the NDRC's implementation has two directions: one, trying

47 For example, Li Keqiang, "Nanhai xingwei zhunze jinzao dacheng, zhongtai, zhonglao tielu jinzao kaigong" [Complete South China Sea Code of Conduct, Start the Construction of China-Thailand and China-Laos Railways], at the ASEAN + China Forum, November 21, 2015; Li Keqiang, "Yatouhang youwang niandi chengli bing yunying, silu jijin yi kaizhan xiangmu touzi" [AIIB Is Likely to Start and Operate in Late 2015; Silk Road Fund Has Already Funded Projects], at ASEAN Plus Three Summit, November 21, 2015.

to come up with acceptable names, scopes, and general standards for the BRI and two, tying the BRI to its domestic priorities, rallying local governments to conduct reform, and reinvigorate growth. Shown shortly, the NDRC's external-projecting efforts faced pushback; its internal agendas moved faster.

In Figure 5.1, in the "Other Ministries" category, the reports are telling. Central agencies in finance, transportation, industry, foreign exchange, customs, and taxation, for example, have passed concrete and potentially significant measures. The Ministry of Finance (MOF) proposed new energy and financial insurance for outgoing companies; Customs adopted sixteen new measures to facilitate international trade; Taxation published ten measures that benefited outgoing companies; and SAFE pledged to support the BRI with foreign exchange reserves while increasing returns on its assets.

Drawing on the opportunity provided by the BRI, the Ministry of Transportation in particular achieved three outcomes: one, it more successfully received support from the State Council, NDRC, MOF, Land and Resources, and Environment; two, it expedited construction of centrally budgeted projects, such as twenty-eight long-distance highways, six large and important ports, and two new long-distance speed rails; and three, it multiplied its funding sources (RMB ¥311 billion central budget + ¥1.8 trillion self-raised funds + ¥100 billion other projects).[48]

In summary, analysis of the BRI documents provides a glimpse into the process and power play in Beijing. First, it seems that the political leadership had become essential to major changes in economic and foreign policies. While many of the policy measures were available in the central state, the leadership intervention via the BRI precipitated their rolling out.[49] Second, it seems that policy implementation in China requires agencies and actors that have power and resources to construct projects and have access to finance. Among the three "gatekeeper" agencies – the NDRC, MFA, and MOFCOM – the NDRC, which has ability to direct

[48] "Jiaotongbu xiada danxiang zijin 3110 yi" [Ministry of Transportation Passed the Allocated Funds of RMB 311 Billion], *Zhongguo xinwen wang* [Chinese News Network], July 16, 2015.

[49] Using the BRI, the State Council published the long-awaited "Guanyu goujian kaifanxing jingji xintizhi de ruogan yijian" [State Council on Constructing a New Open Economic System in China], in which the State Council highlighted the support for Chinese industries going global, developing new competitive sectors in China, and opening new areas and forms to attract "high-quality" FDI. See *Zhongguo zhengfu wang* [Chinese Government Network], September 17, 2015.

local developments and approve large investment projects and whose approval is necessary to access state-financing – emerged as a leading agency in coordinating BRI implementation. The MFA and MOFCOM thus far played important but supportive roles. More important, actors in energy, transportation, and finance – the largest and infrastructural SOEs – acted rapidly and independently from NDRC oversight.

Complex Governance of the BRI

President Xi is central to the BRI's future. Analysis of his speeches helps us detect his vision and policy preferences in the nationalist strategy. A close reading reveals that, first, most of the speeches were nebulous and allowed for flexible interpretation and commercialization by subnational actors. Second, according to different audiences and settings, they illustrated and signaled different agendas. When speaking to multilateral audiences, President Xi emphasized ideals such as openness, inclusiveness, and cooperation.[50] He also stressed the goals to enhance global governance, world development, and regional stability. In bilateral summits, President Xi's messaging was much more concrete and contained strong economic components.[51] In the Middle East, East Europe, and Central and South Asia, the Chinese leader proposed and often signed agreements for economic corridors, bilateral treaties, and infrastructure projects, which combined strategic alignment with expected economic gains. Finally, when speaking to domestic audiences, President Xi emphasized financial incentives and economic development. He launched the Silk Road Fund (at the Central Economics Work Meeting) and mandated that the 13th Five Year Plan include the BRI.

Looking exclusively at President Xi's propositions in a multilateral setting, it is logical to deduce that the driver of the BRI was Xi's ambition to present an alternative vision, regional structure, and balance of power from the status quo system. The bilateral agreements then lead to a conclusion in support of either "economic statecraft" or "state capture," which have been among the main perspectives on the BRI. The analysis here focuses on domestic political dynamics and explains how

[50] For a sample of Xi's multilateral speeches, see "Xi Jinping yidai yilu changyi de zhongyao lunshu huigu" [Remembering Xi Jinping's Important Speeches on the Belt and Road Initiative], Xinhua.net, February 12, 2016.

[51] For good coverage of President Xi's bilateral visits and agreements in the name of the BRI, see "Xi Jinping de yidai yilu zuji" [Xi Jinping's Footprints on the Belt and Road], *Liaowang* [The Outlook], January 6, 2016.

external implementation is likely to be embedded in such internal politics. Fragmentation, mobilization, and globalization work jointly and interactively inside China. Outside, however, they cause confusion, suspicion, and opposition.

Moving to the SLG of the BRI, the data support mobilization, not clear functions to guide implementation. Inaugural chairman Zhang Gaoli was a vice premier with a portfolio in regional development; the SLG has representatives from 23 central agencies. Since its birth, however, no major documents or activities have come out of this body. Zhang's activities were primarily local. He chaired the BRI study sessions and workshops in the provinces of Ningxia, Gansu, Chongqing (twice), Guangdong, Yunnan, and Guangxi. In each province, Zhang focused on mobilizing lower-level governments to participate in the BRI with sufficient enthusiasm.[52] He encouraged Ningxia and Gansu to focus on economic Belt-related infrastructure construction, Chongqing to explore various economic corridors, Guangdong to become a pioneer in high tech, and Guangxi to leverage its trade relations with countries in Southeast Asia. Currently, neither new chairman Yu Zhengsheng nor the BRI SLG has made any new moves or sent any new messages.

Finally, on the NDRC's roles, its Western Development Bureau is the coordinating body for BRI implementation. The agency published the official BRI Macro Planning, the Chinese Standards BRI Action Plan, the Core Principles, and the Industrial Capacity Cooperation Three-year Planning. All of these "official documents" are vague and voluntary. Most of them seem to fold the NDRC's domestic agendas into the name of the BRI. The NDRC's One Belt and One Road Macro Planning, for example, was published in early 2015, but its main contents – administrative reform, corporate reform, investment sectorial guideline, a new budget law, currency marketization, medical provisions, urbanization and hukou reform, new FTA and FDI investment guidelines, and a low-carbon economy – had little to do with the BRI.[53] NDRC, as a super-ministry in the State Council, however, has the power to ask other ministries and local governments to come up with their own

[52] For an example of Zhang Gaoli's local mobilization, see "Zhanggaoli fangwen ningxia, gansu" [Zhang Gaoli Inspect Ningxia and Gansu], *Xinhua News*, July 5, 2014.

[53] "Fagaiwei: Yidaiyilu zongti guihua bianzhi wancheng" [NDRC: One Belt and One Road Macro Planning Document Completed], *Zhongguo xinwen wang* [China News Networks], February 16, 2015, www.ocn.com.cn/hongguan/201503/sqtal23103834.shtml.

plans for BRI implementation. By mid-2015, more than ten ministries had completed their BRI plans; by late 2015, thirty-two provinces had submitted their BRI plans. The plans themselves, however, are vague and nonobligatory.

To summarize, the autocratic intervention in late 2013 inserted the image of cohesion into the state system in order to meet various challenges. In the circle of political leadership, the messages were consistent and stressed the BRI's importance to nationalist ambitions in China. President Xi had clear command over determining the messages, ideas, and importance in the new strategy. The BRI Small Leading Group then focused on mobilization in the localities. At the state level, government-affiliated thinkers were active in inserting their own policy preferences, both amplifying cohesive messaging on the BRI and broadening support from specific interest groups and industries. The NDRC, MFA, and MOFCOM, along with other agencies in the central government, also joined the chorus of support for the autocratic strategy.

"Cohesive messaging," however, masked major differences inside and across the three blocks in the state system (Figure 2.2). There were clearly diverse preferences and interests in the BRI, as well as different resources and powers that agencies could bring to the implementation of the BRI. Among the NDRC, MFA, and MOFCOM, the NDRC with its power to rally other local governments and industrial ministries into compliance assumed more influence in shaping the BRI's implementation. The MFA and MOFCOM became servicing agencies for projects and programs abroad. Furthermore, agencies in foreign exchange, transportation, energy, and so on were able to provide concrete interpretation of the strategy and immediately roll out major projects in the name of the BRI.

REFRAGMENTED IMPLEMENTATION

The mobilization process discussed above demonstrates two aspects of state-mobilized globalization in China. First, the party organization and leadership create "cohesive messages" based on ambitious nationalism – the rise and modernization of the Chinese nation. This message, ambitious and ambiguous, was disseminated by members of the party leadership through major political venues, international events, and state-controlled media. Second, the state agencies, policy experts, and practitioners, moving beyond the ambiguous messages, both sang praises of the strategy and inserted their policy preferences and interpretations into the mobilization of the BRI. Closer reading of those state-level (vs. party-level) "voices" established the salience of state industry, state finance, and local governments, which were predictably the main and immediate implementers of the BRI. In this section, I analyze the reports on the early implementation and map out the main actors and patterns of conducting the BRI in China.

State Capital Going Global

In the DRC's One Belt and One Road Strategic Platform, there is an archival database on the BRI's industrial activities from 2014 to 2016. The data collect titles from online sources and industrial reporting; the titles are typically alarming and confusing – such as "China Ex-Im Bank Invested in 1000 Projects in the BRI" or "Guangdong Nuclear Acquired Nuclear Facilities in Five BRI Countries."[54] I used Baidu to locate the full texts of the titles and analyzed the investors and projects to authenticate the patterns of implementation. After going through analysis of the investors, Figure 5.2 categorizes the 647 reported activities into three categories: national-level state actors, including central SOEs, ministries, and national banks; subnational state actors, including local governments, lower-level SOEs, and local state banks; and private actors, including private firms, associations, media, and so on. Dominance of the state capital is very clear: 47 percent reported activities were by central-level state units; 41 percent were by subnational state units; and only 18 percent were done by private actors such as companies and academics.

Furthermore, the early projects reveal that at both national and local levels, industry-related activities were most salient: Among the 647 total reported activities, 137 were by national SOEs and 108 were by local SOEs. Such a distribution supports the proposition that industrial overcapacities had been the main motivator behind projects and programs in the BRI. The State Council and NDRC had both consistently pushed for this imperative.

In 2015, the State Council passed the opinion on "expediting the development of competitive industries" in which it stressed the support of machinery and equipment producers to go global as part of BRI implementation, and the opinion on "constructing an open new economic system" in which it underscored mutual connectivity and capacities

[54] Upon closer reading, the former report was about "project reserves," not actual investment; the latter was one acquisition by the company, except the acquired company has business in five countries. These reports were not entirely wrong but were mischaracterizations of the true scale and nature of the projects.

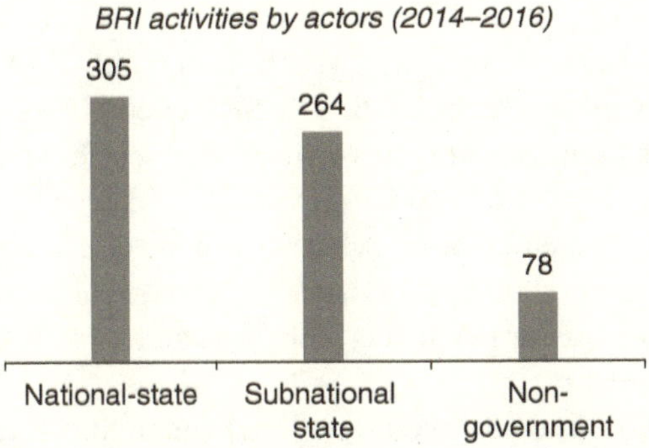

FIGURE 5.2. State in predominance. *Source:* Author, based on archives from DRC, The Belt and Road Strategic Platform, Industrial Reporting, 2014–2016. Available at: http://ydyl.drcnet.com.cn/www/ydyl/Channel.aspx?uid=80091205.

cooperation as the priority of the BRI.[55] The NDRC focused on local governments; in late 2015 it praised provinces – Hebei, Jiangxi, Hubei, Anhui, Yunnan, Shandong, and Gansu – that had made their own internationalization plan for capacity and machinery export guidelines.[56] The policy, however, provided neither specific mechanisms nor clear funds for companies or local governments. Like in the WDP and CGG, they "encouraged" subnational and commercial actors to "improvise" programs and find "bankable" projects.

Now moving to the chief financiers of the BRI projects. In President Xi's BRI announcements in late 2013, he proposed AIIB and SRF as designated financiers for the BRI. In the following two years, the AIIB, under the joint influence of multilateral institutions and more liberal technocrats in the Chinese state, was transformed into a multilateral development bank in the image of the World Bank (WB) and Asian Development Bank (ADB). The terms and procedures of AIIB were improvements over existing rules and practices; the bank-sponsored projects had all been collaborations with either the WB and/or ADB.[57] The SRF has an initial

55 "Guowuyuan guanyu jiakuai peiyu waimao jingzheng xinyoushi de ruogan yijian" [The State Council on Expediting New Competitive Industries in Foreign Trade], *Zhongguo xinwen wang* [China News Network], May 12, 2015; "Guowuyuan guanyu goujian kaifanxing jingji xintizhi de ruogan yijian" [The State Council on Construction of New Open Economic System], *Zhongguo zhengfu wang* [China Government Network], September 17, 2015.

56 "Tuijin guoji channen he zhuanbei zhizao hezuo" [To Promote International Cooperation of Capacity and Machinery Exports], *Zhongguo jingji daobao* [China Economics Guideline], December 25, 2015.

57 Jin Liqun, "Multilateral Approach to Development." Talk at Boston University, Boston, MA, October 18, 2019.

fund of $10 billion, of which $6.5 billion came from SAFE, $1.5 billion from China Investment Corp, $1.5 billion from China's Ex-Im Bank (CEIB), and $0.5 billion from CDB. The SRF exemplifies "conventional" Chinese overseas lending and has prioritized servicing the home market and granting preferences to Chinese SOEs.[58] SRF's funding decisions typically had three elements: (1) whether a project has the participation of a reputable Chinese SOE, (2) whether it provides long-term return on investment, and (3) whether it has joint financing from Chinese and/or international banks.[59]

Clearly, the AIIB and SRF would not have the financial capacity to serve as main financiers for the BRI. For the publicized high price tags – totaling trillions – the likely candidates were the CEIB, CDB, state commercial banks, and local branches of these financial institutions. In the past, CEIB and CDB financed large construction and infrastructure projects outside China, and they have maintained trillions of dollars in project reserves in Eurasian countries. In 2015, CEIB disbursed $80 billion in loans, compared to the ADB's $27.1 billion.[60] In the same year, CEIB publicized that it had stocked up more than 1,000 BRI projects in forty-nine countries, including highways, railways, ports, power plants, resource extraction, pipelines, communications, and industrial parks.[61] The Construction Bank of China, one of the four commercial banks, also claimed to be following more than 400 BRI infrastructure projects and planning to expand into Eastern Europe, Central Asia, and Southeast Asia.[62]

The reports need deep analysis to understand how and how much Chinese financiers have invested in BRI projects. The reported SOE projects have three categories: (1) ambitious yet infeasible "hollow pledges," (2) investment projects in line with business plans, and (3) standard foreign

58 "Jinqi tan jinrong ruhe zhichi yidai yilu jianshe" [Jin Qi Speaks on Financial Support of One Belt One Road], *Jingrong shibao* [Financial Times], May 23, 2016; "Sichou zhilu jijin jihua: zijin conghe erlai" [SRF Plan: Where Is the Money From?], *Jingrong shibao* [Financial Times], May 13, 2016.

59 See "Silu jijin fuzeren jiu xiangmu qidong youguan qingkuang de jizewen" [SRF Director Holds News Conference on Issues Related to Project Launch], world.huanqiu.com, accessed on April 20, 2015.

60 "Jinchukou yinhang yidai yilu daikuang yue chao 5200 yi" [Ex-Im Bank Loans to BRI More than ¥ 520 billion].

61 "Jinchukou yinhang yidai yilu daikuang yuer chao 5200 yi" [Ex-Im Bank Loans to BRI More Than RMB 520 Billion], *Zhongguo zhengquan bao* [China Stocks], January 15, 2016.

62 "Jianhang yuliu 2 wanyi buzhuo yidai yilu shangji" [The Construction Bank Reserved RMB2 Trillion to Seize Business Opportunity in BRI], *Cai Hua She*, April 25, 2016.

aid programs. In the first category, as examples, Southern Grid envisions an electricity connectivity project that builds pipelines across Laos, Myanmar, Russia, and Mongolia; China Rails Construction pledges to construct a network of highways, railways, and housing in Central Asia, Eastern Europe, the Middle East, and Southeast Asia; Southern Airlines proposes to integrate terminals in more than sixty-nine cities in thirty-six nations in Eurasia. All these visions are exceedingly unrealistic and entail no concrete investment plans from the proposers.

In the second category, those in line with corporate business expansion, examples are abundant. China Rails announced a $200 million investment to establish its regional headquarters in Malaysia; China Construction invested in a landmark building in Cambodia and signed a contract to build a China–Malaysia science center; and Shanghai Baosteel proposed an online portal to increase exports.[63] In the full reports, commercial calculations and prior business plans were typically presented. Finally, diplomatically oriented BRI projects mostly took place in Pakistan and Indonesia, and involved public housing, highways, and power plants, as well as a port, a dam, and earthquake relief.

Using the project lists from China Construction and Power China Construction, two centrally affiliated construction contractors and builders in China, Table 5.1 shows that their BRI implementation does not yield strong evidence of an "ambitious projection of power abroad," at least in the near term.[64]

In the table, there are a total of fifty projects, each amounting to more than RMB ¥1.0 billion. The destinations of these projects were more diversified than the BRI priorities indicate. The Belt and Road prioritized three regions in Eurasia: Central Asia, South Asia, and Southeast Asia. In Table 5.1, however, Central Asia is not listed, and South Asia has only six projects, prominently four in Pakistan, one in India, and one in Sri Lanka. Southeast Asia ranked second place, with ten projects.

[63] For example, "Zhongguo zhongtie touzi liangyi meiyuan zai malaixiya jian quyu zhongbu" [China Railways Plans to Establish a Regional Headquarters in Malaysia], ThePaper.cn, March 22, 2016, www.sohu.com/a/64841444_115402; "Zhongguo gangtie zouchuqu: Baogang xiangrang chukouliang de 10% zou tade dianshang pingtai" [China Steel Goes Global: Baosteel Plans to Export 10% on its E-commerce Platform], ThePaper.cn, March 31, 2016. www.thepaper.cn/newsDetail_forward_1451020.

[64] The DRC, BRI Industrial Activities database. For full text, see "2015 nian zhongguo duiwai chengbao gongcheng xinqian hetonge shoupo liangqianyi meiyuan" [2015 China Overseas Construction Projects Reached $210 Billion], *Zhongguo jingji wang*, January 27, 2016, http://money.163.com/16/0127/21/BEC7P1U800253B0H.html.

TABLE 5.1. *Construction in the BRI: Destinations and project types, 2015*

Destinations		Project types	
Africa	18	Power	21
Southeast Asia	10	Auxiliary infrastructure	12
Middle East	7	Real estate	8
South Asia	6	Infrastructure	7
Latin America	3	Resources	1
Others	6		

Source: Author, based on raw data from DRC Belt and Road database.

Africa, on the other hand, topped the list, with eighteen projects out of the fifty. The Middle East and Latin America are also sizable taking up seven and three respectively. Hong Kong, Macao, England, and the United States made up the rest of the projects.

In terms of project types, most investment by the two construction companies were in small-scale infrastructure and power sectors. Considering these two are among China's largest infrastructure builders, the evidence here does not support the BRI's "imperialist" agenda but consistent commercial motivative.

Furthermore, alarmed by the political mobilization, China's banking regulators sought to prevent and cure capital flight from China under the name of BRI. In 2015, China Banking Association (CBA), the liaison between China Banking Regulatory Commission (CBRC) and banks in China, passed five principles for Chinese banks going global, seeking to impose tighter regulation on outbound financing and to more effectively manage investment outflows. According to CBA, BRI-related external financing should (1) expand Chinese bank branches abroad, (2) create innovative financing and products to help Chinese investors explore BRI markets, (3) raise low-cost capital through multiple international channels, (4) coordinate finance and industry to facilitate industrialization in BRI countries, and (5) strengthen bilateral and multilateral financial cooperation.[65]

The overseas financing guidelines were confirmed by BRI-related financial activities. In 2015 and 2016, most finance-related activities

[65] "Zhongzi yinhang jiakuai buju yidai yilu jianshe" [Chinese Banks Speed Up Branch Establishment along the BRI], *Jingji ribao* [China Economics Daily], March 29, 2016, http://finance.huanqiu.com/br/focus/2016-03/8791015.html.

pertained to Chinese banks setting up branch offices in foreign countries, increasing the use of Chinese currency in external transactions, and signing memoranda of understanding (MOUs) between Chinese and foreign bank regulators.[66]

BRI Implementation Inside China

In 2015, the NDRC and CBRC jointly passed the One Belt and One Road Financing Method [*Yidai yilu rongzifa*].[67] The method asks China Development Bank (CDB) to establish project-specific group banks and arrange for Chinese local banks, foreign funds, and the SRF to participate in infrastructure projects *inside* China. The document stipulates that the central government and local governments act as loan guarantors or buy out low-grade equity to ensure profitability for other project investors. It includes examples from central China, such as Hunan, Hubei, and Henan; by contrast, coastal provinces had little demand for infrastructure financing, and western provinces made less business sense. The examples demonstrate that preexisting infrastructure projects, stalled by the economic downturn and credit tightening from 2010 to 2014, were revived by new funding arrangements under the BRI. Furthermore, all these infrastructure projects were closely tied to local governments, SOEs, and banks.

The NDRC and CBRC document opens in this way: "Due to economic pressure, Rails-Highways-Infrastructure is a sure way to stabilize economic growth."[68] In detail, it explains how Hunan's government leveraged the BRI to revive infrastructure and development. In one case, the provincial government provided RMB ¥2.5 billion to purchase low-grade equity in a previously paused rail project; CDB then rallied Postal Savings Bank, Pudong Development Bank, and others to raise RMB ¥7.5 billion to purchase high-grade equity in the project.[69] In another case, a railway project was started in 2008, costing RMB ¥23 billion, of which the Ministry of Railways and Hunan's government would each provide

66 "Jiaqiang hezuo wei yidai yilu tigong jinrong baozhang—zhuanfang zhongguo yinjianhui zhuxi shangfulin" [Enhance Cooperation to Provide Financial Safeguard to the BRI – Special Interview with Chinese Banking Minister Shang Fulin], *Jingji Ribao* [Economics Daily], March 30, 2016, www.financialnews.com.cn/jg/dt/201603/t20160330_94783.html.

67 NDRC and CBRC, "Yidai yilu rongzifa" [One Belt and One Road Financing Method], *Caixin Weekly*, 43, 2015, pp. 36–39.

68 Unless stated otherwise, the examples in BRI financing projects are from NDRC and CBRC, 2015.

69 In 2016, the exchange rate was around RMB ¥6.8 to US $1.0.

25 percent and provincial SOE Hunan Railways would raise loans for 50 percent. The project began to fall apart in 2010 when Hunan Railways could not obtain loans. In 2011, the Ministry of Railways also pulled out. Thanks to the BRI, in 2015, CDB stepped in and formed a group bank consisting of China Construction Bank, CEIB, and a local bank to lend RMB ¥9 billion to Hunan Railways. Construction was fully resumed.

A similar process prevailed in the third case in Hunan. A railway project connecting poverty-stricken mountain areas in Hunan province had depended on provincial SOE Hunan Infrastructure Investment for financing. The project stopped short in 2014 because the SOE accumulated too many bank loans and could not obtain any more. In 2015, CDB's Hunan branch stepped in and, together with the provincial government and the SOE, formed a fund-plus-loans-plus-PPP financing mechanism. Through this mechanism, the local government provided ¥2.5 billion and CDB-led banks contributed ¥10 billion to form the Railway Construction Fund. The rest of the funds came from other financing instruments in the PPP scheme. In line with the practice, by late 2015, CDB's Hunan branch had formed group banks for twenty-five projects in the province, totalling ¥143 billion, including thirty-four highways and eight railways in Hunan.[70] In short, the BRI mobilization revived domestic financing in the localities and served two purposes: to boost GDP growth against economic downturn and help build connectivity inside China.

Zooming into projects in the localities, it became clear that the BRI had allowed some local governments to save loss-making SOEs as well. In Jiangxi, a province in central China, local government set up four funds to save energy chemical companies in the name of exploring overseas opportunities now unfolding with the BRI. Yulin city in inland China also injected funds to save unprofitable coal industry in the name of BRI.[71] Despite overcapacity and pollution, local steelmakers saw the BRI as a "precious opportunity" to stay afloat.[72] In the western province of Gansu, a loss-making state steelmaker received

[70] "Yidai yilu jijian xindai yangben: Guokai hang yanyi zonghe jinrong xietiaoren" [BRI Credit and Loans Sample: CDB Acts as General Broker], *21shiji jingji baogao*, October 26, 2015, www.cdb.com.cn/xwzx/mtjj/201512/t20151211_1114.html.

[71] "Nengyuan huagong duijie yidai yilu yiqicheng" [China's Energy and Chemical Industries Have Started Implementing the Belt and Road], *Zhongguo jingji wang*, October 15, 2015, http://news.youth.cn/jsxw/201510/t20151015_7210198.htm.

[72] "Zhongguo gangtie yingzai yidai yilu shang" [China's Steels Gains from the Belt and Road], *Zhongguo yejinbao* [China Metals Industry Newspaper], July 8, 2015, www.fdi.gov.cn/1800000121_21_81224_0_7.html.

new loans "to go global, purchase raw materials, and establish new factors." Another bank improvised an "overcapacity industry plus 1" financing mechanism – bundling a competitive industry with an overcapacity industry to invest abroad. Although it is clearly difficult to export overcapacity, the local banks reason that in order to export, China has to provide money.[73]

Machinery industries affiliated with local governments were eager to latch onto the BRI. In Deyang city in western China, local governments managed to raise funds in the name of making the city a major supplier of heavy machinery to BRI countries, although machinery makers in the city lacked the technology to do so. The automobile industry is the same. Suffering from sliding overseas sales, CDB set up ¥10 billion to offer customers in Pakistan, Indonesia, Kazakhstan, and Tajikistan so that they could once again order Chinese vehicles. CDB's act, to Chinese automobile exporters, was truly like "sending charcoal [on] a winter day."[74] A metal company in Gansu, which had suffered from overcapacity and financial stress, managed to borrow $1.4 billion from Bank of China's domestic and foreign branches to acquire a metal ore in South Africa. Another company borrowed ¥1.2 billion from China Industrial and Commercial Bank to acquire a gold ore in South Africa.[75] The financier also sent three investment experts to help with the acquisition.

Two dangers loom large in the BRI's rhetorical ambition and localized implementation. Focusing on the BRI's diplomatic ambition, reinforced by loosely reported high price tags, many countries began to have unrealistic expectations of Chinese investment and lending. Such expectations can quickly lead to disappointments and disputes. In Thailand, the host government was surprised at the rather steep rate for China's "concessionary" loans to finance the speed rail that was to be constructed by Chinese railway companies.[76] In Pakistan, the host government was shocked to realize that only Chinese funds spelled out in the

[73] Wu Hong, "Yidai yilu jiannan juejin" [Belt and Road Works Hard to Expand Business], *Caixin Weekly*, No. 50, 2015.

[74] Ibid.

[75] "Yidai yilu zhanlue zhu qiye zouchuqu duguo yandong" [One Belt and One Road Help Chinese Companies Go Global to Overcome Economic Winter], *Jinrong shibao* [Financial Times], November 24, 2015, http://stock.jrj.com.cn/2015/11/24043020122483.shtml.

[76] Interviews of project participants in Thailand.

"early harvest" programs were qualified for concessionary rates, and the remaining financing needed to follow different rate negotiations.[77]

The real danger, as the study here reveals, is in debt-financed infrastructure and industry in Chinese localities. Such debt-financed development in 2008–2012 had been the main reason for China's economic problems in recent years. The BRI, as the early activities show, seemed to have loosened regulation and allowed many loss-making SOEs to stay afloat rather than to phase out. Politically, this might be expedient for the localities; economically, the cost is dear and has to be addressed in the future.

CONCLUSION

The Belt and Road's long-term impact and implications remain to be seen. This chapter investigates its origins, policy formation, and implementation and compares it with the WDP and CGG along the state-mobilized globalization perspective. First, like the WDP and CGG, the BRI's birthing demonstrates that state fragmentation and economic crises have jointly propelled the political leadership to launch nationalist strategies. Then, as the process moves from a set of incongruent proposals to an all-inclusive strategy, the BRI became a political campaign that mobilized major interest groups and subnational states. Finally, the early implementation of BRI, like in the WDP and CGG processes, demonstrates wide gaps and fragmentation between the strategy's political rhetoric and reality on the ground. Stamped with the seals of the political leader, the BRI has paradoxically bolstered major interest groups and lower-level governments that now take over implementation in a highly fragmented fashion.

From 1998 to 2018, differences were also apparent in the systematic comparison of the three strategies. To be specific, in the WDP, top-down mobilization was maintained with reasonably high cohesion at the top layer of the state system. The political leadership and the heads of national agencies converged clearly on internal development priorities. Hence, the political mobilization worked to consistently enhance market-led economic growth in western China. In the CGG, while the

[77] R. Shahbaz, *Pakistan Stops Bid to Include Diamer-Bhasha Dam in CPEC*, November 15, 2017,https://tribune.com.pk/story/1558475/2-pakistan-stops-bid-include-diamer-bhasha-dam-cpec/; "The NDRC Briefs on the Status of China-Pakistan Economic Corridor," December 17, 2017, http://zys.ndrc.gov.cn/xwfb/201712/t20171207_869891.html; A. Jamil, S. Henny, and B. Farhan, "Pakistan Rethinks Its Role in Xi's Belt and Road Plan," September 9, 2018, www.ft.com/content/d4a3e7f8-b282-11e8-99ca-68cf89602132.

political leadership promulgated outbound globalization as a national priority, economic bureaucracies were fragmented into different preferences. Furthermore, subnational actors reinterpreted and improvised the CGG to suit their own needs and often diverged from the strategic intent spoken by the political leadership. Hence, internal investment grew more rapidly than outbound globalization. In the BRI, there seemed to be a general and broad consensus on the need to integrate foreign policy and domestic development, but how to go about it and whether it should be done in a strategy like the BRI are debated and open to different interpretations.

Ambitious rhetoric – critical to overcoming fragmentation in the BRI's birthing – and ambiguous guidelines – critical to incentivize lower units in the state system – are fundamental characteristics of state-mobilized globalization in China. They are perilous outside China, in particular with the country's growing power and increasingly personalistic autocracy. In moving the BRI forward, the Chinese implementers are likely to continue strong business orientation and pursue commercial interests. The recipient governments, however, are likely to view the BRI strategy as diplomatic moves by Beijing, which cares less about profits and returns. The gaps between Chinese actions and recipient expectations will give rise to diplomatic friction between China and the recipients and create backlash against China's outward globalization.

As China rises in the world, "magnanimous power" – to use James Reilly's phrase – may be acceptable and even welcomed; power for profit is certainly not. Unfortunately, the Chinese "political industrial complex" is deeply for profit.[78] As this book shows, prioritizing internal growth has been and will continue to shape Chinese outward investment and lending. However, this "power for profit" might have a silver lining in the meantime. Because of its commercial tendencies, Chinese outward capital has to follow "international norms and principles," as urged by the NDRC statement at the start of this chapter. Such a tendency may limit the BRI's ambition to "project power," but it may just make it more resilient over time. In the end, a "fragmented" rising power that pursues commercial interests is less intimidating than a "cohesive" autocracy seeking regional dominance and global leadership.

[78] James Reilly, "China's Economic Statecraft: Turning Wealth into Power," Lowy Institute for International Policy, University of Sidney, November 2013. www.lowyinstitute.org/sites/default/files/reilly_chinas_economic_statecraft_web_0.pdf.

PART III

SUBNATIONAL ACTORS

6

A Tale of Three Cities

> Economic planning is easier from top down than bottom up. We welcome economic directives from the central government, because once we include our priorities in the central planning, they can be implemented more quickly.
>
> —Remark by an anonymous local cadre[1]

Ambitious strategies launched by the political leadership, such as the WDP, CGG, and BRI, mobilized local governments to implement them in their jurisdictions. Local governments, however, drawing on the strategies ambiguity, improvise projects and program that often diverge from the rhetoric at the strategies and yet conform to their local economic needs. It is in this process of subnational reinterpretation that proclaimed nationalist intent in the strategies is replaced by economic imperatives in the localities. This chapter investigates three cities – Chongqing, Ningbo, and Wenzhou – to evaluate local reinterpretation, diverse implementation, and economic effects in local development, realized and ongoing.

These three cities have been chosen to maximize variables that shape the patterns of localization of nationalist strategies: They have different levels of economic power granted by the national government, different levels of local technocracy, varied economic structures, and varied corporate interests.[2] Furthermore, the cities illustrate three economic

[1] The director of economic planning office of a semiprovincial city in coastal China, August 2016.

[2] These variables constitute of different development constitution across local governments in China. See Thun, *Changing Lanes in China*; Xiaoxiao Shen and Kellee Tsai, "Institutional Adaptability in China: Local Developmental Models under Changing Economic Conditions," *World Development*, 87, 2016, pp. 107–127.

patterns in China that approximate the paradigms in comparative political economy: state capitalism, developmental state, and liberal market. Chongqing has a significant SOE presence, state banks, and a highly politicized local government, thus representing a prototype of state capitalism. Ningbo has a diverse economic structure and highly competent local bureaucracies that more or less conform to the developmental state model. Wenzhou, with its dominant private capital and a weak local state, is rather similar to the liberal market model.

The comparative cities confirm that different political–economic conditions lead to completely different interpretations of the same nationalist strategies. In Chongqing, local SOEs and state banks led implementation of the strategies and adopted measures that primarily served to revive and revitalize local state sectors. In Ningbo, economic bureaucrats utilized the national strategies to devise local economic planning and inaugurated new policies that aimed to upgrade local industry. Implementation in Wenzhou demonstrated a market-led response to economic challenges, with private enterprises adopting measures that served short-term business interests.

In terms of which city is best at tackling the twin challenges in China – rebalancing the economy from investment to consumption and upgrading from low-tech industry to high-tech manufacturing – there are no clear winners. The city and policy that are better at one task can be counterproductive at the other. Wenzhou, for example, is the least effective among the three in state-led industrial upgrading, and yet is most effective in market-driven restructuring.

COMPARING CITIES

The three cities chosen for comparison represent different economic regions in China, each with a distinct set of historical and socialist legacies, local government capacities, and relative strength of private economies. Chongqing is a representative and leading city in western China. Ningbo exhibits political–economic legacies and institutions surrounding Shanghai, including southern Jiangsu and northern Zhejiang. Wenzhou, by contrast, belongs to the economic region surrounding southern Zhejiang and Fujian province.[3] Table 6.1 summarizes the political–economic

3 Also see Barry Naughton, *The Chinese Economy: Adaptation and Growth*. Cambridge, MA: MIT Press, 2018, p. 31.

TABLE 6.1. *Comparing cities at a glimpse*

	Location	Political status	Market structure	Technocracy
Chongqing	Western China	Provincial level	SOE-dominated	Medium
Ningbo	Eastern China	Semiprovincial	Diverse capitalism	High
Wenzhou	Southeastern China	Prefecture level	Private-dominated	Low

Source: Made by Author.

characteristics of the three cities. Therefore, even though China has a centralized system, different local institutions – political status, market structure, and technocracy – have shaped different means of interpretation and implementation of national strategies in different cities.

Chongqing is one of the four provincial cities – on par with Beijing, Shanghai, and Tianjin – and has the highest economic power among the three compared cities. SOEs dominate the local economy, followed by large MNCs, with private capital coming a distant third. Ningbo is one of the twelve "specially designated" cities [*jihua danlie shi*] and has significantly more economic clout than regular prefecture-level cities but less than provincial cities in China. The Ningbo government can implement local lending, tax, and land policies that are more favorable than those implemented nationally. Private enterprises have contributed to the majority of local GDP, yet the city also has significant numbers of SOEs and foreign companies. Wenzhou is a prefecture-level city and, compared to Chongqing and Ningbo, does not have particular economic power in financing, fiscal policies, or land provisions. Wenzhou's local economy is predominantly private – private firms contributed more than 90 percent of industrial output in the city.

Table 6.1 presents the levels of technocracy among the local governments. Focusing on educational attainment and exposure to external information – defined by experiences in other Chinese cities and abroad – Ningbo's bureaucrats display high expertise and exposure, followed by Chongqing, with Wenzhou bringing up the rear. Expertise is measured by academic degrees received by city bureaucrats, in the order of PhD, MA, BA (or BS), and associate degrees. Furthermore, in each city, I observed the foreign education and experience of local bureaucrats, think-tank networks in the city and beyond, and informal networks between city

TABLE 6.2. *Local reinterpretation of national strategies*

	Programs participated in	Key local actors	Economic agendas	Outcome
Chongqing	WDP; BRI	SOEs	Infrastructure; financing; SOE revenues	Strengthening of SOEs
Ningbo	CGG; BRI	Economic bureaucracies	Industrial upgrades, rebalancing	Strengthened local state and FDI
Wenzhou	WDP; CGG; BRI	Private entrepreneurs	Exporting markets	Expanded markets

Source: Made by Author.

officials and external advisors. It is clear from field observation that the Ningbo government has high exposure to external information, Chongqing officials have medium-level exposure, and Wenzhou officials have the least.

Distinct local economic and political contexts correspond to marked differences in localized implementation of the national strategies, such as whether the city creates programs to implement, who the key local implementers are, what the specific programs are, and what effects the programs have on local development (see Table 6.2). In Chongqing, the local government boasts slogans such as being the "strategic pillar" of the BRI and "new high ground of openness" [*kaifang xin gaodi*] in western China throughout its interpretation of the BRI strategy. Both slogans, however, came from Beijing's think-tank scholars rather than from the city government. Instead, during interviews, local state agents were generally careful and refrained from discussing the city's BRI projects and programs. The most salient implementers and most eager supporters of the BRI were local SOEs, which spun off new – usually online – businesses to earn new revenues and access new financing.[4]

The local government in Ningbo was most proactive and strategic among the three. Leveraging the BRI, the city came up with a transnational investment consortium, a new free trade area, and a new maritime trading index that purported to rival foreign maritime indexes. Main

[4] Determination of local dynamics rely significantly on field surveys and interviews with local governments and companies. In these cases, I also collected online materials to support and verify interviews.

implementers in Ningbo, in contrast to Chongqing, are well-trained economic bureaucrats who aspire to upgrade local industry, diversify the local economy, and boost the city's global profile. In Wenzhou, the local government was passive toward the BRI: Local cadres, preoccupied with social stability and public goods provision, no longer treat economic growth as a priority. Individual private entrepreneurs, however, strategically utilized the BRI to organize an annual trade expo in Western Europe, where they have had strong business interests.

Furthermore, cities can also choose to participate in one nationalist strategy but not another. In Table 6.2, Chongqing has actively implemented the WDP and BRI, both of which helped reform and revive SOEs in the city. Ningbo actively implemented the CGG and BRI, both of which aimed primarily to attract inbound FDI to new economic zones in the city. In Wenzhou, despite an inactive government, private entrepreneurs have participated in all three strategies. In the case of the WDP, Wenzhou's private entrepreneurs saw market opportunities in western China and expanded investment and manufacturing into the hinterlands. In the case of the CGG, Wenzhou's private entrepreneurs expanded export markets and investment in the world. Furthermore, in the BRI, Wenzhou's manufacturers and entrepreneurs wanted to find new markets for existing industries rather than moving into high-tech sectors as identified by the national and local governments.[5]

To summarize, these cities provide findings that go beyond the national analyses in the earlier chapters. First, diverse and localized implementation presents compelling evidence that ambitious and ambiguous strategies have mobilized local state entities and corporations into action while permitting local actors to reinterpret and deviate from national guidelines. Second, contributing to the study of Chinese central–local relations, the chapter updates whether and how central–local interactions have evolved and been challenged during China's globalization.

In Chongqing, continuity is all-important. State capital, after rounds of corporatization and privatization, still plays a leading role in defining and implementing national policies in the city. In Ningbo, the local state has been versatile and agile in matching national programs with local industrial ambitions. In Wenzhou, while private economy dominates the market, the city leadership can help or hinder local development: When city leadership leveraged national strategies and private capital

[5] See Lin Li, "Xin changtai, xin Wenzhou" [The "New Normal" and the New Wenzhou], *Wenzhou Xuekan* [Wenzhou Research Magazine], No. 3, June 2014, pp. 19–25.

successfully, the local economy thrived; when city leadership acted on national programs but *against* local business, the economy suffered. Most of the time, however, city heads merely waited to be promoted out, with little effect on local development.

Chongqing Playing Catch-up

Chongqing is a historic and economic center in western China. Before China's economic reform, Chongqing's economy and industry were ahead of both Ningbo and Wenzhou. However, from 1978 to 1998, as reform and openness generated rapid growth and globalization in coastal China, western industrial heavyweights like Chongqing fell behind. The 1999 WDP strategy was launched to expedite economic growth in western China in order to allow the region to catch up with coastal regions. Comparing economic performance in Chongqing with Ningbo and Wenzhou (Figure 6.1) using GDP growth rates and FDI inflows suggests

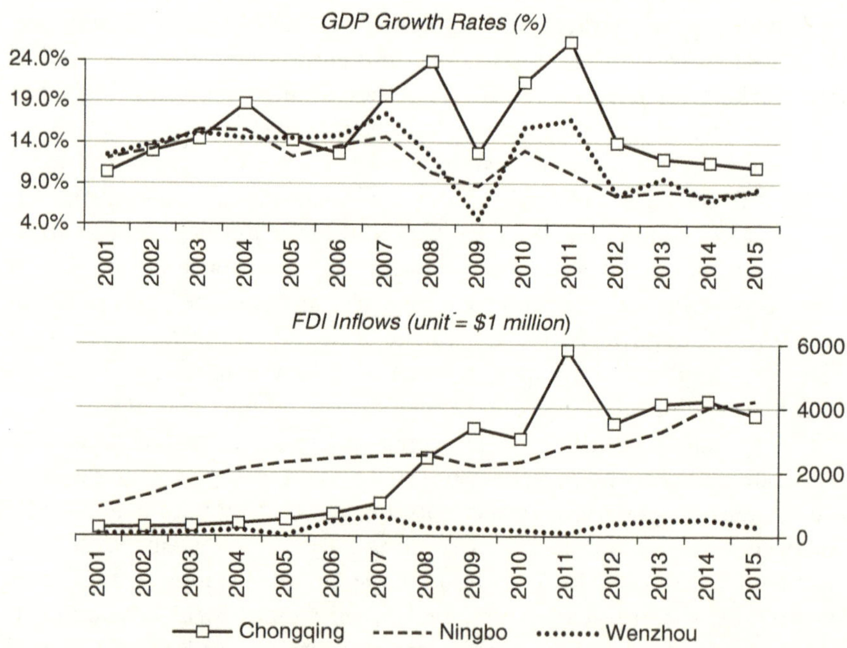

FIGURE 6.1. Chongqing, Ningbo, and Wenzhou: Growth and globalization. *Source:* Author, computed from raw data in Statistical Yearbooks of Chongqing, Ningbo, and Wenzhou, various editions. *Note:* FDI inflows serve to measure the rate of globalization in the city.

that the WDP was somewhat effective in narrowing the gaps from 2001 to 2007, but Chongqing's superior performance compared to the other cities occurred after 2008.

Specifically, in 2001, Chongqing's GDP growth was lower than that of Ningbo and Wenzhou and continued to be the lowest among the three until 2004. Nonetheless, GDP growth rates in the three cities were all extraordinarily high: In 2003, Chongqing's GDP growth was 14.5 percent, while growth rates in Ningbo and Wenzhou were more than 15 percent. Starting in 2004, GDP growth in Chongqing surpassed the other two cities and reached as high as 18 percent. After the 2008 global financial crisis, which impacted export-oriented economies more severely than others, Chongqing's GDP growth was substantially better than its coastal counterparts. In 2009, for example, Wenzhou's growth rate was 4.7 percent, its lowest in decades. Chongqing also experienced lower growth, but remained at a reasonably high 12.7 percent.

As the Chinese economy entered the "new normal" under the current administration, starting in 2012, growth rates in the three cities were all significantly lower than they were at their peak, yet Chongqing performed better than the others. In terms of inbound FDI, as demonstrated in the lower chart in Figure 6.1, Chongqing performed better than Wenzhou but was far behind Ningbo from 2001 to 2008. From 2009 to 2014, Chongqing's inbound FDI also surpassed that of Ningbo.

Chongqing's industrial catch-up from 2000 to 2015 demonstrates mutual enhancement between the state and market, as well as strong links between top-down strategies – such as the WDP – and local government initiatives. To be specific, in implementing the WDP, the Chongqing government was granted considerable power pressure to restructure and reform loss-making SOEs. To help Chongqing in this task, Beijing appointed former vice mayor of Shanghai Huang Qifang to the city in 2001. Huang, with decades of experience and business networks in Shanghai, replicated many of Shanghai's financial measures and endeavored to attract foreign electronics producers to relocate from coastal China to the western city. Drawing on Shanghai's earlier experiences in reforming SOEs, Huang's measures precipitated SOE reforms in Chongqing.

In short, the WDP strategy greatly expanded the role of markets in Chongqing by appointing market-oriented local officials, incentivizing SOE privatization, and enhancing the trend of globalization. Under the WDP, Chongqing's SOE shares in local GDP dropped significantly.

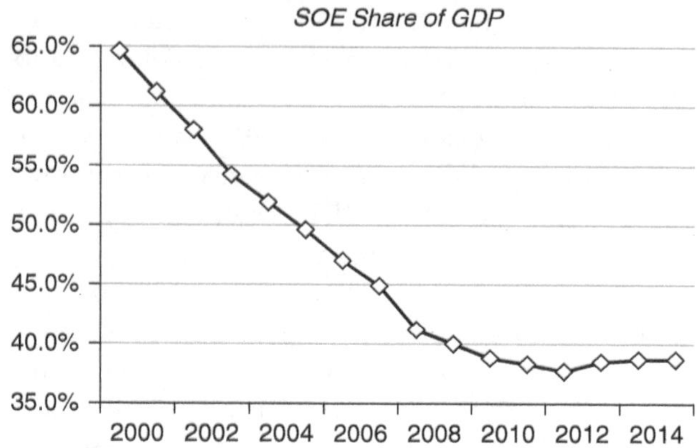

FIGURE 6.2. WDP and declining SOEs in Chongqing. *Source:* Author, based on raw data in Chongqing Statistics Yearbook, annual editions.

As can be seen in Figure 6.2, from 1999 to 2004, which constituted the first phase of the WDP, the share of SOEs in local GDP declined from 65 to 52 percent. In the second phase, from 2005 to 2008, the SOEs' share continued to decline rapidly, from 50 to 40 percent. Then the rate of SOE privatization stagnated; from 2012 onward, SOEs' weight in the local economy climbed slightly, from 37.7 to 38.7 percent in 2015.

Moving to the BRI, field research demonstrates that SOEs remain the main economic actors in Chongqing and enjoy robust support from the local government. Although there is a general consensus on the need for restructuring SOEs, there are no calls for sweeping privatization or reduction of SOEs' roles in the city. Chongqing's dependence on SOEs to implement nationalist strategies differs from the patterns in Ningbo and Wenzhou, but it is similar to many cities in the western, central, and northeastern regions of China, where SOEs continue to serve as leading players in the local economy. State capital in general, however, have been transformed to pursue commercial interests. They have emerged as active market actors engaged in globalization. Indeed, in Chongqing, reinvigorated state capital has been the source of high growth.

State, Market, and Capital during the WDP

The WDP, launched by former president Jiang Zemin against the backdrop of the economic crises of 1999, served as a major turning point in Chongqing's development. Chongqing was granted by the central government the status of provincial city and received preferential policies to conduct growth and globalization measures. Furthermore, the WDP provided special latitude for western China to expedite privatization of SOEs and offer incentives to attract foreign and private capital into the region. In 2001, the Chongqing government set up the Yufu Asset Management Group to resolve heavy nonperforming loans in the state sector and help restructure SOEs in the city. In the following years, Yufu Asset Management used land formerly occupied by SOEs as collateral to borrow from China Development Bank and commercial banks to buy out debts in the state sector. To promote the restructuring of state capital, Chongqing's government then established eight competitive SOEs that had strong market potential to conduct infrastructure investment, including transportation, energy, water, industrial and commercial real estate, and public housing.[6]

Under the WDP, Chongqing's government was able to apply exceptional incentives to foreign and private investors in the city and thereafter enhanced market forces. In the early 2000s, the city established several industrial zones and provided them with generous incentives and preferential policies. In the electronics high-tech zone, for example, the city government strived to attract Hewlett Packard (HP) to establish a production base. In addition to tax concessions and rebates, the government pledged to purchase more than 100,000 HP notebooks per year for three years. Furthermore, in order to attract and retain a skilled workforce from outside Chongqing, the city constructed subsidized public housing and invested in healthcare and education, which also relieved companies of social burdens. Because a large part of the workforce in coastal China had been migrants from the western region, Chongqing's industrial catch-up helped drive the labor force's return. Such return migration helped companies in coastal China relocate to Chongqing. Among them, Taiwanese manufacturers such as Foxconn were prominent; along with electronics component makers, other electronics brands also expanded into Chongqing.[7]

In the process of the WDP and Chongqing's resurgence, political strongmen helped integrate central power and local policy initiatives.

[6] This case draws on Liu Weidong, Michael Dunford, Song Zhouying, and Chen Mingxing, "Urban-Rural Integration Drives Regional Economic Growth in Chongqing, Western China," *Area Development and Policy*, 1(1), 2016, pp. 132–154.

[7] See Gao Boyang et al., "Capturing Gains by Relocating Global Production Networks: The Rise of Chongqing's Notebook Computer Industry, 2008–2014," *Eurasian Geography and Economics*, June 2017, pp. 1–27.

Chongqing's party secretary (from 2007 to 2012) Bo Xilai was the former minister of commerce (MOFCOM), and upon arriving in Chongqing, he brought major MNCs to visit and invest in Chongqing.[8] HP established a production site there in 2003, but in order for it to truly embed itself in the fabric of the city, it needed connectivity between Chongqing and Germany, HP's global distribution center. Bo Xilai, who had powerful connections in Beijing, arguably helped secure the national government's support for a transnational railway originating in Chongqing and crossing Xinjiang on its way to Germany. Named Yu-Xin-Ou [Chongqing–Xinjiang–Europe] Railway, the company involved the Ministry of Railways, Customs, MFA, MOFCOM, and their counterparts in Kazakhstan, Russia, and Germany. With the commitment of the Eurasian railway, HP relocated its manufacturing base to Chongqing. Along with HP's relocation, 5 large-brand notebook manufacturers, 6 large assemblers, and 800 parts and components suppliers all came to Chongqing. By 2011, Chongqing had emerged as the largest computer-manufacturing base in China.[9]

Furthermore, lower-level government officials in Chongqing had drawn on the WDP to attract private capital from the coastal region. In 2003, Bi County in Chongqing sent a delegation to Wenzhou, where shoemaking was one of the main industries. The delegation spoke to business leaders in Wenzhou and attracted interest from one of the largest shoemakers in China. To persuade the Wenzhou company, the county delegation carried a personal letter from Chongqing's party secretary. In addition, they offered 2,600 mu land – equivalent to 173 hectares – for the company to build a Shoe City [*xiedu*] in western China. Construction of Shoe City started in 2004, and it opened for business in 2005. However, the Wenzhou company production in Bi County remained small, using the site as a springboard to expand sales into interior China. Furthermore, the company constructed module factories in the Shoe City and rented them out to other shoemakers. As one of the earliest capital investors in the locality, the Wenzhou company soon became a key player in the emerging real estate market.

In the comparative literature on state capitalism in China, the focus is often on the state – how political priorities shape corporate behaviors and how the state provides subsidies to benefit SOEs – and has not

[8] Calder and Ye, *Making of Northeast Asia*, pp. 176–181.

[9] Gao et al., "Capturing Gains by Relocating Global Production Networks."

been on capitalist behaviors in state capitalism.[10] Chongqing's industrial catch-up and the WDP strategy demonstrate that state capitalism can coexist with market rationales, with the local state providing facilitative conditions to attract market-based investors. They also demonstrate, for a latecomer in growth and globalization, the state has special roles to play in helping market grow. The western region, compared to coastal China, had advantages in land, labor and resources. Yet it needed the government to invest in infrastructure and connectivities to make it a feasible manufacturing center. When governments provided preferential incentives to attract private and foreign capital into the western region, former migrants to coastal cities began to return, making this place a viable destination for industrial relocation and expansion of coastal production in China.

BRI as New-Round Opening in Western China

The BRI's domestic proportion – from Xi'an westward to Xinjiang – overlapped with the coverage of the WDP; the BRI's governing agency was the same Western Development Bureau in the NDRC. Policy specialists in Beijing, in mobilizing local implementation, called upon Chongqing to develop itself into BRI's "strategic pillar" and urged the city to construct infrastructure to connect western China more closely with the eastern region, thereby facilitating implementation of the BRI.[11] In a 2015 edition of *People's Daily*, an editorial read, "Development of a region must fully comply with strategic development of the nation, to serve the nation while improving itself."[12] In line with top-down mobilization, the Chongqing government publicized its BRI slogan, "Make Chongqing a new high ground of openness in interior China," and set up an offshore center for whole-car imports, three tariff-free zones, and new technology policies.

To mobilize the Chongqing government, in 2015, the head of BRI Small Leading Group Zhang Gaoli asked Chongqing to devise local

[10] Kellee Tsai, "The State of China's Economic Miracle," *Asia Policy*, 20, July 2015, pp. 144–148.

[11] "Chongqing: tongda jianghai xibu kaifa de zhongyao zhicheng" [Chongqing: Connecting River and Sea, a Major Pillar of Western Development], Phoenix International Think Tank, March 28, 2016.

[12] "Quanmian rongru yidai yilu he changjiang jingjidai zhanlue" [Fully Comply with One Belt and One Road and Yangtze River Economic Belt Strategy], *Remin Ribao* [People's Daily], November 10, 2015.

programs that would integrate the BRI with the Yangtze River Economic Belt [Changjiang jingjidai]. In the same year, the All China Customs Conference and the Quality Supervision and Inspection Conference – involving many industries and central agencies – were held in Chongqing. In January 2016, President Xi personally visited Chongqing to promote the BRI, and following Xi's visit, the central government approved the Sino-Singapore Financial Park in Chongqing. Facing such intense mobilization, economic planners in the city have been surprisingly passive. In all their discourses on the BRI's implementation, they underscored the centrality of market forces, *not the state*, to the achievement of industrial upgrading.[13] Their relative aloofness was due to the fact that the BRI offered few concrete incentives for major local projects – the Sino-Singapore Park in Chongqing, for example, was a new "title" on an existing facility, not a new zone for investors.

Compared to the state, state capital in Chongqing had been more active and used the BRI as an opportunity to provide *selective* rescue to struggling SOEs. The Ex-Im Bank branch in Chongqing passed a myriad of financial instruments, including export insurance and import credit to Chongqing's exporters and importers and funds for Chongqing's trading companies, machinery makers, and high-tech exports. As Chongqing's signature BRI scheme, CEIB's Chongqing branch launched "3 + N" to support local SOEs' attempts to go global (the "3" in the scheme refers to Chongqing's CEIB, Chongqing's MOFCOM, and Chongqing Foreign Trade Group – a provincial SOE). Such an arrangement promoted exports and overseas investment made by SOEs in Chongqing. Actual projects may diverge from such agendas. The well-known programs in the early phase of the BRI belonged to low-risk business expansions.

In 2014, Chongqing Foreign Trade Group founded a subsidiary company named Yu-Xin-Ou [Chongqing-Xinjiang-Europe] Ecommerce. The ecommerce company, although not affiliated with the China-Europe railway, drew significant publicity and prestige by using this name. In interview, it was clear that the company's main mandate was to generate profits to its parent SOE. Leveraging the BRI, the e-commerce company started business and expanded quickly. It thrived by *buying* consumer goods from Western Europe and selling them to consumers in western China, thanks to tariff relief through two new zones passed in Chongqing in the backdrop of BRI. In short, while at the national level, the BRI urged Chinese companies to sell Chinese products abroad,

[13] Interviews in Chongqing, summer 2016.

in the locality, Yu-Xin-Ou Ecommerce did just the opposite and helped bring more foreign goods to China, but at a more competitive price.

The centrality of the state and state capital to Chongqing's globalization and industrial resurgence was well captured by a long-term director of the Foreign Investment Promotion Bureau in the city. "Chongqing's success was due to state companies' leading roles, followed by influx of private capital, and then foreign capital," observed the director. "Were there no SOEs to get the market ready, what can foreign capital do?"[14] This observation was quite remarkable, considering that the director's job was to promote FDI in Chongqing.

In summary, the WDP process shows that underneath the nationalist strategy, Chongqing's government conducted SOE reforms and implemented pro-business policies. Relying on state banks and SOEs, the local government was able to construct infrastructure, public housing, and other social provisions, all important conditions for private and foreign investors. Leveraging the BRI, the local state acquired power to set up preferential zones and provided favorable policies to investors, thus leading to expansion of internet-based commerce in the city. The chief economic effect of the BRI in Chongqing was expansion of the internal market, not so much external extension. The political effect, of the nationalist strategies, however, can be regressive. The director of the Foreign Investment Promotion Bureau put it best when he confessed, "I am nothing without the platform provided by the government." In Chongqing, successful implementation of the WDP and BRI has enhanced state capitalism, with state agencies and private companies playing less salient roles in the local economy.

TECHNOCRATIC PLANNING IN NINGBO

It was a delight to conduct academic research in Ningbo. Government officials are professional, knowledgeable, and articulate. They explain clearly what they do, take your questions, and are happy to provide their own opinions; meanwhile, they are respectful of scholars and are eager to solicit external advice. They have a striking resemblance to economic technocrats in Japan and South Korea, who proactively interact with specialists when making new policies. Of the seven interviewed city bureaucrats, three of them have overseas master's degrees; three have master's degrees from top schools in China and are presently enrolled in doctoral

[14] Interviews in Chongqing, summer 2016.

programs at Zhejiang University and Fudan University. The remaining one was a senior director in the Customs Bureau who graduated from a highly regarded economics program in China.

I also interviewed managers of three SOEs based in Ningbo. Compared to the government bureaucrats, SOE managers had less impressive educational backgrounds and had risen in their companies through decades of work experience. Clearly, they understood their companies' history, business, and clients, yet they had little international exposure and showed no interest in speaking on issues beyond their immediate responsibilities. Neither were they interested in taking scholarly questions, nor seeking scholarly advice. In 2016, asked about the BRI, the SOE managers were pragmatic and supported the strategy in principle but had yet to allocate concrete resources to facilitate its implementation. The projects that the SOEs listed as relevant to the BRI were in line with business needs that preexisted the launch of the strategy.

CGG as Inbound Globalization

The CGG strategy aimed to encourage Chinese companies to find overseas markets and invest abroad. In Ningbo, the city government identified and interpreted the strategy as an opportunity to attract inbound FDI and develop an export-processing economy. The CGG's critical importance to Ningbo's globalization did not lie in any specific policy content – other than the ambivalent wording "going global" – but in enhancing the role of local states in making inbound globalization policies. According to a long-term manager of Ningbo's most famed export processing zone, the State Council approved the proposal for an export-processing zone in 1992 but it took until 2002 for construction of the zone to be completed; the CGG helped with the tail end of this process.

Drawing on the CGG, Ningbo's government provided highly favorable incentives to the zone management office.[15] First, the city government only exercised a formal jurisdiction over the zone, providing neither budget nor oversight. The zone management thus operated with high-level autonomy. The zone and local government's revenue sharing was 6:4 in favor of the zone, in which the zone management had discretion over 32 percent of its tax revenues. To attract more foreign companies

[15] The case is drawn from interviews with managers of Ningbo's export-processing zones, as well as zone policies and materials provided by the managers.

to register in and relocate to the zone, the zone management typically rebated the discretionary revenues to the companies. Such incentives were important to lure a set of suppliers for Taiwanese electronics makers. To best serve these firms, the zone management set up a new office specifically to search for workers from outside Ningbo.

By 2008, however, development based on inbound FDI and processing exports had become unsustainable in Ningbo because the eastern city had a very limited labor force of its own. And due to rapidly rising housing cost, zone management has faced significant challenges in retaining migrant workers from outside Ningbo. Furthermore, FDI-led processing trade resulted in structural imbalance in the local economy. Exports were concentrated in consumer and light manufacturing goods; imports consisted of resources and raw materials. Such imbalance rendered Ningbo vulnerable to fluctuations in the global market. In 2012, in order to diversify its trade structure, Beijing selected Ningbo as one of five experimental e-commerce cities. Like in Chongqing, Ningbo's e-commerce business focused on imports of consumer goods and grew rapidly from 2013. However, in 2016, with some RMB ¥2 billion ($0.3 billion) of business, e-commerce accounted for 2 percent of total trade. Clearly, e-commerce was in no position to make up for losses in FDI-led export-processing industries; Ningbo had to find new sources for local development.

Against this economic backdrop, the local government proactively searched for new industries that could revive growth in the city. Economic planners studied nearby Shanghai and Hangzhou for models and aspired to replicate these cities new-tech manufacturing in Ningbo. The planners recognized that the main hurdle to Ningbo's high-tech aspiration was the city's "low global profile," which made it difficult to attract "high-quality" foreign capital that could bring advanced technology and management, help grow new sectors in Ningbo, and attract global talent and a high-caliber workforce.

Even before the BRI, Ningbo had pursued two-pronged industrial policies. First, the city set up a new office of inbound FDI Promotion in the Commerce Bureau, headed by a returnee who had worked in Ningbo's NDRC for more than a decade. This office focused on attracting investment from companies on the world's *Fortune 500* list. Second, the city expanded a new industrial zone in the Plum Mountain area, which was provided with "world-class" facilitates and services to attract new investors. The BRI's launch became a facilitative juncture for bottom-up economic planning in Ningbo.

BRI as Industrial Planning from Below

In summer 2017, Ningbo's new economic zone Plum Mountain acquired its status as Zhejiang province's BRI experimental site and is in the process of seeking national recognition. Among coastal cities, Ningbo has consistently leveraged the BRI and churned out many well-publicized programs to implement the strategy. One of the early programs was the Central and Eastern Europe (CEE) Project, in which the city designated a sizable building to serve as a permanent site to exhibit and sell goods from CEE countries. In addition, the city budget subsidized trade and exchange between Ningbo and CEE countries; average tariffs for foreign goods were 2 percent in Ningbo, and tariffs for similar goods from CEE were halved to 1 percent. Furthermore, a Ningbo company (including private ones) could apply for travel expenses for business exploration trips to CEE markets. Finally, Ningbo proposed hosting a CEE Trade Fair as a nationally recognized international trade consortium, which could boost Ningbo into a "global" city that could host "international" events.[16]

Why did Ningbo's planners come up with the CEE project as its key program to implement the BRI? Three factors were at play. First, city planners had clearly listened to specialists and strategists from Beijing and recognized that among regions covered in the BRI, central and eastern Europe are both economically stable and strategically available for China to increase influence. Second, eight of Ningbo's top ten trading partners were actually in the CEE region, due to significant energy trade between China and CEE countries over the preceding period.[17] Reviving commerce with CEE regions was viewed as important to stabilizing the city's foreign trade. Finally, the rationale of industrial planning was clear. The launch of CEE helped Ningbo construct and expand the new economic zone of Plum Mountain. Simply put, the Ningbo government used the BRI as an opportunity to plan a new industrial policy that would facilitate the city's shift from a diverse economy toward more advanced FDI, from low-tech manufacturing to high-tech industry, and from a port-dominated economy to services.

Ningbo's BRI projects deviated from the rhetoric of the BRI as espoused by the political leader. For example, the top-level BRI proclaimed to

[16] Only cities that receive support from the national government, in particular the Ministry of Foreign Affairs and Ministry of Commerce, can host international events and thus assume a "global" profile that appeals to foreign capital.

[17] For a study of energy linkage between China and Eastern and Central Europe, see Kent Calder, *The New Continentalism: Energy and Twenty First Century Eurasian Geopolitics*. New Haven, CT: Yale University Press, 2017.

encourage Chinese capital to invest abroad; Ningbo's BRI endeavors were mostly to attract inbound FDI to help local industrial upgrading. In order to attract more advanced FDI, the BRI projects in Ningbo strived to raise the city's global profile. Should the CEE cooperation be routinized as a multinational gathering, Ningbo may be able to match up with other Chinese cities – such as Guangzhou and Hangzhou – as host cities for transnational organizations.

Applying the same logic, the Ningbo city government delegated a local SOE – Ningbo's Logistic Company – to devise a Maritime Silk Road Shipping Index, which was included in the nation's 13th Five Year Plan (FYP) in 2016. The Maritime Silk Road Shipping Index, touted as the second of the world's only two maritime trade indexes – the other being the Baltic Exchange Index – was a boost for Ningbo's global profile. The architect of the index – also CEO of the city SOE – took great pride in designing and promoting the index at the national level; in the meantime, he was under pressure to find healthy, sustainable revenues for his company. Presently, the city government financed the index as part of a branding drive for the city, but sooner or later, the government will apply pressure and ask the index to stand on its own. Under such pressure, the SOE worked tirelessly to provide services and products that other companies could buy later. The CEO himself was enrolled in a computer science PhD program at Zhejiang University in order to expand business links between Ningbo and Hangzhou, the heart of internet-enabled services in China, and to develop marketable products for the company.

Industrial planning was clear in the Plum Mountain New Zone in Ningbo. Leveraging the BRI, the New Zone was expanded significantly as a new platform of globalization. In order to copy practices and build connections with companies in Shanghai, Ningbo's government hired a professor from Fudan University who previously served as an expert consultant in the planning for the Free Trade Zone in Shanghai. To further draw on experiences in Shanghai, one planner for the Plum Mountain New Zone was enrolled in the economics PhD program at Fudan University.

It is clear from these cases that the Ningbo government had proactively implemented the BRI as a new round of inbound globalization and industrial transformation, and it looked to Shanghai and Hangzhou as policy models and business links. In 2017, Plum Mountain was granted the status of Belt and Road Experimental Site in Zhejiang province, and a proposal was submitted to the State Council to present Ningbo as a national experimental site for the BRI. Whether Ningbo will succeed in this round of globalization remains to be seen. Thus far, the expanded and upgraded Plum Mountain zone is underutilized and its market links with Hangzhou and Shanghai have yet to be developed.

To summarize, Ningbo's interpretation and implementation of nationalist strategies reveal a strong and strategic local state that resembles the developmental state in Japan, South Korea, and Taiwan. In all these states, government officials were well trained and had good external exposure. They focused on policy learning and made "rational" planning decisions to achieve cohesive developmental goals. In Ningbo, the local state identified the weaknesses in the local economy and strived to attract high-tech FDI as a key program to upgrade the industry. To achieve this, it improvised the CEE, Maritime Silk Road Index, and Plum Mountain New Zone, all in an attempt to boost the city's global profile and attract technologically advanced foreign MNCs.

This developmental state pattern in Ningbo is quite different from the pattern of implementation in Chongqing, where state capital – banks and SOEs – improvised programs that helped struggling SOEs revive and expand revenue. It is also different from the pattern in Wenzhou, where private capital used the BRI banner to help expand business in line with market needs.

PRIVATE CAPITAL IN COMMAND IN WENZHOU

China has about 700 cities, more than half of which have the same administrative ranking (prefecture level) as Wenzhou. As a prefecture-level city, Wenzhou does not enjoy the kind of economic autonomy that Chongqing and Ningbo do. It cannot, for example, make drastically more favorable fiscal, financial, or land policies in the locality than those specified in the national regulations. Prefecture-city governments can approve zone projects and real estate deals, and they can provide credits and grants, but in zones of prefecture cities, national regulations are applied. Lacking autonomous economic power, Wenzhou and other prefecture-level cities cannot compete with specially designated cities such as Ningbo – or provincial cities such as Chongqing – in engineering industries or attract desirable companies.

Wenzhou is an anomaly among Chinese cities in many ways. It was the early pioneer of private economy in Communist China; its household-based and township-clustered manufacturing became the exemplar for such cities in the 1980s, earning the city the "model" status, in juxtaposition to Guangdong and Jiangsu.[18] Compared to robust private

[18] Naughton, *The Chinese Economy*.

capital, the local state had been more or less minimalist before 2000. Then as state capital and globalization rose in prominence in China in recent decades, the local government and state–business relations in Wenzhou also experienced changes. The development outcomes have been uneven: When a city leader integrates national strategies with indigenous capital, the local economy thrives; when a city leader implements national strategies against indigenous capital, the local economy suffers; in general, city leaders are inactive, leaving local capital in control.

BRI and Business in Wenzhou

The BRI encourages Chinese companies to invest in and export to emerging markets in Eurasia; some of the places were even politically risky and underdeveloped. Adventurous entrepreneurs in Wenzhou had conducted such business in line with the BRI, yet without portraying it as implementation of the BRI. For example, prior to the BRI, Wenzhou's private capital had established sixteen specialized markets in Brazil, Cameron, Russia, Emeritus, Holland, the United States, and Finland. In Southeast Asia and Africa, Wenzhou capital had also established two national-level and two provincial-level industrial parks prior to the BRI.

Since the launch of the BRI in late 2013, entrepreneurial participation has followed two distinct paths. On the one hand, individual entrepreneurs devised business plans in the BRI's name, thereby securing support from national agencies. The target markets in these programs, however, were not necessarily typical BRI countries. On the other hand, while private manufacturers explore market potential in underdeveloped BRI nations, they typically do not openly proclaim the connections with the top-down strategy.

Research on Wenzhou's implementation of the BRI quickly led me to Mr. Wu, founder of *China-Europe Business News*, a Chinese-language paper based in Italy. Wu launched the annual Belt and Road Trade Expo from 2014 to 2016. The BRI Expo received endorsement from five ministries in Beijing. While the expo was branded as showcase for China's BRI strategy, annual events only took place in Italy, where Wenzhou merchants had a strong immigrant and business presence. The BRI Expo typically displays hundreds of brand names and products for free or minimal fees, but only one or two corporate sponsors receive specially arranged investment contacts, business networking, and publicity in Italy. In 2016, the sponsor was a large LED light producer in Wenzhou. Asked about his motivation to support the BRI Expo, the entrepreneur downplayed politics and explained simply, "Our biggest export market is in Western Europe, and we hope to expand our market shares in Italy."[19]

In addition to Mr. Wu's BRI Expo, several other companies in Wenzhou have participated in and championed the BRI strategy. Just as at the BRI Expo, business interests, rather than politics, have shaped these corporate BRI projects. Wenzhou's largest power device maker was among the strong supporters of the strategy. The company was outspoken in publicizing its BRI projects, including growing sales in Pakistan and Iran and a newly built facility in Xi'an.

Smaller private enterprises typically steer clear of the nationalist strategy, although many business behaviors are very much in line with the directions and regions identified in the BRI. During field surveys, an unidentified textile exporter was critical of the strategy and argued that underdeveloped regions were unlikely to become markets for products made in China. Nonetheless, the exporter's next big trip was to Sri Lanka, an identified BRI nation in South Asia, to "enjoy the beaches and explore possible investment opportunities." Another private entrepreneur with long-term international business experience was also evasive in commenting on the BRI, remarking, "To small companies like ours, the nationalist strategy is really not on our radar." His recent international business trips, however, were all in less-developed regions; and his company identified its top target market in the next five years to be Pakistan.

Wenzhou local government, in contrast to Ningbo and Chongqing, showed little interest in the BRI, focusing instead on an industrial transition to innovative sectors. As private capital leveraged the BRI strategy to facilitate business expansion, the city government could not even envision feasible programs that might tie local industrial restructuring with the national strategy. Party Secretary Chen Yixin emphasized high-tech industries and merely recited nebulous slogans parroted from the central documents, such as promoting "socialism with Chinese characteristics, unleashing social productivity, and improving the governing capacity."[20] Grassroots cadres, revealed in interviews, appeared to focus more on social provision than economic

[19] Interview at BRI Expo planning session, Wenzhou, August 2016.

[20] Anonymous, "Luelun wenzhou moshi shengminli de neizai genju" [On Inner Vitality of the Wenzhou Model], *Wenzhou xuekan* [Wenzhou Journal], No. 2, April 2014, p. 12.

growth in their jurisdiction; the nationalist strategy cannot be further from their local concerns.

According to a party official in an industrial district in Wenzhou, "the most important concern [for us] now is social stability – *bu chushi* [avoidance of social turmoil], not economy." As far as the economic downturn was concerned, he continued, "Growth is the concern of superior governments, not grassroot cadres." Despite a sliding economy, the district has actively expelled low-skill factories for fear of potential labor and environmental issues. Asked about the district's revenue base that might shrink from factory shutdowns, the official explained that grassroots government no longer depends on business revenues for expenditures because operating budgets, such as salaries for civil servants and social welfare expenditures, are allocated from superior governments. Furthermore, infrastructure and development projects are almost entirely financed by bank loans – tacitly guaranteed by the local government.

Unable to latch onto the BRI, the Wenzhou government focused instead on e-commerce and adopted a program called mass entrepreneurs and mass innovation [*wanzong chuangye, dazong chuangxin*]. To promote computer-based industries, the government established a small leading group, a government bureau on the internet, a research institute, an expert commission, and an internet-companies association. In 2015, it passed a three-year action plan on Wenzhou's internet economy and an internet development Five Year Plan (2015–2020). It also adopted preferential policies with considerable subsidies for e-commerce companies.[21] Government efforts to develop high-tech industries to upgrade traditional manufacturing in the city, however, caused problems for private capital in the city. One shoemaker observed, "We can still make money by manufacturing shoes, but we will die immediately if we start on a new internet company."[22]

Wenzhou's economic turnaround, if it happens, is unlikely to come from implementing these national policies. As demonstrated at the end of this section, while ongoing state programs in Wenzhou are slow moving, the market has already started the process of readjustment.

21 Ye Zi, "Wenzhou dianzi shangwu yanjiu" [Wenzhou E-commerce], *Wenzhou xuekan* [Wenzhou Journal], No. 2, April 2016, pp. 12–13.

22 Revealed in a dinner with a Wenzhou entrepreneur, who's been in the shoe business for thirty years, summer 2016.

State and Market in Tandem or in Tension in Wenzhou

Wenzhou's entrepreneurs have participated strongly in the CGG. Drawing on this nationalist strategy, the local state mobilized private capital and implemented major development initiatives, with positive development outcomes in the city. Wenzhou and the WDP were more complicated, however. Private capital participated actively – and successfully – in western China's development. Within Wenzhou, the local government latched onto the WDP after the 2008 Stimulus Plan and, relying on loose credit, the city leadership forced through some large-scale urbanization projects that worked against small business in the city. The contrast between the two strategies reveals how political leadership can play a critical role in a city's economic development; when a city leader integrates a national strategy with local market conditions, local development can benefit from the strategy.

Li Qiang – President Xi's protégé, former party secretary of Jiangsu, and current party secretary of Shanghai – served as Wenzhou's party secretary from early 2002 to late 2004. A native to Wenzhou, Li Qiang left important imprints on the city's development. Drawing on the national CGG strategy, Li launched the "one port and three cities" [*yigang sancheng*] program, aiming to build Wenzhou into a free trade port, light industry city, open coastal city, and culturally renowned city.[23] This program cleverly drew on Wenzhou's strength as a major producer and exporter of light industrial goods; it also integrated the city's severe market fragmentation by setting up industrial clusters and infrastructure that would grow the economy. During that period, Wenzhou's government revenues and state-led financing were quite limited, and thus Li pulled private capital and extensively used public–private partnerships (PPP). In the PPP schemes, private entrepreneurs took on infrastructure equity-holders or purchased public projects such as highways, railways, bridges, and public buildings.[24]

Under Li's push, Wenzhou also constructed high-tech and development zones to attract FDI, like other cities in China; yet such efforts to attract inbound FDI were not as successful. A former bureaucrat

[23] See Li Qiang, "Shishi haishang Wenzhou jianshe, jianshe haiyang jingji qiangshi" [Realize Oceanic Wenzhou Construction, and Develop a Strong Maritime Economy in Wenzhou], *Zhejiang jingji* [Zhejiang Economy], No. 16, 2003.

[24] Li Qiang, "Nuli ba Wenzhou jiancheng quanguo zuiju huoli de chengshi" [Strive to Develop Wenzhou into the Most Vibrant City in China], *Jingri zhejiang* [Today's Zhejiang], No. 23, 2002, pp. 12–13.

at Wenzhou's FDI Bureau recounted, "Wenzhou just could not attract real FDI." He continued, "Emigrant entrepreneurs made up for most of FDI in the city." The reasons, as he explained, were twofold: On the one hand, Wenzhou as a prefecture city could not offer preferential policies like Ningbo, Hangzhou, and Shanghai could; on the other hand, Wenzhou itself had abundant private capital – if there were good projects that needed capital injections, local capital would step in, not FDI.[25] Furthermore, Wenzhou's entrepreneurs – drawing on their emigrant networks in Europe and the United States – had been active in going global. In the early 2000s, Wenzhou's light products exported strongly to global markets, in particular Western Europe.

Indeed, among the three cities – Chongqing, Ningbo, and Wenzhou – only Wenzhou had carried out the "real spirit" of the CGG, that is, promoting Chinese goods and capital to go global, while the other two cities focused on inbound globalization.

The WDP strategy pertained more to western China; Wenzhou's initial connection to it was through private capital that leveraged the strategy to expand business into western China. Concurrent with the WDP's third phase unleashed by the 2008 Stimulus Plan, many cities in China experienced massive state-funded infrastructure development and urbanization. Wenzhou was also profoundly affected. Party secretary Chen Derong endeavored to construct greenspace parks, major transportation arteries, and large urban renovation, measures prevalent in western cities but not yet in Wenzhou.[26] Financing came from bank loans that were guaranteed by state-owned land. In this process, private capital was excluded and small business suffered from rapid increases in operating costs.

Chen Derong was also a Wenzhou native. He arrived in 2009 after a successful tenure in Shaoxing, a neighboring city that shares similarities to Ningbo, but not Wenzhou. Chen's development program was called the Six City-Strive Project [*liucheng lianchuang*], in which Chen sought to revamp Wenzhou into a green, civilized, sustainable, and beautiful city. The city leadership looked at Ningbo, Shaoxing, Suzhou, Wuxi, and Qingdao, all coastal cities with strong state roles

[25] See also Ye, *Diasporas and Foreign Direct Investment in China and India*, pp. 109–110.

[26] Chen Derong, "Renzhen guanche luoshi sheng dangdaihui jingsheng, nuli tuijing Wenzhou jianshe" [To Implement Provincial Party Committee's Principle and Implement Wenzhou Development], *Zhengce liaowang* [Policy Outlook], No. 7, 2012, pp. 10–12.

in the economy, as inspiration for Wenzhou.[27] As part of the comprehensive "reboot" of the city, Chen ordered the citywide demolition of factories and buildings that had been constructed without proper permits. Since Wenzhou's small businesses and manufacturers had depended on affordable rents and the low costs of these "illegal" buildings, the crackdown immediately decimated large numbers of small businesses.[28]

In summary, Party Secretaries Li and Chen were both capable and ambitious local leaders. They represented two phases of economic development in China. The first was led by rapid liberalization of the local economy and export growth in consumer products. Wenzhou, with abundant private capital and dense overseas links, participated in such development effectively. Party Secretary Li leveraged the national strategy and enhanced state–business networks in the city. By contrast, during Chen's tenure, the Chinese economy entered the phase marked by state-led infrastructure and heavy state financing. Such a phase was at odds with the private capital-dominated market in Wenzhou. By replicating what other cities were doing, Chen antagonized local business and brought about his own political downfall – he was forced out before the end of his tenure without promotion.

In the aftermath of Chen's downfall, party secretaries in Wenzhou had exchanged terms frequently and were passive toward economic engineering; market forces have regained the dominant roles in Wenzhou's business landscape. Economic rebalancing and industrial restructuring in the city are hence likely to differ from localities with strong states or state capital.

Rebirths on Vacant Factory Floors

During economic downturns, new business in Wenzhou came and went very frequently. On any given day, in every shopping mall, new stores were open and not so new ones were closed; on streets, children's activities centers were demolished while specialty liquor stores were thriving; after-school programs were opened in one summer but did not survive until the next. In a city teeming with limitless entrepreneurship, the next new business is always around the corner, and yet profitable business

[27] See "Liucheng lianchuang, Wenzhou look for economic transition," *Zhejiang ribao* [Zhejiang Daily], November 7, 2010, pp. 8–12.

[28] In interviews, professionals in the city cheered for the program, but most business was critical of the government.

is hard to sustain. This section presents three rebirthing examples in Wenzhou and demonstrates that while the local state was ineffective in upgrading industrial sectors, the market has precipitated a switch from industry to consumption during economic recession, a task which most localities and the national state are still struggling to keep up with.

Case 1 is Water Margins Paidang, a small and delightfully decorated restaurant near Wenzhou's largest shopping center, Wanxiang City, a signature development by China's national SOE Huarun. The restaurant's name is taken from a classic Chinese novel set during the late Song Dynasty. Paidang was a popular street eatery in Wenzhou in the 1980s and 1990s, but a combination of industrialization and real estate development made urban space for Paidang increasingly hard to find. Paidang eatery was therefore pushed to the margins and perched along highways on the outskirts of town. Concerns about food safety prevented Wenzhou residents from consuming Paidang's food – who could cherish street food alongside noisy and dusty highways? The new Water Margins restaurant, however, nestles cozily in urban life; food is prepared in an open and modern kitchen, and the interior is decorated comfortably with a nod to popular entertainment – the main floor showcases a wall-size TV, which at one point during a recent visit was showing a dragon boat race and at another a soccer match, two extremely popular sports in the city.

Water Margins Paidang signifies a new way of providing old street food to middle-class clientele and enlivens a much-loved but squeezed sector. Moreover, the restaurant was born to economic recession; its success was precisely due to industrial failure in the city. Before the recession, industry was booming, and local government had leased land to factories at very low rents.[29] As industry declined, many factories were abandoned and became inexpensive sites for other businesses. Water Margins Paidang was housed in such an abandoned factory. The land belonged to a village that was more than happy to rent out the space at the (low) industry rate. The restaurant's rent was a small fraction of that in Wanxiang City just across the street (RMB ¥19 vs. ¥300 per square meter). Labor costs, on the other hand, accounted for the largest expense of the restaurant, followed by food purchases. Leveraging the cheap rent, the Water Margins restaurant provided better food at lower prices than those in the mall.

[29] Chinese land policy follows a two-tier system. The cost of land used by industry is much lower than that for land used for commercial development.

Case 2 is Sunrise Swimming Camp, a sports training facility for children of middle- and low-income families. The facility was constructed from a vacated shoe factory in an old industrial district. Due to regulatory tightening and increased labor costs, shoemaking was no longer viable in Wenzhou's urban setting – the factory owner had moved away. In 2013, drawing on the district's efforts to promote recreational sports – a part of governmental social provisions, Sunrise's founder, a first-time entrepreneur and a physical education teacher, saw the space and rented it for a bargain. Like the Water Margins, Sunrise is an adaptive way to bring a traditional lifestyle back to a city that had been largely destroyed by industrialization and commercialization.

Prior to the 1990s, children in Wenzhou were used to swimming in rivers and lakes – the city was marked by numerous small rivers and lakes that cut through different communities. However, with urbanization came water pollution; it became impossible to swim in such water. High-end sports stadiums that featured swimming pools were constructed in the city, but these were extremely limited and very expensive. For children from middle- and low-income households, swimming – a common pastime for Wenzhou kids before 1990 – became out of reach. Sunrise, drawing on industrial decline in the city, was able to provide a facility and swimming lessons at a very reasonable price. Like the Water Margins restaurant, it showcased a market-led transition from industry to consumption.

Case 3 is the huge newly built Trampoline Theme Park that was packed with children on a visit in the summer of 2016. Like the Waters Margin restaurant and Sunrise Swimming Camp, the Theme Park was a reincarnation of an industrial space – this time, the former Furniture Exhibition Center in Wenzhou. The city had been a major producer, marketer, and exporter of furniture in southern China. Overcapacities and declining exports in recent years had rendered furniture making unprofitable; the Exhibition Center was abandoned in 2012. It was remarkable to see this enormous five-story building repurposed into a Trampoline Theme Park – the largest of its kind in southern China. When the Theme Park was opened for business in August 2016, its reconstruction was not complete. The parking lot was a mess, and the road leading to the building was not even paved. Yet the price of admission was affordable for middle- to low-income households because the vacant building was almost rent-free. The entrepreneur who made this transformation spent most of his investment on repurposing the interior of the furniture center to allow for a maze of trampolines.

With a reasonable pricing structure, the entrepreneur expects to recoup his investment within three years.

Research on Wenzhou's economic transition led to a grassroots cadre who had worked in the city for more than three decades and had never intended to leave his district – even refusing to accept a promotion out of the locality. He explained that Wenzhou's industrial districts had long lost competitiveness in low-skilled manufacturing: Land was too expensive, labor was too expensive, and government policy was too restrictive toward small business. Neither could Wenzhou develop high-tech sectors, he observed, because it was impossible for the city to compete with Hangzhou, Shanghai, or some inland cities in attracting high-skilled labor. "This [industrial hollowing out] is ok," he remarked, "as long as we make households in Wenzhou a bit wealthier and their life a bit easier – considering the high cost of education and healthcare, Wenzhou will be okay."[30]

CONCLUSION

Central–local relations have been important to China's reform experiences since the late 1970s; they are also debated among China specialists. Some are convinced that elite politics – the central state – is the main determinant of China's reform trajectory, while others argue that local governments play a stronger role. Furthermore, some scholars claim that the Chinese central state was too weak, to the detriment of the national economy and power,[31] while others convincingly argue that due to top-down political organizations, local governments are inevitably weaker than the national authority.[32] In the SMG framework, the central-local relationships are dynamic and interactive; they are both mutually reinforcing and mutually checked.

Investigating the local implementation of the three strategies, the chapter demonstrates that first, whether the power structure is provincial, semiprovincial, or prefecture-level, a city has considerable autonomy in choosing what central directives to follow and what directives are to be ignored. Here the decisions were as much shaped by local

30 Interview from Wenzhou, August 2016.

31 Hu Angang and Wang Shaoguang, *The Chinese State in Crisis: State Capacity and Tax Reforms in China*. Abingdon, UK: Routledge, 2001.

32 Yasheng Huang, "Administrative Monitoring in China," *China Quarterly*, 143, 1995, pp. 828–844.

markets as by the local states. Second, cities have different instruments rooted in their local conditions. In using some instruments and eschewing others, the cities can endure decentralized autonomy against the general trend of centralization in contemporary China. Chongqing, Ningbo, and Wenzhou today still retain considerable differences despite various top-down strategies. Third, across diverse approaches to the nationalist strategies, Chinese cities are geared more toward local economic growth than carrying out strategies on behalf of Beijing.

As a whole, the chapter supports that "foreign" strategies such as the CGG and BRI have lasting effects inside China. They help local governments and market actors promote their preferred economic and business plans. Since local governments are important elements in the triblock state system, Chinese foreign policy's external effects are also deeply shaped by domestic and local players, whom foreign observers typically are least familiar.

7

Typologies of Chinese Companies

> Listen to the central government, learn from Europe and America, and do your own job.
>
> —A private entrepreneur

Companies, private and state-owned, are the main commercial actors, employers, and revenue generators in China; they are of central concern in studies of China and globalization. How they approach nationalist strategies sheds light on the nature of Chinese capitalism, the characteristics of business–government interactions, and the prospect – distant or otherwise – of political liberalization in China. China specialists have conducted in-depth research on corporate behaviors in 1990s China, including Bruce Dickson's surveys on "red capitalists," Kellee Tsai's informal adaptation of private capital, and Scott Kennedy's work on business lobbying across different sectors.[1] In the new millennium, political studies seemed to focus less on companies, while burgeoning business studies have primarily concerned themselves with technology and management issues.[2]

This chapter draws on long term observations of three companies, as well as multi-rounds of interviews with the managers. The companies

[1] Bruce Dickson, *Red Capitalism in China: The Party, Private Entrepreneurs, and Prospects for Political Change*. New York: Cambridge University Press, 2003; Kellee Tsai, *Capitalism without Democracy: The Private Sector in Contemporary China*. Ithaca, NY: Cornell University Press, 2007; Scott Kennedy, *The Business of Lobbying in China*. Cambridge, MA: Harvard University Press, 2008.

[2] See Shaun Rein, *The End of Copycat China: The Rise of Creativity, Innovation, and Individualism in Asia*. Hoboken, NJ: John Wiley & Sons, Incorporated, 2014; Lin Zhang, *Venture Capital and Corporate Governance of Chinese Listed Companies*. New York: Springer, 2012; George Yip and Bruce McKern, *China's Next Strategic*

were born and grew during China's economic reform era. They are key members of China's economic miracle in the recent history. The three companies are engaged in heavy and light manufacturing and have state and private ownership. Their experiences reveal how Chinese companies, private and state-owned, have grown and been challenged by globalization in and outside China.

In research for this chapter, I used interviews to discover the companies authentic experiences with globalization and actual approaches to the nationalist strategies.

Archives were employed to fill gaps and corroborate findings from the interviews. Investigations for this chapter was helped by also, the nationalist strategies' high political status, which provided safety for corporate managers to speak their minds with external scholars. Thus, at each company, I was able to conduct interviews with different managers, at different sites, with different perspectives.

The government–corporate patterns that emerged from this research confirm neither "crony capitalism," in which companies "capture" state power and assets,[3] nor "strategic capitalism," in which the state compells companies to fit nationalist strategies.[4] Rather, the companies – both state-owned and private – have genuine commercial interests, and the government has genuine been supportive of companies' market-based behavior. On the other hand, successful companies – including private ones – seem to have depended on the state for varieties of support, in particular in their dealings with foreign capital and expansion abroad. Such developments have resulted in what could be characterized as "codependent" state and capital interactions in globalizing China.

A SKETCH OF CHINESE COMPANIES

In the late 1990s, in preparation for China's WTO membership, the central government launched sweeping reforms of state-owned enterprises (SOEs). Widely characterized as "grabbing the big and letting go the small" [*zhuada fangxiao*], the reforms demanded the restructuring and privatization of all but 1,000 large and infrastructural SOEs. These 1,000

Advantage: From Imitation to Innovation. Cambridge, MA: MIT Press, 2016; Joel Backaler, *China Goes West: Everything You Need to Know about Chinese Companies Going Global*. London: Palgrave Macmillan, 2014.

[3] Carl Minzner, *End of an Era: How China's Authoritarian Revival Is Undermining Its Rise*. New York: Oxford University Press, 2018, pp. 79–83.

[4] Economy, *Xi Jiping and the Third Revolution in China*.

TABLE 7.1. *Comparative trends in Chinese state and private firms*

		2000	2005	2010	2015
Number of companies	SOEs	53,500	27,500	20,300	19,300
	Private	22,100	123,800	273,300	216,500
Industrial output (¥100mn)	SOEs	40,600	83,800	185,900	228,400
	Private	N/A	47,800	213,300	391,600
Employment (10,000)	SOEs	3,000	1,900	1,800	1,800
	Private	300	1,700	3,300	3,500
Revenues (¥100mn)	SOEs	42,200	85,600	194,300	241,700
	Private	4,800	45,800	207,800	386,400

Source: Author, based on raw data from MIIT, *Zhongguo gongye nianjian* [China Industrial Yearbook], 2005–2016 annual editions.

"grabbed" SOEs were later consolidated into 169.[5] In 2003, the government set up the State Assets Supervision and Administration commission (SASAC) to act as state ownership and regulate behaviors of the reformed SOEs. However, major reforms rarely succeed through the stroke of a pen, particularly in a large country such as China. As noted in Chapter 6, the peak of SOE reform in Chongqing actually took place from 2003 to 2007; thereafter, SOEs remained dominant economic and political players in the city. In the coastal city of Ningbo, local government has flexibly created various SOEs to accomplish economic agendas in the locality.

These phenomena do not mean that SOE reform was a mere cosmetic exercise inside China. Rather, by various indicators, SOEs have declined in importance in the Chinese economy, and private firms have gained significantly. This section first establishes general trends in corporate China and then provides an overview discussion of the selected companies. To follow are three sections that conduct in-depth studies of the three companies' relationships with Chinese government and experiences with globalization.

As Table 7.1 shows, there were more than 50,000 SOEs in China in 2000. Five years later, this number had had been cut nearly in half. From 2005 to 2015, the number remained steady, such that in 2015, there were 19,300 SOEs in China. Private companies gained significantly in numbers: 22,000 in 2000; 124,000 in 2005; and 273,000 in 2010. In employment, a similar pattern holds, but in industrial output and revenues, slightly

[5] For the process of SOE reform, see Ye, *Diasporas and Foreign Direct Investment in China and India*, pp. 112–116.

different trends are discerned. SOEs and private companies both achieved impressive growth from 2000 to 2015, although the rate of gains at private firms was greater. Thus in 2015, while SOEs were greatly outnumbered by private firms, they were smaller but comparable to the latter in industrial output and revenue contributions.

Such aggregate data mask significant variations inside SOEs and private firms. Among SOEs, for example, there are four tiers, roughly corresponding to administrative ranks in the Chinese state system. The highest tier, centrally affiliated SOEs, typically has China [*Zhongguo*] in their names. They are the largest state banks, as well as companies involved with infrastructure, energy, and other resources. SOEs in this category have enjoyed special provisions in "going global." They typically have more investible resources and political latitude to operate abroad. The companies' nominal regulator and owner in the state system is SASAC. Yet in power rankings, the party secretary of a central SOE may be equal to or higher than the chairman of the SASAC. Hence, in specific cases, the companies seem to act above the SASAC in interpreting and implementing nationalist strategies.

In the second tier are national-level SOEs that are typically engaged in heavy and infrastructural industries such as telecommunications, steel, and automobile manufacturing.[6] Just as with the central SOEs, national-level SOEs are regulated by the SASAC, but the regulation and oversight are clearly stronger. Compared to central SOEs, national SOEs do not have special provisions related to investing abroad, although they generally have better access to state financing than private firms do. The third-tier SOEs are affiliated with provincial governments; and the bottom tier consists of SOE spinoffs and those created by city-level governments. Bottom-tier SOEs are difficult to capture because they come and go in order to deliver certain functions or generate specific revenues for their parent organizations.

In this book, information on central SOEs was garnered through archives and informal contacts and conversations at various meetings in China. In terms of the other tiers, research was carried out at selected companies via primary and structured interviews. Precious Steel, the first company researched here, is a national SOE owned by the State Council

[6] Some scholars combine the central and national SOEs as one tier. See, for example, Margaret Pearson, "State-Owned Business and Party-State Regulation in China's Modern Political Economy," in *State Capitalism, Institutional Adaptation, and the Chinese Miracle*, edited by Barry Naughton and Kellee S. Tsai. New York: Cambridge University Press, 2015.

and regulated by the SASAC. During the late 1990s, the company was corporatized to be responsible for its own economic performance and profit margins. Among the companies interviewed, Precious Steel is the most critical of state interference in corporate decisions. It suggests that national SOEs can experience "double whammies" – being responsible for their own returns in the marketspace and yet being expected by the state to shoulder political and social burdens. The analysis of corporate history also shows that SOEs and the state are in a long-term codependent relationship – where Precious Steel incurred losses in one transaction with the state, it often got them back in another.

In the localities, Chongqing Foreign Trade Group (CFTG) and Ningbo-Zhoushan Port Group (NZPG) were provincial-level SOEs that reported to Chongqing and Zhejiang governments, respectively. Ningbo Logistics Company and Yu-Xin-Ou Ecommerce are city-level SOEs. The former is an instrument established by Ningbo's city government; the latter is a spin-off of CFTG. It is clear that provincial SOEs have been corporatized and their behavior has been largely business-driven. Their relationships with provincial governments, however, can be rather different. In state capital–dominant Chongqing, SOE–government relations are close and symbiotic – SOEs seem to define many of the economic priorities in the city while the government relies on SOEs to conduct myriad economic functions. In private capital–abundant Zhejiang, the relationship between SOEs and the government is quite autonomous. Zhejiang government in general appeals to private capital in its economic regulation and governance; SOEs are also eager to partner with and serve private capital's needs.

Such diverse patterns of corporate behaviors and SOE–government relations are informative and more nuanced than uniform views of SOEs. Indeed, state ownership does not preordain a SOE's dependence on the state, or necessarily make a SOE do the government's bidding all the time. Rather, the institutional environment in which the company operates greatly shapes its behaviors and its interactions with the home state. Furthermore, the research shows that there are constant tensions and conflicts between the state and SOEs, but in general the state relies on SOEs to carry out its development programs while the companies leverage the state to expand their business interests. The long-term codependency relations are clear.

The other two companies examined in detail are private companies based in Zhejiang: Safety Electric and Health Shoes. Safety Electric makes power devices and operates in the regulated energy sector.

Companies such as Safety Electric face considerable competition with manufacturers in advanced countries. In the last few decades, Safety Electric has been dependent on government support to grow its domestic business and expand globally. On the other end of the spectrum is Health Shoes from the footwear sector. Light manufacturing sectors in China are close to free market conditions; the government regulates the sector through macroeconomic policies as a whole. Yet in Health Shoes' corporate history, its expansion inside China drew on regional economic policies launched by the central government to encourage local governments to provide preferential incentives to investors in the target region. Furthermore, the management at Health Shoes skillfully redeploys the central leadership's rhetoric and slogans to manage labor relations within the company. In short, private companies – whether heavy manufacturing or light industry – and the government are mutually reinforcing, with the government serving as a kind of "benefactor" of business in China.

SOES, THE STATE, AND GLOBALIZATION

Precious Steel (PS) is a national-level SOE with a mandate to implement top-down strategies. After the launch of the BRI, the company established a new unit called the BRI Strategic Investment Office that was headed by a veteran manager. To implement the strategy, the manager led a delegation to Beijing and met representatives of CDB, SRF, NDRC, MOFCOM and others. The delegation focused on finding out whether, how much, and under what conditions the central government had provided investment support to SOEs' implementation of the BRI. During the visit, the delegation discovered that, there were no particular funds allocated to SOEs in 2015. Rather, the central financiers urged Precious Steel to search for "bankable" projects abroad. When Precious Steel managed to do so, the central financiers promised that they would consider funding such bankable projects as part of the BRI.

Returning to Shanghai, the BRI Office evaluated the countries covered in the strategy and identified India as a strategic target market. At the time, India was among vocal critics of and resisters to the BRI strategy. Precious Steel's BRI director explained that the choice of India was based on commercial considerations. First, India has a large potential market for steel; second, its infrastructure and auto manufacturing are in rapid growth and will remain so in the near future; and finally, India's GDP growth rate just surpassed that of China in 2015. The Indian market, however, can be challenging to Chinese state steelmakers, particularly given the troublesome and fragile political relationships between the two Asian giants in recent years. Aware of these challenges, the BRI director planned to find an Indian company as its localization partner. Precious Steel is the world's largest steelmaker, but in venturing into India, the BRI director preferred to form an alliance with a medium-sized Indian steel maker, eschewing larger companies because, as he explained, the company did not want publicity as it moved abroad.

As a whole, in the process of the BRI, the state company displays clear commercial drive and risk aversion. Throughout the interviews, the managers downplayed the political and strategic implications of the new strategy. Instead, in the BRI director's words,

> Precious Steel, as a SOE, has taken over too much responsibility from the state. In the BRI implementation, we cannot think about the strategic and political significance but to focus on BRI's economic rationale and how it helps our business strategy.[7]

SOE–State Codependency

Precious Steel's wariness of ambitious rhetoric and political mobilization was rooted in its past experiences with top-down government strategies, such as the WDP and CGG. As a state company, it has had a complicated relationship with government mandates. During the company's recent history, although the government provided resources that facilitated the company's domestic growth, the government also repeatedly asked the company to shoulder heavy social burdens from other SOEs. For example, in Shanghai in 2001, the company was asked to absorb thousands of workers from another national SOE that was privatized. It took PS a whole decade to recover from the social burden of that takeover. The manager interviewed for this book explained bluntly that were it not for that politically pressured takeover, Precious Steel's performance would be more impressive than it was after China's admission into the WTO.

The other major case was Precious Steel's acquisition of Eight-One Steel Plant in Xinjiang, a border province in China, with the backdrop of the WDP. To promote SOE reforms in western China, the central government urged competitive coastal SOEs and international companies to participate. In January 2007, arrangements were made for Precious Steel to take over Eight-One, a massive manufacturing facility and the

[7] Interviews in Shanghai, August 2015.

largest employer in Xinjiang. By this time, Eight-One had incurred long-term financial losses and experienced multiple rounds of unsuccessful reforms. In taking over the plant, Precious Steel signed a contract worth RMB ¥3 billion (equivalent to $0.4 billion) with Xinjiang provincial government and acquired land, facilities, equipment, and corporate restructuring of the acquired company. Thanks to preferential policies toward investments in western China – and also due to rapidly growing steel demand – Precious Steel enjoyed a period of success in the ensuing years. As overcapacities became rampant after 2010, however, the Western subsidiary became unsustainable, and manufacturing in western China was no longer profitable.[8] In subsequent years, Precious Steel tried multiple rounds of rescue packages, all to no avail.[9]

Despite decade-long corporatization and commercialization, Precious Steel, as a state company, still cannot fire employees flexibly. In a recent takeover case in central China, the subsidiary manager was so frustrated with employees at the acquired SOE that he said he would rather "pay them not to come to work." In 2010, the subsidiary manager devised a business plan to establish an e-commerce company, but deliberately avoided financial injections from the parent company. Concerned about interference from the parent company, the manager delayed the launch of the e-commerce platform for years. It is clear from repeated interviews with multiple managers that commercial interests have consistently driven Precious Steel's behavior and that state ownership has afforded both advantages and constraints on the company's domestic and global expansion.

Precious Steel's business orientation is similar to that of provincial SOEs such as Chongqing Foreign Trade Group and Ningbo-Zhoushan Port Group. Yet the lower-level SOEs, paradoxically, seem to have more flexibility in expanding abroad. Prior to the BRI, the Chongqing SOE had invested in small-scale power stations and infrastructure projects in Vietnam and Pakistan, and with the BRI, it quickly launched an e-commerce company that delivered rapid returns. Similarly, the Zhejiang SOE was careful not to commit to potentially uncertain

[8] Li Zhiguo, "PS: yingnan ershang mou zhuanxing fazhan" [Precious Steel: Face Up to Difficulties and Seek New Development], *Jingri Ribao*, February 27, 2012.

[9] See a lengthy interview with former energy director Zhang Guobao of the NDRC, "Gangtie gongye channen yanzhong guosheng," *Gangzhijia* [House of Steel], September 30, 2015, http://futures.hexun.com/2015-09-30/179584998.html; MIIT, "Zhongguo gangtie chanye guojihua rengzhongdaoyuan," March 2, 2012, www.xzbu.com/2/view-416379.htm.

projects. For example, when the China Investment Group invited the company and other major port groups to participate in the Gwadar Port project in Pakistan, the Zhejiang SOE declined, explaining that the cycle of return took too long. Instead, it explored the connectivity between river and rail transportation inside China, as well as investment in servicing a port in Saudi Arabia. Both projects were closely aligned with the company's business structure and promised predictable returns. Similarly, in the CGG strategy, the Zhejiang SOE acquired several iron ore mines as well as agricultural land in South America and joined in overseas industrial zones because those investments promised steady and significant returns.

In summary, the state–SOE relationship is more complicated than either "state capture" – SOEs control the government policy – or "statecraft" – SOEs serve as political and strategic tools of the government. Rather, the state and state capital are both closely interactive and operationally autonomous. The state and SOEs are playing a repeated game in which payoff structures are different from transaction-style, single-shot games.[10] Out of mutual dependence and the need for survival, the state largely leaves SOEs alone in their pursuit of commercial interests. It is very much in the state's interest not to interfere with or blindly subsidize state capital. While it is true that a SOE is sometimes asked to carry out political mandates that do not fit with its immediate business interests, these troublesome operations do – in the long run – help the company acquire new assets and expand into new areas. In the repeated and codependent gameplay, the state and SOEs are in constant negotiations that adapt to the evolving needs and interests of both.

Bifurcated Globalization

Precious Steel was product of China's globalization; it symbolized high-level collaboration between China and Japan in the 1980s. In the company's early years, Japan's Nippon Steel provided technology, management know-how, and initial funds. Because of this heritage, Precious Steel was among the first of the Chinese SOEs to start globalization early with visible success. During its first period of globalization, Precious Steel focused on expanding its presence in advanced economies overseas; and this business strategy paid off. In 1985, the company

[10] Robert Axelrod, *The Evolution of Cooperation*. New York: Basic Books, 1984.

began to export products, and by 1990, many of its products had entered Japan and Germany. In 1988, the company established a joint venture in Japan, and by 2004, it had set up ten subsidiaries abroad, with foreign sales accounting for 14 percent of total sales.[11]

In the early 2000s, as President Jiang Zemin – who was the party boss of Shanghai before assuming the central leadership – launched the CGG and urged large SOEs to actively go global and seek external markets and resources. In responding to this top-down mobilization and growing market demand in China for steel and raw materials, Precious Steel ratcheted up its efforts to invest and acquire assets abroad, with such movement intensifying in the mid-2000s. Unfortunately, some of the company's high-profile acquisitions did not go well and generated negative press inside China. In a self-study conducted in 2009, Precious Steel recognized that among comparable global players, the company was slow and limited in globalization.[12]

The company's largest – and troubled – investment in Brazil demonstrates vulnerability in Precious Steel's outward globalization. In going global, the SOE was susceptible to complex politics both at home and abroad. In 2005, the company formed a joint venture (JV) with Brazil's Companhia Vale do Rio Doce (CVRD) and Australia's Rio Tinto to jointly explore iron ore mines that could serve its steel production in China. This move made clear commercial sense at the time: China was quickly becoming a major market for steel production and its demand for iron ore was rising fast. Lacking equity in global iron ore, the Chinese steelmaker had little pricing power. The company was unfamiliar with the Brazilian market and with acquisition and mergers in general. The corporate leadership initially planned the project as a relatively modest investment.

Two political conditions helped enlarge the project at Precious Steel. In China, as the CGG entered an intensified second phase, the central government – represented by the MOF and SAFE – were pressing for and enabling large acquisitions of resources and raw materials. More important, inside Brazil, the ruling party at the time was engaged in difficult political reelection campaigns. The incumbent government therefore pressured the Chinese firm to increase investment to $1 billion, the highest investment from China at the time. Precious Steel signed a large production JV with CVRD in Brazil and held 80 percent of equity shares.

[11] MIIT, "Zhongguo gangtie chanye guojihua rengzhongdaoyuan."

[12] Min Ye, "China Invests Overseas: Regulation and Representation," *Modern China Studies*, 21(1), 2014, pp. 173–204.

In reciprocity, the incumbent government conceded a large parcel of land and facilities to the company.

The deal was leaked to the Brazilian media and quickly became a campaign scandal that was exploited by the opposition party. Apparently, the land concession was in violation of a local land use clause in Brazil. To save its own neck, the Brazilian government let Precious Steel and its corporate partners in Brazil take the blame. Under such an intensely politicized atmosphere, the project was paused indefinitely. Back in China, Precious Steel's Brazilian project was viewed in an extremely negative light. Both the Chinese media and scholars described the investment as both a waste of state funds and a disgrace on the national image abroad. Precious Steel's leadership suffered politically from this globalization endeavor.[13]

This overseas acquisition scarred the SOE's globalization team; the company has since been extremely cautious in launching overseas ventures, particularly in unfamiliar markets. After 2010, as Chinese domestic conditions changed dramatically in terms of industry, labor costs, and environmental pressures, Precious Steel became more active in restructuring, research and development, and globalization. In its general manager's words, "Precious Steel, as an infrastructural industry, had to follow other manufacturing industries. If those industries such as appliances, shipbuilding, machinery, and automobiles are moving abroad, Precious Steel had to go abroad too."[14] Inside China, the company started to compete in the high-tech segments of the industry in order to reduce production and still maintain profit margins. In 2012, while its production was only 7 percent of China's total steel production, it accounted for 27 percent of revenue in the industry.

Before the launch of the BRI, Precious Steel's restructuring had focused on using online tools to better access international markets. In June 2013, the company unveiled its six-year business plan and refocused its priorities on exporting to the US market. The company was actively searching for partners in the United States and aimed to provide products to American automakers. Responding to the US auto industry's demands for new materials, Precious Steel had started research and development

[13] The case draws on the author's interviews in summer 2010, Shanghai; Ye, "China Invests Overseas."

[14] Zhang Xiangdang, "PS xin liunian guihua jiedu" [How to Read Precious Steel's New Six-Year Plan, Focus on America Again], June 25, 2013, *Jingji guanchawang* [Economics Observation Network], www.eeo.com.cn/2013/0621/245550.shtml.

to produce materials other than steel. Its slogan of the year in 2015 was to "use [the] internet to increase values in steel production and to create an Alibaba in the steel industry."[15]

Precious Steel's globalization experience illustrates the advantages and disadvantages in Chinese state capital. On the one hand, drawing on codependent and repeated interplays with the government, the company has achieved rapid growth in the domestic market. Because of this domestic advantage, the company has been less inclined than their global counterparts to expand global business endeavors; its overseas investment seems to primarily serve domestic production. On the other hand, SOEs face real vulnerabilities outside China, because the "game" structures abroad are quite different from domestic ones. The players are more diverse, and the payoff structure tends to be transactional in nature. Coupled with politics at home and in the host country, the outcomes can be extremely unpredictable. Ultimately, SOE leadership consists of politicians who do not like risks and uncertainties. In general, however, the interviewed SOE managers show that economic nationalism is not prevalent at SOEs; rather, they are open and eager to study and emulate norms, practices, technology, and management from counterparts in advanced mature markets.

Precious Steel is but one company among many. Yet in large-*n* studies of SOE behaviors, commercial and market tendencies were also clearly established. Among them, two were particularly worth noting. One was a statistical testing of SOEs and private firms in trading with North Korea during political crises. The author finds that SOEs' behavior is quite commercially sensitive.[16] The other was a study of Chinese SOEs' behavior in global trade following WTO membership and provides compelling results in line with market tendencies.[17]

Furthermore, Precious Steel's behavioral patterns have parallels to other SOEs observed throughout this project, including China Construction, a centrally affiliated SOE involved in infrastructure investment and construction, and Construction Bank of China, one of the four commercial banks. Commercial tendency is also clear in provincial-level SOEs Chongqing Foreign Trade Group and Ningbo-Zhoushan Port

[15] Zhang,"PS Xinliunian guihua jiedu".

[16] Xiaojun Li, "China's Geoeconomic Strategy: China as a Trading Superpower," *IDEAS Report*, 2012, http://eprints.lse.ac.uk/44204/.

[17] Christina Davis and Meredith Wilf, "Joining the Club: Accession to the GATT/WTO," *Journal of Politics*, 79(3), 2017, pp. 964–978.

Group, city-level SOEs Yu-Xin-Ou Ecommerce and Ningbo Logistic Company, and many other SOEs that I approached in informal conversations over the past decade.

To conclude, the state and state capital in China have complicated interactions that go beyond common perceptions of state capture and statecraft. They conform to the repeated game structure in which the players are mutually dependent for survival, and reputation is at stake for future iterations. Thus, despite lots of disagreement and (even) distrust, cooperation between the state and SOEs seem to prevail. Under normal circumstances, the state expects and pushes SOEs to be efficient commercial actors that focus on profits and returns on their investment decisions. In politically dire situations, SOEs are asked to shoulder public and social responsibilities. The two mandates are often in tension; in each specific round of the gameplay, both functions typically cannot be achieved at optimal levels.

In the long term, however, the repeated game structure prevails; and the system muddles through. On the one hand, the state puts SOEs on a long leash to enable their commercial performance and then pulls the strings when circumstances threaten social stability in key areas. On the other hand, SOE managers understand the dynamics and engage in constant negotiation and resizing of state imperatives and intentions. They seek to maximize commercial interests even if it means compromising short-term economic gains for longer returns.

LOYALIST CAPITAL

Safety Electric (SE) is a private company that operates in a state-controlled sector – that of electrical device production. It has been compliant in implementing national strategies launched by the political leadership. In both deeds and words, Safety Electric had "loyally" participated in the WDP, CGG, and BRI. For a long time, the company has openly championed key ideas from the ruling party and adopted Communist organizational skills to manage its employees. During interviews, managers of the company displayed nationalist sentiment and were critical of global capital and Western ideas. Driving such nationalist outlook are the company's long-term positive relationships with the home government and quite negative experiences with foreign competitors both within China and abroad.

Safety Electric's behavior patterns have parallels with other private companies with whom I have interacted in the past decade. For example, Hangzhou-based Legend Chemical concentrated business in chemical production and bio-agriculture. Both sectors were regulated by government licenses. Thus, corporate–government relationships were important to the leadership of the company. Legend Chemical's founder was the chairman of Zhejiang's Association of Industry and Commerce at the same time President Xi Jinping served as the provincial party secretary. After Xi became national leader, Legend Chemical's founder became the chairman of All China Association of Industry and Commerce.

A research trip to the company in 2014 revealed a corporate headquarters showcasing its loyalty to the ruling party. Red posters of party doctrines and photos of political leaders could be seen everywhere. Furthermore, the company has a CCP Party Committee that regularly organizes study sessions for employees on party doctrines and new government policies. On one occasion, the company organized group dating and group weddings for their employees, reminiscent of a common practice in the socialist past. In the meantime, the company was both dismissive and distrustful of global ideas and practices. Managers deemed that "Western learning" was incompatible with the Chinese business environment.[18]

Communist loyalty was also clear in another company I researched in 2015. Rejuvenation after Quake was an earthquake detection device maker in Sichuan whose founder had studied in the United States and returned with proprietary technology and initial venture capital. However, turning technology into marketable devices required considerable and continuous financial injection. Those typically came from state banks. The company's orders were also filled with government procurement. Treated as an exemplary case [*dianxing*] for returnees with advanced technology who found successful business in western China, the company was meticulous in demonstrating its loyalty to the Communist regime and Communist values generally. In the company's meeting room, two conspicuous flags – the national flag and the PLA army flag – adorned the massive conference table. On the walls were red posters with famous quotes from Communist leaders, including Chairman Mao and President Xi, as well as enlarged photos of government officials who visited the company. Both cases demonstrate that the firm's loyalty to the ruling party is quite real, but also rooted in real interest.

Safety Electric (SE) originated as a rural factory in Wenzhou in the 1980s and grew rapidly in the domestic market during the 1990s. During its growth, SE expended much energy in developing close relationship with the government. In Wenzhou, it routinely hired retired

[18] Interviews with the long-time aid to the company founder and three middle-level managers at the headquarter office in Hangzhou during August 2014.

officials to serve as consultants for the company. In 1993, SE established a CCP Party organization – the first private firm to do so in Zhejiang; in 1995, it expanded the role of the party organization. In 1998, the company established an internal CCP Party Congress, the first among private firms in Wenzhou. It sees the Party Congress as "the backbone of the company that guides our path forward."[19]

In 2015, SE's founder Mr. Nan became chairman of Zhejiang's Association of Industry and Commerce. Acting as a corporate leader in the province, Nan championed the BRI strategy on various occasions and closely followed the political leaders' progress and pronouncements abroad.[20] His well-known mantra was "listen To the Center, Look at Europe and America, and Act According to Our Own Conditions" [*Tin zhongyang de, kan oumei de, gan ziji de*].[21] As China was rapidly changing vis a vis the domestic economy and outward globalization in recent decades, Safety Electric adapted to such challenges and opportunities by leveraging nationalist programs and strengthening ties with the government. Such state-dependent adaptation was driven both by its troubled experience with foreign companies and favorable relations with the home government.

Troubles with Global MNC's

Safety Electric's globalization started in the early 1990s. In the beginning, the company relied on Wenzhou's immigrant networks abroad and exported products in such countries as Italy, Spain, and Brazil, where Wenzhou business associations were most vibrant. Nonetheless, the company's main growth and expansion occurred in China. By the mid-1990s, several of the company's electrical devices had captured the lion's shares of domestic markets. As China opened the sector and domestic markets to foreign goods and manufacturers, SE emerged as a competitor to incoming global players. Competition and rivalry developed rapidly.

19 Ibid. "Zhengtai jituan gongsi kuayueshi fazhan de jingyan yu qishi" [Experience and Lessons of Safety Electrical Leap Frogging Development], 2004. www.ced-ceda.org.cn/yjbg/content.php?id=39.

20 "Nan cunhui: women zheng buju sanda zhanlue rongru yidaiyilu" [Nan Cunhui: We Are Planning Three Strategies to Participate in the Belt and Road], Xinhua Net, March 10, 2015, www.xinhuanet.com//politics/2015lh/2015-03/10/c_1114588710.htm.

21 "Nan: tin zhongyangde, kan oumeide, gan zijide" [Nan: Listen to the Center, Look at Europe and America, and Do Your Own Thing], *Zhongguo gongshang shibao* [China Industrial and Commercial Daily], September 9, 2008, http://business.sohu.com/20080911/n259504293.shtml.

In 1994, French manufacturer Schneider Electric emerged as a player on the scene. It began by proposing a joint venture (JV) deal with Safety Electric but asked for 80 percent equity in the JV, a proposal that SE quickly rejected. This provoked Schneider to lodge an intellectual property (IP) lawsuit against Safety Electric. The case would drag on for years, and in 1998, Schneider proposed another joint venture in which equity shares would be distributed at 51 versus 49 percent in slight favor of the French maker. This was an offer that was again rejected by SE. This resulted in three more IP lawsuits by Schneider. Animosity between the French and Chinese rivals became intense.[22]

After China joined the WTO in 2001, Safety Electric increased exports to international markets, particularly in Italy, Germany, and France, where Schneider products were traditionally dominant. As SE's exports grew, Schneider proposed the third joint venture with equity shares 50–50. By this time, however, SE had deemed Schneider as its chief rival and again rejected the proposal. Relations hardened further; Schneider lodged multiple lawsuits against key SE products in different European countries. SE found itself embroiled in costly legal battles, with its products banned from the European market. Inside China, Schneider also launched extensive legal wars against SE. From 1994 to 2007, Schneider lodged a total of 24 lawsuits against the Chinese company.[23]

In response, Safety Electric stepped up investment in indigenous research and development and aggressively filed IP licenses in China. By 2005, SE's IPR licenses in China had surpassed those of Schneider; it also strived to participate in attaining global standards and filed hundreds of licenses abroad. In 2006, in retaliation, Safety Electric even filed an IP lawsuit in a Wenzhou court against Schneider's subsidiary in Tianjin, China. The first ruling was in favor of Safety Electric, a ruling that Schneider appealed to a higher court. This court then mediated a deal between Schneider and Safety Electric in 2009, with Schneider agreeing to pay a RMB ¥160 million (roughly $30 million) indemnity to the Chinese company. Following the agreement, the Chinese and French makers reached a peace accord worldwide, agreeing not to file lawsuits against each other as a business tactic.

[22] From interviews; also see "China's SE Accuses French Rival of Seeking to Block Its Expansion," Agence France Presse, December 18, 2008, www.sinodaily.com/2006/081218194352.1wnlz1m2.html.

[23] Ibid.

However, the damage was already done. To senior managers at the Chinese firm, Schneider – a global giant – had ruthlessly used its hegemonic status to choke SE's business in China and abroad. Inside China, the legal battles with the French company earned SE empathy and support in the media and with government agencies, who one way or another stood with the Chinese firm against the foreign rival. In retrospect, Safety Electric, due to its founder's lack of global business experience, might have made missteps in its competition with Schneider. Nonetheless, the decades-old rivalry arguably contributed to deep nationalism and distrust of Western capital in SE's corporate culture.

The rivalry also tragically contributed to an ill-prepared alliance with America's General Electric (GE). In this case, eager to save its domestic market and expand into new foreign markets, SE was unusually flexible in its negotiations with GE. The American company, on the other hand, was a latecomer to China and faced hurdles from earlier European and Japanese entrants. Anxious to compete with other global players – Schneider being one – GE was attracted to Safety Electric's extensive sales networks throughout China. In 2005, the Safety Electric–General Electric joint venture was established. The Chinese maker accepted an equity distribution in favor of GE (51% vs. 49%), giving the American partner controlling shares in the JV. It is worth noting that just a year earlier, the Chinese maker had rejected an equal-partner venture with Schneider. However, marriage based on convenience does not tend to last. In the ensuing GE–SE venture, distrust and false expectations were pervasive. After three years' heavy losses on both sides, the two companies agreed to dissolve the venture.

The GE–SE venture demonstrates the inherent difficulties in alliances between global MNCs and indigenous capital in emerging markets.[24] During the process of negotiation, the Chinese firm was under considerable pressure to make concessions. GE represented a global giant with a long corporate history; SE was born to a low-tech rural enterprise not long ago in southern China. Not only did SE compromise its initial insistence on majority shares in the new venture, it also give up its ability to intervene in the design, manufacture, and marketing of jointly branded products. Furthermore, the jointly branded product line was a direct offspring of an already failed GE line in China. Without any input from SE's indigenous expertise, the product was doomed to another round of failure. The problem also lay in the fact that SE's sales representatives

[24] The case is based on interviews of managers at SE.

were neither invited nor incentivized to participate in the JV negotiation and operation. The sales therefore continued to prioritize marketing for SE products to the jointly branded line Neither did they provide timely feedback on sales to GE management.

On GE's side, the management did not trust its Chinese partner and was careful to hold full control over the joint brand. When sales were lackluster, GE management blamed the Chinese firm for not pressuring its sales representatives. The truth was that although SE provided products and licenses to its nationwide sales channels, the sales representatives were independent entities who did not take direct orders from SE's management. Being excluded from the GE–SE venture, they merely took in supplies of jointly branded products without actively promoting their sales. After the joint venture was dissolved, SE was left with considerable unsold inventories and incurred huge losses in order to absorb these inventories.

Safety Electric's negative experiences with both Schneider and GE reinforced the company's nativist approach to globalization. The company leadership was convinced that successful globalization had to follow its own way and ensure autonomy from external influence. In recent decades, in order to upgrade technology, SE invested heavily in R&D based in Shanghai and Hangzhou. In order to expand international sales and name recognition, SE invited foreign ambassadors and consuls in Beijing and Shanghai to tour SE's facilities and corporate headquarters. Since 2005, it has also held a biannual international marketing forum where the company invites major foreign sales representatives to exchange information and networks. In 2009, some 190 sales representatives from sixty countries attended the SE International Marketing Forum. Since 2013, SE's founder has accompanied President Xi and Premier Li's overseas trips.

Over the past decade, SE achieved more success in overseas markets by partnering with Chinese SOEs. Previously, SE's foreign sales had been mostly carried out by supplying local partners in foreign markets. This practice saw foreign sellers capturing the main profit margins. Beginning in 2006, SE joined forces with Chinese companies in machinery imports and exports, international engineering contractors, and energy companies. Jointly, they participated in bids for energy and infrastructure contracts in international markets. In 2006, SE outbid established foreign rivals – including Schneider and Swedish-Swiss maker ABB – to supply €60 million worth of equipment to Italy's national electricity company. SE also won energy contracts in Saudi Arabia, Cuba, Kenya, and Greece.

In short, Chinese state-led investment and infrastructure projects in less-developed regions offered opportunities for SE's expansion of its global footprint.

Currently, SE's globalization strategy seeks to maintain core autonomy and technology. It is reluctant to make investment in overseas manufacturing; instead, it has acquired research teams in advanced countries, such as in the United States and Europe, to guide the company's R&D and high-end manufacturing facilities in China. Thus far, according to senior managers, this practice is now paying off. The company has set up overseas branches in five continents and plans to grow its international sales to represent one-third of total sales by 2020. In this planned global expansion, SE differs from Precious Steel and Health Shoes in that it does not deem Western business consulting as useful because, as the managers explained, the corporate culture and business environment are so different between China and the West. Instead, the company concludes, quoting a senior manager in Shanghai, "Going global must be done; and going global has to work with the government."

SE's globalization experience is not unique. When China opened itself up to foreign capital in the 1990s, Chinese firms were thrown into intense competition with global players from both within and without. Many rural firms lacked basic technology and expertise and were ill prepared for the turbulence of competition. Their subsequent dealings with foreign competitors were often flawed. Negative experiences served to enhance nationalist tendencies at these companies; instead of converging with global practices, companies intensified their dependence on the Chinese state. Thus, instead of becoming a liberalizing force in political democratization in China, loyal private capital has become both the preserver and enhancer of the Communist autocracy.

Domestic Expansion

Safety Electric has a robust and long relationship with the Chinese government in their decades of domestic expansion. It pays close attention to the nationalist strategies launched by the central leadership. During the WDP, SE leveraged new industrialization in western China and expanded sales networks in inland cities. In 2004, to demonstrate its service and commitment to western development, Safety Electronic joined the CCP Youth League and National Students' Association and provided scholarships to college students from western China. The company actively sponsored activities in this poorer region and worked closely with local governments. These public and government relationships paid off: by 2008, Safety Electric had established 2,000 licensed stores in western China. Furthermore, it earned the much-coveted license to supply power devices to the West to East National Grid – a signature infrastructure project in the WDP.

China's 2008 Solar Industrial Development Strategy also helped Safety Electric's domestic expansion. Entering the new sector, the company led a delegation to America and Europe to acquire information, technology, and human talent. It eventually hired Chinese technologists in Silicon Valley who agreed to return homeland to help the company establish a solar panel manufacturing base. The company then negotiated with the Hangzhou government and received special permission and favorable policies toward the technologists' resettlement and other related issues.

After 2012, however, China's solar industry was in severe overcapacity, and the company's production in Hangzhou became too costly due to a rapid rise in labor and land prices. These factors drove Safety Electric to aggressively explore interior markets. In Gansu, in 2012, the company launched a new manufacturing site where labor and land were much cheaper, and where it received endorsement from the provincial government and the national energy agency. It was against this backdrop – severe overcapacities and an imperative to find cheaper production sites – that the company received and interpreted the top-down BRI strategy. Preexisting business plans along the BRI routes were greatly expedited and expanded – more so inside China than abroad.

BRI and Business

Safety Electric has been a vocal champion and supporter of the Belt and Road. From 2014 to 2017, Safety Electric showcased several key projects in the name of the BRI, demonstrating how firms interpret the strategy and how the strategy assists the firm's market behaviors. SE's BRI implementation has two directions. Externally, it continues and expands participation in infrastructure and energy subcontracting on which it had already collaborated with Chinese SOE projects. Following political rhetoric, the company increased its business exploration in emerging markets, many of which were undeveloped.[25] Pakistan is the main example here. Internally, the company continues and expands its efforts

[25] For some cases abroad, see "SE Promotes M&A Strategy," *China Daily*, December 12, 2016.

to penetrate inland markets and relocate manufacturing from costly coastal sites to western China.

Unlike SOEs that prefer more developed markets in the BRI, private companies such as Safety Electric prioritized Pakistan, Iran, the Czech Republic, and Southeast Asia, all underdeveloped target markets outlined in the BRI. This tactic seemed to work for the company: In 2015, thanks to orders related to the China–Pakistan Economic Corridor (CPEC), global sales of electrical switches rose rapidly, accounting for 70 percent of sales growth at the company.[26]

According to the managers interviewed, economic complementarity between China and Pakistan and business incentives had existed before CPEC, but the launch of CPEC fermented those nascent business ideas into new investment plans. Previously, the company had preferred an arms-length business strategy in Pakistan, choosing to rely on local subcontractors to conduct sales there. With CPEC, however, it began to reevaluate manufacturing in Pakistan seriously. As one manager put it,

> CPEC, with its endorsement from leaders of the two countries, eased our company's uncertainty in establishing a factory in Pakistan. Such risk reduction effect was not due to any specific regulatory change or new incentives provided by [the] Pakistani government, but [rather it was] due to [the] strong presence of Chinese power in the country. [...] We do not trust promises or policies from the Pakistani government but we can trust guarantees from our own leadership.

Safety Electric's willingness to expand business in uncertain emerging markets was arguably shaped by its corporate history. Established in rural China during the early 1980s, the company was used to underdevelopment and chaos. Even as it grew, the company did not break from its humble roots. To a large extent, its business model had been about expanding products to less developed regions where competition was less fierce. Interviewed managers observed that poor countries such as Cambodia and Myanmar were a lot like China in the 1980s when power and infrastructure were severely undersupplied, and the political authorities were extremely hungry for economic growth. After SE established a power plant in Cambodia, the Cambodian king awarded a national medal to the Chinese company.[27]

[26] The Pakistan case was based on interviews of senior managers in Shanghai.

[27] "Yijia kuaguo qiye de chengzhang" [The Growth of a Multinational Company], *Zhejiang zaixian* [Zhejiang Online], 2009. http://zjnews.zjol.com.cn/zjnews/zjxw/201809/t20180908_8218100.shtml.

Just as in Pakistan, the BRI enhanced Safety Electric's business in Sri Lanka, another South Asian nation. The company formed a joint venture with Sri Lanka's electricity company CED and established Safety Electric Power in 2006. Over the years, it steadily localized its operations and built strong business networks in the country. It came to occupy more than 10 percent of the power market in Sri Lanka in 2014. The BRI boosted SE's business interest in Sri Lanka. In April 2015, SE held a Grand Products Expo in the South Asian nation and invited a vice party secretary of Zhejiang to give a keynote speech. At the opening ceremony, Mr. Nan pledged that private companies should participate in the construction of Belt and Road, expedite the pace of "going global," and improve competitiveness in the world market.[28]

As a loyal entrepreneur, Nan had followed overseas trips by President Xi Jinping and Premier Li Keqiang, including trips to South Korea, Germany, and other countries in Europe and Asia. In November 2014, he also accompanied Zhejiang party secretary to Singapore and India and donated solar power equipment to these countries. In connection with these visits, the company signed overseas projects in South Korea, Finland, and Germany. Furthermore, the company led the creation of a private investment fund, called the Green Silk Road Fund, to be used for environmental and solar power development in the BRI countries. The company is also an active force in the Zhejiang Private Investment Fund, which claimed to closely follow investment opportunities in the BRI.

Despite these well-publicized BRI activities abroad, Safety Electric's largest and fastest-growing project in the name of the BRI took place within China. This was the creation of its newest manufacturing base near Xi'an – the starting point of the Silk Road Economic Belt. Negotiations for the project were concluded in 2014, and by 2017, the new site already had a 300 mu (20 hectare) facility; the local government committed to providing a further 3,000 mu of land. During interviews, the company emphasized how the city's status as "the pillar and starting point of the Belt" had precipitated the project, and because of that, the company could more effectively capture China's interior markets, move into Central Asia, and eventually relocate its manufacturing production from coastal sites to the interior. In short, prior to the BRI, the company

28 "Nan: women zhengzai jihua jiaru Yidai Yilu de Sanda zhanlue"[Nan: We are planning three strategies to participate in BRI implementation] March 10, 2015, http://news.xinhuanet.com/politics/2015lh/2015-03/10/c_1114588710.htm; "Safety Electrical Display at Xinjiang Electrical Exhibition, Internationalize via One Belt and One Road," www.xinjiang.gov.cn/tzxj/tzdt/2016/262972.htm.

had a solid business plan that was driven by market forces and had entered negotiations with the local government in Xi'an. The launch of the BRI both expedited and expanded the preexisting business project.

In 2012, Safety Electric began to approach local governments in Xi'an in an effort to locate a major manufacturing site in western China, an area the company identified as having both "land and demand" that would facilitate its expansion and growth in the next decade. Among the different sites compared, SE decided on Xi'an for three reasons: one, the local economy was relatively diverse and robust; two, the location was advantageous as it connects with five provinces in western China and is close to Central Asia; and three, the city has abundant human capital, with well-established universities, research institutions, and R&D centers. Furthermore, the local government was willing to offer favorable tax rates, concessionary land, and construction of an industrial park for SE and its suppliers. In short, the decision to invest and construct a new manufacturing facility near Xi'an was based on business and market calculations.

The BRI expedited the process of the project and enlarged the scope of commitment from the company and local government. According to the site manager, the Belt earmarked Xi'an as a starting point and enhanced investors' confidence in the city. Safety Electric and a range of other firms had shown interest in investing there. SE initially treated the Xi'an site with more caution – as an experiment for potential expansion into less developed western China; the BRI's launch boosted the company's commitment. SE increased investment from RMB ¥100 million to ¥3 billion, a 30-fold enlargement. On the local government side, the approval and construction of the new industrial park were much quicker; by 2017, the new park had already attracted several large electrical device makers in the country. The increased clustering of producers made the city a more viable site for large-scale production of electrical devices. Indeed, compared to coastal sites, manufacturing in Xi'an would save SE at least one third of labor and land expenses.

To conclude, the growth patterns, vulnerabilities, and government relations as captured in the case of Safety Electric apply to other private firms in regulated sectors. For example, Legendary Chemical, Rejuvenation after Quake, Sanyi Heavy Machinery, and Yutong Automobiles have all exhibited dependence on government policy and displayed loyalist approaches to the ruling party. Due to overcapacities, private producers had to expand markets abroad, but they faced major hurdles in overseas expansion. In mature markets, Chinese private companies had neither brand nor technology advantages. In less developed markets, they had little experience or expertise. Hence, many of them rely on government programs to make investment decisions. As one experienced international business consultant in Shanghai observed,

> Corporate China is a latecomer in the global market. In order to go global, it has to improvise different routes from those by early globalizers. These routes, in varying degrees, all involve working with governments at home and in the host [nation].[29]

FREE MARKET AND UNFREE MANAGEMENT

Globalization has complex and diverse effects on different types of Chinese companies. Precious Steel, a national SOE that was in a propitious position to partner with Western capital, conforms to what Edward Steinfeld describes as "playing our game" in which the SOE seeks to be more like MNCs from advanced countries.[30] Safety Electric, a private enterprise that faced immense challenges and hostility from foreign companies, demonstrates dependence on its home government and adopts a nationalist stance against foreign capital. Health Shoes, a private producer in a highly liberalized sector, has demonstrated a different pattern. Its interpretation of nationalist strategies is twofold. First, its managers view top-down strategies as important for the nation but having little obligatory power over the company's decisions. Second, the company proactively and flexibly embraces global partnerships and technologies, including soft knowledge and experiences. Here, "markets, not Mao" have driven corporate behaviors.[31] In the meantime, the managers revere nationalist leaders and adopt tactics prevalent in party ideology and organization to manage their workers.

Health Shoes, headquartered in Wenzhou and stock-listed in Hong Kong, is the largest fashion shoe maker in China, with household brand names in the country. It has 5,000 chain stores across the country, and its direct employment reached 22,000 in 2015. The company in general is low-key and seldom takes interviews or requests for study. In its home city, the company has a long-term lease on a massive site, which it acquired in the 1980s; it also has many real estate assets on its books. Different from the leadership of Safety Electric, the shoe company's founder never

[29] Interview, Shanghai, August 2016.
[30] Steinfeld, *Playing Our Game*.
[31] Lardy, *Market, Not Mao*.

sought affiliation with the ruling party or took on honorary posts in the government. Arranged by close personal ties, interviews with veteran managers at the company were carried out in an open-ended, conversational style and proved invaluable in penetrating the rather opaque business world in China.

Learning from Foreigners

China's entry into the WTO and the rapid rise of foreign companies in China have shaped Health Shoes' perception and experience of globalization in the past two decades. As an indigenously branded fashion shoemaker, the company focused on the domestic market; globalization helped the company grow inside China. In 2001, the company acquired exclusive sales rights from the American shoe brand Geox. More important than the sales rights, though, the Chinese shoemaker emulated Geox management style and skills. The interviewed manager admitted that the partnership, for the first time, turned Health Shoes into a "modern" company and helped it outperform other shoemakers from Wenzhou. In 2010, leveraging its shares in the Chinese market, Health Shoes acquired exclusive sales rights in China from American brand Skecher. The Chinese firm focused on learning about more advanced brand promotion and innovative design in shoemaking; its goal remains to expand its brands in the home market and compete with both domestic and foreign competitors inside China.

Also in 2010, Health Shoes hired Roland Berger Management Consulting – a German company with global operations including China – to conduct extensive research and develop a business strategy for Health Shoes' growth going forward into the next decade. By drawing on the experiences of shoemakers in advanced nations, the consulting company devised a three-step business strategy: increasing the sale of Health Shoes' own brands, focusing on design and manufacturing its own brands, and expanding sales of other brands in Health Shoes chain stores. This plan, claimed the consultants, could double Health Shoes' sales from 2010 to 2020.

Unlike Safety Electric, which saw Western experience as irrelevant and ineffective in helping its business expansion, the shoemaker followed the Roland Berger ten-year business plan to the letter. The applicability of Western experience to Chinese shoemakers demonstrates that in light manufacturing industries, which had experienced profound market liberalization during the reform era, globalization has resulted in a high degree of convergence between China and foreign countries. As elsewhere, market forces dominate China's light industries, with the government playing a minimal role.

This contrast between Health Shoes and Safety Electrical – both private companies originated from rural entrepreneurs in Wenzhou, like the contrast between provincial SOEs Chongqing Foreign Trade Group and Ningbo-Zhoushan Port Group, demonstrates that ownership of a company does not determine the company's relationship with the home government and patterns of globalization. Rather, it is the institutional environment of the sector, or the host society, in which the company concentrates and operates that has greater impacts.

In relation to the BRI, the strategic implications do not have much relevance to Health Shoes, but the market rationale also works for the company. For example, the shoemaker began to explore overseas sales in Southeast Asia prior to the BRI. In 2013, just before the launch of the strategy, Health Shoes opened seven chain stores in Vietnam, which turned out to be in line with the BRI. The company also invested in Light in the Box, a business to business (B2B) platform for e-commerce in Central Asia. In 2015, the company became the largest shareholder of the e-platform and began to actively explore business opportunities in Central Asia, moves that were again in line with the geographic coverage of the BRI.

In a way, the example of Health Shoes demonstrates that the BRI strategy, which was mainly viewed as an external expansionist strategy, does have economic rationality. With or without the BRI, market forces have already influenced corporate behaviors in similar directions. With the BRI, such behaviors are expedited.

Domestic Expansion

The WDP strategy was most pronounced in mobilizing western governments to reform SOEs and attract foreign capital. However, in the context of expedited market reform, local governments – in particular below the provincial level – were proactive in attracting private capital from coastal China. Health Shoes, as a well-known shoemaker in China, was approached by a county in Chongqing, which offered concessionary land and tax benefits. The company then established a large shoemaking industrial zone in this county and expanded into western markets from this new zone. As the WDP entered the stage of rapid urbanization and infrastructure development in the mid-2000s, Health Shoes extended its business into commercial construction and real estate. After 2012, as the Chinese government stepped up efforts to tighten environmental standards and crack down on polluting shoemakers, Health Shoes consolidated business in the western region and acquired smaller shoe manufacturers in the Chongqing environs.

When interviewed, Health Shoes managers made it abundantly clear that in today's China, their relationships with local governments do *not* have a huge impact on the company's business. The company does not need to covet ties with or cozy up to local officials; rather, local officials increasingly rely on large companies to fulfill regulatory targets. Environmental and labor standards, for example, need the cooperation of large companies. The managers also made it clear that national regulations remain important as they often carry direct tax ramifications. Thus, as the central government passed high-tech tax credits, Health Shoes adopted new machines on its assembly lines. When new environmental regulations came out, the company used cleaner – and significantly more expensive – glue in its shoemaking to qualify for a new tax credit. In short, even when operating in a profoundly free sector, firms still respond quickly to national regulations; corporate elites are geared toward programs passed by the central state.

Furthermore, through interviews, it was clear that Health Shoes management was enamored with the ideas and messages of the new leader Xi Jinping, not because they enhanced any particular business projects (as in the case of Safety Electric) but because they encouraged the cohesive management of its workers. The management asked all workers, divided into small groups, to study the president's speeches and regularly submit reflection papers for exchange inside the company. In 2016, inspired by President Xi's speech at the ninety-fifth birthday of the CCP, the company held its annual leadership meeting in the birthplace of an ancient philosopher frequently referred to by President Xi. Drawing on the leader's speeches, the company worked to enhance a cohesive corporate culture. According to one senior manager, the sessions studying President Xi's speeches helped instill a common vision in all floor managers at Health Shoes. They are part of the company's "virtual university" that – in addition to political learning – provides employees with regular vocational education on government policies. Furthermore, by copying from the standard playbook of the CCP, the company is routinely selecting exemplary cases/individuals [*dianxing*] to reinforce preferred behaviors and induce conformity within the company.

In summary, "free" enterprises in China such as Health Shoes still develop rather cordial and filial relationships with the government and national strategies. Three dynamics are at work. First, the government policies and regulations have more or less worked to help the companies grow. Ambiguity in the nationalist strategies allowed the enterprises to interpret them in ways that strengthen their business. Second, regulations that seek to change corporate behaviors – in terms of high-tech contents or higher environmental standards – were passed in incentivizing conformity, thus not necessarily causing resistance. Finally, social norms underpinning authoritarian party politics are familiar and similar to corporate management in these companies. Companies are therefore attuned to political programs and slogans to manage labor issues. Workers, who grew up and were educated in the same social milieu, are quite used to it. These practices, in a way, make free enterprises agents of an "unfree" state.

CONCLUSION

In theory, market reforms make capitalists more autonomous from an authoritarian state, thus facilitating political liberalization. Similarly, economic globalization is theorized to bring about liberal convergence across globalizing nations, with autocracy increasingly succumbing to the pressure of democratization.[32] In the past four decades of market reform and globalization, however, the Chinese corporate experiences demonstrate surprising interactions that involve indigenous firms, home government, and foreign capital. Diversity in such experiences across types of companies and sectors is consistent and compelling; it reveals the true colors of Chinese capitalism – they all have close relationships with the state, but for different reasons.

The examples of the firms investigated here establish that corporate interpretations of nationalist strategies have been driven by market conditions and corporate needs, not proclaimed strategic rhetoric. The national SOE – Precious Steel – was risk averse in interpreting and implementing the Belt and Road. The SOE was also involved in the WDP and CGG strategies, but these experiences were shaped by government pressures to serve domestic priorities, such as taking over social burdens from failed SOEs. Private companies in market-dominant sectors, such as Health Shoes, did not make specific plans to implement the BRI. Nevertheless, the shoemaker was effective in leveraging the WDP, during which time the company penetrated markets in western China, and

[32] Gallagher, "How FDI Delayed Democratization in China," pp. 338–340.

the CGG, in which the company adopted newer skills and technology from foreign partners. Private capital in regulated sectors, such as Safety Electric, was the most eager implementer of the BRI, which expedited and expanded preexisting projects in China and abroad.

In studying the political effect of globalization, Mary Gallagher observed in 2002 that liberalization and integration with the global economy had differential effects over time, and that "political change [democratization in China] has been *delayed*, not stopped."[33] The conclusion in this chapter, based on corporate–government interactions in recent decades, is less promising. It is clear that in adopting nationalist strategies, the state and market have reinforced each other in the economic realm and jointly maintained high growth in the country for an extended time. It is also clear that given authoritarianism and deep globalization, corporate nationalism has been strengthened in China; relationships between the authoritarian state and companies are becoming increasingly symbiotic. Were China to pluralize, it is *unlikely* to come from the corporate sector.

[33] Ibid., p. 372.

8

Global Implications: Roads and Roadblocks in China and Beyond

> The West was sure the Chinese approach would not work. It just had to wait. It's still waiting.
>
> —Philip P. Pan, "The Land Failed to Fail"[1]

In 1998, Communist China was trapped in crises. The Asian financial crisis precipitated sharp falls in incoming foreign investment and outgoing exports in China; violent protests against the United States brought Sino–American relations to near a halt; nationwide crackdowns on the religious movement Falun Gong pitted the state against its own society. Deng Xiaoping had just passed away a year earlier. Against this backdrop, Beijing's decision to join the World Trade Organization was almost like "raising a white flag"; both liberals and conservative members of the ruling elite felt that "doomsday" was near.[2] People of that era could not have expected that the Chinese economy could go so far so fast.[3]

Perhaps that was why scholars on China moved away from the earlier focus on the Chinese state and how it adapts to economic transition to new research interests related to civil society, social movements, the environment, rule of law, and political cooptation.[4] In each of the new

[1] Philip P. Pan is the Asia editor of the *New York Times*. His quote is from "The Land That Failed to Fail," *New York Times*, November 18, 2018.

[2] Remark by speakers at the conference "China's Reform and Openness at 40," the Fairbank Center for China Studies at Harvard University, November 7, 2018.

[3] Joseph Fewsmith, *China Today, China Tomorrow: Domestic Politics, Economy, and Society*. Lanham, MD: Rowman & Littlefield Publishers, 2010.

[4] Bruce Dickson, "Integrating Wealth and Power in China: The Communist Party's Embrace of the Private Sector," *The China Quarterly*, 192, 2007.

areas, strident discoveries have been made by China scholars.[5] The study of the Chinese experience in a globalized economy, on the contrary, has become deeply divided, and not much progress has been made.

This book formulates the state-mobilized globalization (SMG) framework to capture policy making and implementation of the Western Development Program (WDP), China Goes Global (CGG), and Belt and Road Initiative (BRI), during the period 1998–2018. It focuses on the Chinese state and unpacks it into three "blocks" – the party leadership, the national agencies, and the commercial and developmental arms (state capital and local governments). In this state system, power and interest fragmentations are inherit in the structure at party-state institutions and the complex webs of interpersonal relationships. Explained in Chapter 2, such deep and broad fragmentation make it impossible for the state to come up with effective responses to important needs in changing market and society. During critical jundures opened up by major crises, the autocratic leadership launched nationalist strategies to coordinate state behavior and help regain internal growth momentum.

These strategies are ambitious and ambiguous. While mobilizing subnational and commercial actors into implementation, the strategies also allow them to self-interpret and reinterpret the strategies to serve localized economic needs. With state-mobilized globalization from 1998 to 2018, both markets and globalization have expanded inside China, with positive effects on sustaining the high-growth economy. The political outcomes, by contrast, are much less positive and much less certain.

Synthesizing the theoretical and empirical analyses in the earlier chapters, this concluding chapter reflects on findings in this book against broader political–economic debates regarding China, Chinese roles in the world, and trends in global development and shifting power. On China, the book speaks to, first, the political future of Communist China, in particular the popularly perceived stagnation or reversal in the recent period, and second, the rise of Xi Jinping in the Chinese state system. Going beyond China, first, the chapter stresses the importance of *both* state and market for economies to succeed in today's globalization, and second, it covers concerns in world development and shifting power as a

5 Andrew Mertha, *China's Water Warriors*. Ithaca, NY: Cornell University Press, 2010; Rachel Stern, *Environmental Litigation in China: A Study in Political Ambivalence*. New York: Cambridge University Press, 2014; Mary Gallagher, *Authoritarian Legality in China: Law, Workers, and the State*. New York: Cambridge University Press, 2017; William Hurst, *The Chinese Worker after Socialism*. New York: Cambridge University Press, 2012.

result of globalization *by* China. The chapter ends with an echo back to the motivating strategy, the Belt and Road, and points to different pathways of implementation as well as potential roadblocks.

DEBATES ON CHINA

Globalization and China's Nondemocratic Future

When the United States agreed to admit China into the WTO, it justified the decision on the expectation that China, with economic globalization, would experience democratization and converge more with the US-preferred liberal system.[6] In a liberal globalist view, globalization is "not an economic fad. It is not a passing trend." Rather, it represents "an international system – the dominant international system that replaced the Cold War system after the fall of the Berlin Wall."[7]

China scholars, to a large extent, shared or had been influenced by this view. Bruce Gilley wrote in 2003, "The end of communist rule and the embrace of democracy in China will be one of the most important events of the twenty-first century. It will mark for the world the virtual end of a remarkable yet tragic experiment in utopianism known as Marxist-Leninism."[8] Mary Gallagher, after explaining why foreign direct investment helped sustain the rule of the Chinese Communist Party, remarked clearly, "A very important qualification of the general argument presented here is the conclusion that political change has been *delayed*, not stopped."[9]

Lately, facing political stagnation or liberal reversal, scholars have blamed individual leaders;[10] others focused on the tactics of coercion and cooptation employed by the ruling party.[11] More important, it has become a popular belief that the tradition and culture of China are impossible to change, despite the country's participation in economic globalization. Represented by the writings of Henry Kissinger, the endpoint of China's contemporary globalization can be anything but "integration" into "any global order not of its own creation".[12] "China is singular.

[6] Wasserstrom, "China and Globalization."
[7] Thomas Friedman, *The Lexus and the Oliver Tree*. New York: Farrar, Strauss and Giroux, 2000, p. 7.
[8] Bruce Gilley, *China's Democratic Future: How It Will Happen and Where It Will Lead*. New York: Columbia University Press, 2003, p. ix.
[9] Gallagher, "Why FDI Delayed Democratization," p. 372.
[10] Minzner, *End of an Era*.
[11] Bruce Dickson, *Dictators' Dilemma*. New York: Oxford University Press, 2018.
[12] Wasserstrom, "China and Globalization," p. 163.

No other country can claim so long a continuous civilization, or such an intimate relationship to its ancient past and classical principles."[13]

China's democratic future is not the central concern of this book; the SMG framework was set up to study economic globalization in China, not political liberalization. Yet by investigating globalization politics and policies from 1998 to 2018, the period that the democratic convergence expectation gradually gave way to growing conviction in China's authoritarian divergence, the book demonstrates patterns of Chinese adaptation to globalization and political–economic consequences of such adaptation that have impacted political regime dynamics in China.

For example, in the background of the WDP, cross-regional inequalities, a result of "successful" economic globalization in coastal China, generated persistent and powerful pressure on the political leadership to react. That political motivation was important in the launch of the top-down WDP, as shown in Chapter 3. Similarly, against the background of the CGG, successful expansion of private foreign capital created major losses in the state sectors in China. The "losers" included not only state-owned enterprises (SOEs) and their managers but also professionals, scholars, and civil servants who experienced relative deprivation in social status and income levels. These groups mounted pressure on the national leadership to protect the state sectors. In Chapter 4, the CGG birthing process demonstrates that political leaders employed the state-led strategy to ease such concerns while sustaining the trend of globalization in China.

On top of the political pressures generated by income and developmental inequalities, globalization also made the national economy vulnerable to crisis. A globalized economy is porous to swings and volatilities in the world market, and oftentimes the state is thrown into crises because of such global recessions. In China, the economy expanded rapidly in the mid-1990s because of global inflationary swing, and then suffered severely when the AFC struck in 1998. Factory shutdowns and unemployment became threats to social stability in the country. It was shown in Chapters 3 and 4 that the crisis and overcapacities were the main motivators behind the launch of the WDP and CGG in 1999 and 2000, respectively.

In 2008, the global financial crisis (GFC) posed severe challenges to China's exporting industries. Moreover, western China experienced an

[13] Henry Kissinger, *On China*. New York: Penguin Press, 2011, p. 2.

unprecedented earthquake disaster, which claimed massive human losses and infrastructure in the region. The combined crises led to passage of a massive stimulus plan that contributed to rapidly accumulated industrial and infrastructure overcapacities in China. Thus, as the new administration began in 2012, domestic overcapacities and a shrinking global market, coupled with diplomatic and strategic conflicts, became strong motivations behind the Belt and Road, which was officially launched in late 2013 (see Chapter 5).

Just as globalization made economic crises a recurrent phenomenon, the national government's ability to respond to crises seemed to be in decline. As economic exchange between the global markets and domestic actors decentralized to localities, as amply shown in the three SMG cycles in China, national agencies such as the NDRC, MOFCOM, and MFA experienced more limited power to come up with widely acceptable national policies or implement their sectoral policies effectively. Against the background of the WDP, for example, the SPC proposed well-planned programs to address cross-regional inequalities, but was repeatedly opposed by other agencies and local governments in coastal regions. Similarly, in the origin of CGG, before it became an autocratic, nationalist strategy, there was considerable opposition to Chinese SOEs going global. Furthermore, in the formation of the BRI, three different functional bureaucracies offered practiced proposals to address the crises, but none of them gained cross-agency support.

It was in these critical, crisis-laden, moments that autocratic leaders intervened and staked their personal authority on the nationalist strategies, the WDP, CGG, and BRI. In promoting these strategies, the autocrats relied on political mobilization based on nationalist rhetoric, rallied cross-state support through control of information and party organizations, and incentivized participation by decentralizing economic powers and resources to SOEs and local governments. Under the banners of these nationalist strategies, different state actors and interest groups then flexibly interpreted and improvised economic programs that work for their own business interests. Yet by "nominally" conforming to the messages and mobilization from the top, they reinforced the perceived power of individual leaders, including Jiang Zemin and Xi Jinping.

This political process of globalization, discovered through the SMG analysis, complements other factors of authoritarianism that are underscored in the regime literature as driving authoritarian resilience or reversal in the recent era.[14] The regime literature, however, is confined to domestic political considerations and has not incorporated the politics and process of globalization.

Drawing on China's twenty years of globalization, it is clear that separation between the two fields – domestic versus global studies – is insufficient to explain the trajectory of regime change in China, or elsewhere. In fact, the politics of globalization – inequality, crisis, and declining state capacity as shown in China – is common in many countries around the world. Just in recent years, personalistic autocratic leaders have swept into power not only in autocracies but also democracies, such as Narendra Modi in India, Rodrigo Duterte in the Philippines, Donald Trump in the United States, and Mohamad Mahathir, who was reelected in Malaysia.

In short, the liberal globalist view, as expressed in terms such as "the end of the history,"[15] "the world is flat,"[16] and "playing our game,"[17] not only has gotten political democratization wrong but has also gotten economic globalization wrong.

Xi and the Chinese State

In an article in *the Economist* in early 2018, referring to Chinese leader Xi Jinping, it was observed, "Not since Mao Zedong [has] a Chinese leader ... wielded so much power so openly."[18] This description was quite true. Since President Xi's coming to power, he has organized and led seven Small Leading Groups in the party leadership organs – ranging from finance to law to regional economies. In his second term, Xi achieved an even greater concentration of power. Of the seven-member Politburo Standing Committee (PSC), Xi is one above all others; few of the other members have their own power bases. Also, in a departure from long-standing convention in reformist China, Xi changed the Constitution to allow him to stay in power for more than two terms.

[14] Dickson, *Dictators' Dilemma*; Minzner, *End of an Era*; Jennifer Gandhi and Adam Przeworski, "Authoritarian Institutions and the Survival of Autocrats," *Comparative Political Studies*, 40(11), 2007, pp. 1279–1301; Martin K. Dimitrov, "Popular Autocrats," *Journal of Democracy*, 20(1), 2009, pp. 78–81.

[15] Francis Fukuyama, *The End of History and the Last Man*. New York: Free Press, 1992.

[16] Thomas Friedman, *The World Is Flat*. New York: Farrar, Straus and Giroux, 2005.

[17] Stenfield, *Playing Our Game*.

[18] "How the West Got China Wrong," *Economist*, March 3, 2018, p. 9.

In pushing for concentration of such political power and policy authority, President Xi and his close associates constantly justified the changes based on the fragmented Chinese state system. They have repeatedly argued that the concentrated "superstructure" [*dinceng sheji*] was necessary to coordinate effective cross-governmental actions and to achieve "grand" tasks of domestic development and the international rise of China.[19]

Does this mean that the leadership now has enough power to enforce his vision upon the Chinese state and impose changes that he deems important to China's rising ambition? Has President Xi successfully overcome state fragmentation in ruling China? Is fragmentation a time-specific equilibrium that can pass when circumstances change, or is it an enduring institutional characteristic of the Chinese state system?

Answers to these questions cannot be certain. Yet the *whole* process of the BRI – President Xi's brain child – shows that fragmentation is still quite present and powerful despite the concentration of the president's power. First, the original ideas were provided by three preexisting practices and proposals from central agencies – infrastructure diplomacy associated with the Ministry of Foreign Affairs, the Chinese Marshall Plan proposal advanced by financial technocrats, and the China Goes West strategy supported by security specialists. We can observe that these agencies and agents have "edged" President Xi into launching the Belt and Road strategy. However, as the strategy gained popularity, the political autocrat was viewed to have more power because authoritarian leaders, lacking institutionalized power indicators, can demonstrate "certainty of power" only by subordinates' support of their policies.[20]

Then as the BRI strategy was being formulated in the central government, fragmentation took over. Regardless the leader's "vision," agencies with resources became the main actors in devising specific projects and programs; agencies that did not gain power and incentives from the strategy became passive servicers of the BRI.[21] During the mobilization process, in particular, government policy preferences were communicated in disparate ways – conferences, publicity events, news broadcasting, and so on – yet few obligatory guidelines were passed from the central government.

[19] According to interviews with Chinese scholars and government officials.

[20] Shih, *Factions and Finance in China*, p. 4.

[21] The Ministry of Commerce, for example, was incredibly inattentive to movements in the BRI, despite being one of the three agencies that drafted the 2015 Action and Vision Plan.

Furthermore, the BRI's implementation reveals significant decentralization and divergence from the nationalist ambition proclaimed by the political leadership. Local governments, leveraging ambiguity in the BRI, reinterpreted the strategy to facilitate local markets – in Chongqing, it led to rescue packages for struggling SOEs; in Ningbo, it helped local planners pass policies to upgrade the local economy; in Wenzhou, it enabled private entrepreneurs to strengthen traditional markets in Western Europe, not new markets as identified in the BRI (see Chapter 6). Companies, including SOEs, implemented the BRI only when it helped preexisting business plans and in ways that aided these plans as well (see Chapter 7).

Finally, BRI implementation may even intensify fragmentation in China, compared to the previous two strategies, the WDP and CGG. In the two earlier strategies, national agencies – NDRC, MOFCOM, and SAFE, for example – have passed regulatory changes that shaped lower-level behaviors, although lower-level governments also gave input on those regulatory changes. In the BRI, few regulatory changes were made, and local implementation often disregarded rhetoric from the central government. For example, while the State Council and NDRC consistently pushed for industrial capacities going global, city-level governments and SOEs became the main actors and decision makers with regard to specific projects and programs in the BRI. More than ever, *city* governments submitted special zone proposals to the State Council and had them approved.

In short, it may be impossible to gauge how much power President Xi has over the Chinese state. The process analysis here suggests that the perception of Xi's unprecedented power over the state is likely exaggerated; the fragmented state is still quite alive.

However, fragmentation in an authoritarian system may not be a bad thing. Because of fragmentation, no single interest group can "capture the state" and predominantly shape government policy. This helps ensure the continual existence of "public purpose" in autocratic China. Workers' groups check the business interest; landlocked provinces check the influence of the coastal region; ultra-nationalist groups check the globalists' influence on economic policies, and vice versa. In an authoritarian system, lacking rules-based checks and balances, were it not for state fragmentation, special interests would shape the polity in one way or the another.[22]

[22] The distorted tendency is also true in mature democracies. See Thelen, "The American Precariat"; Katherine Levine Einstein, Maxwell Palmer, and David Glick, "Who Participates in Local Government? Evidence from Meeting Minutes," *Perspectives on Politics*, 17(1), 2019, pp. 28–46.

Fragmentation, however, is not the only defining feature of the Chinese state system. Twenty years of SMG, as this book reveals, demonstrate consistent ideology, organization, and the polity's ability to rally nationwide programs, despite complex interactions and bargaining inside the state system. First, the more or less consistent ideology has three tiers: nationalism pertaining to modernization and the power of the Chinese nation at the highest level; prioritization of rapid economic growth in the middle level; and a general consensus on markets and globalization as the means to rapid economic growth on the ground level. Second, in combating severe economic crises, the SMG analysis shows that the party and state leaderships repeatedly fall back on using "old" tactics of political mobilization to coordinate their preferred state behaviors. And finally, entering implementation, markets and globalization then take over as instruments to revive the economy.

The analysis of SMG cycle – from fragmentation to autocratic intervention then to re-fragmentation – has parallels to the long-standing insight of "fragmented authoritarianism" in Chinese politics, which was originally proposed by Kenneth Lieberthal and David Lampton in 1992 and then adopted by subsequent scholars in various fashions.[23] Fragmentation in the SMG is a structural characteristic rooted in the Chinese state system – a gigantic apparatus with multiple power and policy clusters and relational nodes. Unless the state withdraws from society in significant measures, at which point some state elements and functions will be migrated out of the state system and be left to rules and institutions, fragmentation is almost impossible to overcome in China. Then again, fragmented authoritarianism is better than totalitarian authoritarianism in political life and policy outcomes.

IT TAKES TWO TO SUCCEED IN GLOBALIZATION

The State–Market Debate

In mainstream economic theories, a separation between state and market is consistently upheld.[24] The idea behind it is that the market, as an invisible hand, balances supply and demand of commodities and channels resources to the most efficient sectors and actors, while the state has political, public, and strategic purposes that diverge from market mechanisms.[25] When a state intervenes in the market, it is typically

[23] Mertha, "Fragmented Authoritarianism 2.0."

[24] Bob Jessop, "The 'Return' of the National State in the Current Crisis of the World Market," *Capital & Class*, 34(1), 2010, pp. 38–43.

[25] Kahler, "External Ambition and Economic Performance."

ineffective and inefficient. Therefore, to the extent the state plays a part in the economy, the roles should be the provision of services to market actors or supply of institutions to correct risky market behavior.[26]

Such thinking has influenced debates on China's economic growth among scholars. Countering state-capitalist observations, Nicholas Lardy contended in 2014 that it was markets that have driven China's economic miracles.[27] Yet again in 2019, he had to reverse his characterization of Chinese economy as "the end of reform."[28] Kellee Tsai, who published a seminal book on the emergence of private capital in Communist China in 2006, has lately been arguing for the term "state capitalism" to describe the Chinese economy.[29] Barry Naughton, whose long-time scholarship has been about gradualist, convergent reforms in China, has recently been testing out the framework "China as a socialist."[30]

Addressing divergence, but convinced of market-led achievements in China, political scientist Edward Steinfeld stresses that market institutions, available in the West, have helped the Chinese economy. Thus, despite outdated state institutions in China, the Chinese economy is actually "playing by our rules."[31] Business professor Yasheng Huang explicitly retorted that China's economic success was not due to the state but *in spite of* the state.[32]

The SMG framework in this book speaks to this state–market debate by unpacking the policy processes of three nationalist strategies. In doing so, it consistently establishes the mechanism of mutual enhancement between the state and market during China's globalization. More important, it demonstrates patterns of state–market interactions during different stages of the strategies. During the birthing process, the political leadership (as one element of the state) was vital to launching a strategy to coordinate state behaviors and counter economic crisis. Then entering the formation phase, the central agencies made general policy guidelines to empower and encourage market activities. Finally,

26 Martin Wolf, *Why Globalization Works*. New Haven, CT: Yale University Press, 2004.

27 Lardy, *Markets over Mao*.

28 Nicholas Lardy, *The State Strikes Back: The End of Economic Reform in China?* New York: Columbia University Press, 2019.

29 Tsai, *Capitalism without Democracy*; Tsai, "The State of China's Economic Miracle."

30 Barry Naughton, "Is China Socialist?" *Journal of Economic Perspective*, 31(1), 2017, pp. 3–24.

31 Steinfeld, *Playing by Our Rules*.

32 Yasheng Huang, *Capitalism with Chinese Characteristics*. New York: Cambridge University Press, 2008.

during full-blown implementation, local governments and companies interpreted and improvised programs and projects almost entirely based on their own market conditions. As a whole, because of the state and market's *adaptive interaction*, these nationalist strategies seem to have helped overcome economic crises and revive the high-growth economy in China.

China Compared to Historical Cases

The phenomenon in the SMG is drawn from China's experiences, but in the past, state *and* market have jointly driven economic rises of major powers. Economic historian and writer Pankaj Mishra observed, "economic history reveals that great economic powers have always become great because of activist states. Regardless of the mystical properties claimed for it, the invisible hand of self-interest depends on the visible and often heavy hand of government."[33] The United States, while industrializing, was the bastion of modern protectionism, with average tariffs in the late nineteenth century reaching as high as 45 percent.[34] The philosophical father of the American financial system, whose pupils included the Germans, the Japanese, and indirectly, the Chinese, Alexander Hamilton was a strong advocate of "infant industry protectionism."[35] Hamilton's formula of industrial protection, as juxtaposed to free trade in Britain, arguably contributed to the United States becoming the world's fastest-growing economy in the nineteenth century and into the 1920s.

Hamilton's nationalist industrial policy also influenced other nations coming late to international economic competition in the nineteenth century. For example, one of Hamilton's most influential followers was German economist Friedrich List, who wrote a book titled *Outlines of American Political Economy*.[36] Then the German state applied List's lessons from the United States and moved the country with spectacular

[33] Pankaj Mishra, "The Rise of China and the Fall of the Free Trade Myth," *New York Times Magazine*, February 7, 2018, http://nyti.ms/2BKdhbo.

[34] Paul Bairoch and J.-M. Limbor, "Changes in the Industrial Distribution of the World Labour Force, by Region, 1880–1960," *International Labour Review*, 98, 1968, pp. 311–336.

[35] Alexander Hamilton, Report on the Subject of Manufacturers, 1791, www.gilderlehrman.org/content/hamilton's-report-subject-manufactures-179.

[36] Friedrich List, *Outlines of American Political Economy*, available at Paul & Co Pub Consortium, 1996.

speed from an agrarian to an industrial economy.[37] Following the German example, Meiji-era Japan heavily subsidized its first factories, and the Japanese state not only protected its business from excessive competition but also guaranteed them a minimum profit.[38] This Meiji-era experience was incorporated into Japan's "developmental state" after World War II, which in turn gave birth to developmental states in South Korea and Taiwan.

To what extent is the SMG framework similar to historic "nationalist" development experiences, in particular, in the developmental states in China's near neighbors? They all feature strong states and quite vibrant markets during their economic successes. Yet considerable differences have prevailed. As revealed in the WDP, CGG, and BRI, the Chinese state is much larger and far more fragmented than states in the other cases, where the government was either democratically elected or staffed with institutionalized agencies. In 2019, the Chinese ruling party has 89 million members who fill the central and local governments, major companies, and research institutions. Coordination in such a massive state apparatus is almost impossible. Furthermore, the gigantic population and vast and diverse territories present severe challenges to governance and make nationwide policy coordination extremely difficult. Political leadership in China, different from the developmental states, relies heavily on political mobilization, drawing on nationalist ideology, *not* institutions or "rational" planning that have defined the state intervention in the earlier risers.

Second, the degree of globalization and penetration by foreign forces during China's rise are much greater and far more overwhelming than the historical periods of American, German, and Japanese ascendency. In those cases, exchange of goods was the main content of globalization; and raising tariffs served as an effective means to protect infant industries. Past globalization also covered fewer segments of population; therefore, changes in the global market brought less destruction to domestic stability. In the current era, globalization has enmeshed almost all groups and regions and intensified, in the Chinese case, divisions between coastal provinces and interior ones and between capitalists and

[37] Mishra, "The Rise of China and the Fall of the Free Trade Myth."

[38] Mark Borthwick, *Pacific Century: The Emergence of Modern Pacific Asia.* New York: Westview, 2014.

workers, as well as recurrent economic crises that allow very short response times. During deep globalization, national economies have become deeply dependent and porous to volatilities in other countries.

Finally, although historic records are patchy, there is reason to believe that the level of development in Communist China before opening was extremely low compared to industry and technology levels in the United States, Germany, and Japan prior to their takeoff stages.[39] Furthermore, as many developing countries were ready for industrial takeoff in the 1980s, competitive pressures that reformist China faced were severe; and the time allowed for China's industrial catch-up was arguably short. In other words, Communist China had to leapfrog its economic ladders with very backward technology and know-how. Globalization, enabled by diaspora entrepreneurs in East Asia, provided a shortcut and was a necessary condition for the Chinese economy to take off.[40] It is also volatile and challenging, bringing new values and ideas that threaten the ruling ideology and government system. Going back to points one and two, the rise of China is very stressful to the Communist state. Adaptation to such constant stress has not only prolonged economic growth but also strengthened Communist rule and made regime change toward liberalization difficult in China.

To synthesize, it is the argument here that Communist China has risen since the late 1990s under conditions such as massive challenges in governance, a high degree of external penetration, and extremely backward technology and institutional levels. The state-mobilized globalization came to embody patterns of state–market mutual enhancement that departs from past experiences elsewhere. In SMG, political campaigns, not institutionalized rules, have provided coordination across agencies and levels of the government.[41] Local governments and state-affiliated capital with direct incentives and resources in policy implementation came to be dominant players in the marketspace and operate more or less in accordance with commercial rules, rather than strictly following directives from national agencies and technocratic industrial planning.

39 Alice Amsden, The Rise of "the Rest" : Challenges to the West From Late Industrializing Economies. New York: Oxford University Press, 2003.

40 Min Ye, "Policy Learning or Diffusion: How China Opened to Foreign Direct Investment?" *Journal of East Asian Studies*, 9(3), 2009, pp. 399–432; Min Ye, "Utility and Conditions of Diffusion by Diasporas: Foreign Direct Investment in China and India," *Journal of East Asian Studies*, 16(2), 2016, pp. 261–280.

41 For characteristics of American state building, see Stephen Skowronek, *Building a New American State: The Expansion of National Administrative Capacities, 1877–1920*. New York: Cambridge University Press, 1982.

GLOBALIZATION *BY* CHINA

The previous sections focused on political–economic debates on the globalization of China. That is, how have participation in and expansion of global trade and investment taken place in China and how has such globalization changed politics and the state system in the country. With the rise of China in the world economic system, globalization *by* China is growing rapidly and is likely to significantly impact shifting power and world development trajectories.

Shifting Balance of Power

Historically, the rise of a major economic power has major impacts on the global system. In the eighteenth century, economic expansion of the British Empire pulled a large part of the world into its trading orbit, with colonialism as one key and lasting outcome. US-led globalization has also deeply shaped the world's economic and political order; many developing economies drew their initial growth engines from this new superpower.[42] The economic renaissance of Japan after World War II significantly contributed to industrialization in East Asia and resource-rich nations in the Middle East and Africa.[43] Now, with China's economic rise through state-mobilized globalization, it is natural for students of global politics to ponder – and heatedly debate – its impacts on geopolitics and global development.

In East Asia and US – China relations, debates and discourses on rising China have been persistent since the 1990s.[44] After the 2008 global financial crisis, even global specialists began to examine such issues. In 2013, UK- and US based scholars published a joint volume arguing that global power has shifted to Asia with the decline of Europe and the United States.[45] In the volume, UK scholar Shaun Breslin clarifies that

[42] John Ruggie, "International Regimes, Transactions, and Change: Embedded Liberalism in the Postwar Economic Order," *International Organization*, 36(2), 1982, pp. 379–415.

[43] Mitchell Bernard and John Ravenhill, "Beyond Product Cycles and Flying Geese: Regionalization, Hierarchy, and the Industrialization of East Asia," *World Politics*, 47(2), 1995, pp. 171–209.

[44] For example, David Kang, "Getting Asia Wrong: The Need for New Analytical Frameworks," *International Security*, 27(4), 2003, pp. 57–85; Calder and Ye, *Making of Northeast Asia*; Calder, *The New Continentalism*; David Kang, *China Rising: Peace, Power, and Order in East Asia*. New York: Columbia University Press, 2007.

[45] Wyn and Wilson, *The Consequences of the Global Financial Crisis*.

the 2008 crisis showed the robustness of the Chinese economic system and the state's ability to mobilize resources to support national goals. He notes that the crisis increased China's relative financial power and firmly established it both at the center of global politics and as a key nation in any multilateral attempts to reform the structure of global governance.

In 2014, US and Canadian scholars produced another volume on China's global roles. Focusing on financial issues, Eric Helleiner and Jonathan Kirshner declared that "China's growing power in international monetary relations is multidimensional." They observe that China's power is enhanced by it "playing a larger role" in a game governed by existing rules, "demanding significant reforms to that status quo," and "demanding wholesale transformation or by exiting that system to create its own arrangements."[46]

This book speaks to and corrects this global power-shift perspective and argues that via state-mobilized globalization, China has revived domestic development after global recessions, yet it faces profound disadvantages in power projection outside China.[47] As shown in the implementation of the CGG and BRI, state salience and political mobilization are counterproductive as China pursues global leadership because foreign state and society are genuinely wary and skeptical of "politicized" investment and infrastructure projects. Even when outbound projects are devised in commercial terms, foreign counterparts are concerned about potential interference from the Chinese state.

Mistrust of China-led globalization runs deep in many parts of the world. In fact, for China to more effectively expand global power, it has two likely options: either (1) adopt prevalent global rules and norms that can make its outbound expansion more acceptable, that is, *bind* its own hands, or (2) spend resources on political–security terms irrespective of commercial gains, that is, *buy* political influence. Both institutional binding and interest buying are incompatible with the SMG dynamics revealed here. On the other hand, China's outgoing capital is often promoted through nationalist mobilization; on the other hand, it prioritizes commercial gains in overseas projects. Such dual characteristics have helped globalization in China from 1998 to 2018. They are insufficient, and can be disadvantageous, in globalization by China.

46 Eric Helleiner and Jonathan Kirshner (eds.), *The Great Wall of Money: Power and Politics in China's International Monetary Relations*. Ithaca, NY: Cornell University Press, 2014, p. 8.

47 See David Shambaugh's thorough evaluation of Chinese and American leadership in Southeast Asia, "U.S.-China Rivalry in Southeast Asia: Power Shift or Competitive Coexistence?" *International Security*, 42(1), 2018, pp. 85–127.

Prospect for the Latest Industrialization

Other than power-shift concerns, development specialists have focused on whether and how outbound China can help or hinder economic growth in countries that are attempting to catch up with industrialization and globalization, the latest industrializers in world development history. The answers have been divided and often debated.

In Africa, Deborah Brautigam paints a fairly balanced picture showing that while the PRC has become the largest economic presence on the continent, development outcomes are uneven across countries. Chinese banks and companies provide investment, infrastructure, and industries in some areas but not others. Furthermore, development outcomes are multidimensional: In places with economic gains, social and political consequences can still be damaging. More important, Brautigam observes that the Chinese pattern is not so different from past patterns between Africa and external powers, including the United States and Japan.[48] Will China do it better this time around? Only time will tell.

In Latin American countries (LAC), Kevin Gallagher observes that China–LAC economic relations leapt exponentially from 2003 to 2013; China's entry gave rise to a "resource boom" in the LAC region.[49] He notes, however, that these China–LAC relations are highly uneven, with economic benefits going to only a few countries and concentrated in a few sectors.[50] More important, Gallagher finds that governments in LAC have squandered much of the benefits from their "China boom." Instead of leveraging new capital from China to transform their domestic economies and upgrade industry, as China itself did during its globalization era, LAC spent most of their gains on social expenditure and consumption. With the China boom waning in recent years, these LAC economies are now deeply indebted and have slumped into recession.

State-mobilized globalization reveals that China's economics success had been embedded in its unique political–economic conditions. The framework worked in China because of a combination of strong autocracy *and* vibrant market economy, which has been growing rapidly since 1978. Coexistence of strong state and strong market can be hard to achieve elsewhere, in particular the latest industrializers.

48 Brautigam, *The Dragon's Gift*, p. 13.
49 Gallagher, *The China Triangle*.
50 Rebecca Ray and Kevin Gallagher, "China-Latin America Economic Relations Bulletin," GEGI Working Paper Series, Boston University, 2013.

Furthermore, like the Japanese "circles of compensation," Chinese commercial actors – state banks and SOEs – formed close and exclusive networks, which worked well to generate high investment-based growth inside China. Yet moving outward, these networks are likely to continue to operate within themselves; actors in recipients hence cannot be included deeply. As a whole, due to the mismatch between the Chinese framework and external environments, state-mobilized globalization is *unlikely* to lead a worldwide industrialization wave, although pockets of economic success are achievable.[51]

Potential of Global Governance

In terms of China's place in global governance, although rising powers inevitably lead to rising influence, outgoing China is *unlikely* to offer new institutions and norms to replace existing ones. The Chinese SMG is a mobilization framework and is weak in building institutions. Ambiguity in the SMG may allow Chinese actors to assume preexisting norms and institutions, such as in the case of BRI-associated AIIB. Such "institutional outsourcing" cannot spread to the entire package of globalization by China.[52] This does not mean that foreign actors – particularly from advanced Western societies – have no role to play. The flexibility that Chinese actors enjoy during implementation of these strategies means that external actors can contribute to the major evolution of China's outbound globalization and shape Chinese influence toward better outcomes in the future.

For foreign actors to fulfill such roles, they need to have an adequate understanding of the process and mechanisms of China's globalization strategies. As security expert Thomas Christensen writes, "To shape Beijing's choices so as to channel China's nationalist ambitions into cooperation rather than coercion ... will require us to better understand the meaning of China's rise and the domestic challenges Chinese leaders face."[53] Or, as political scientist Peter Hall remarks, "if we want to know where we are going, it is useful to know from where we have come."[54]

51 See examples in Doig, *High-Speed Empire Chinese Expansion and the Future of Southeast Asia.*

52 Steinfeld, *Playing by Our Rules*, 2010.

53 Christensen, *The China Challenge*, p. xxii.

54 Peter Hall, "The Political Origins of Our Economic Discontents: Contemporary Adjustment Problems in Historical Perspective," in *Politics in the New Hard Times: The Great Recession in Comparative Perspective*, edited by Miles Kahler and David Lake. Ithaca, NY: Cornell University Press, 2013, p. 129.

To understand today's China, we should trace how it got to where it is; to anticipate its role in the world, we ought to examine the inner workings of the Chinese state. This is precisely where the SMG framework has important roles to play in understanding China's ongoing and future foreign strategies.

ROADS AND ROADBLOCKS IN THE BRI

Now coming back to our core strategy that motivated the book project, the BRI. The ongoing strategy has experienced twists and turns in many rounds since its birth. From late 2013 to mid-2015, Chinese leadership was busy building up broader support; different state agencies were busy leveraging the strategy to insert their own policy priorities. In the formative two years, however, external attention to the new strategy was limited and dismissive.[55]

Then from mid-2015 to 2016, as the Chinese began to roll out projects and programs in the name of the BRI, external attention was suddenly intensified. In 2016, China's outbound investment reached almost $200 billion – the highest in its history – and its construction contracts reached more than $110 billion.[56] They represented a 34 and 25 percent increase, respectively, over the prior year. Such rapid jumps in BRI outbound projects resulted in major apprehension and resistance from the global powers and receiving countries. In 2017, both outbound FDI and construction contracts shrank significantly, reducing by 36 and 11 percent, respectively. Entering 2018, debates on drivers and impacts of the BRI remained pervasive and unsettling in many parts of the world.

The future remains uncertain. Yet it is good time, after five years, to synthesize where, the "roads" in the BRI lie and what are the "roadblocks."

The Roads

The first set of "roads" under the BRI are inside China. Leveraging the nationalist strategy, the Ministry of Transportation constructed two super-long speed rails, from Shanghai to Kunming and from Hangzhou to Changsha. In the localities, from the coastal city of Ningbo to the western city of Chongqing and to the western border city of Urumqi,

[55] The US government was dismissive of the strategy and persuaded its allies not to engage with it.

[56] See UNCTAD statistics and China Investment Track by Heritage Foundation.

local governments have proposed and implemented important projects and programs that help the cities achieve their development aspirations. Some local projects entail large physical infrastructure and investment, such as the new Customs and Development Zone in Urumqi that featured large buildings, facilities, and roads, and to a lesser extent, the greatly expanded new Plum Mountain zone in Ningbo. Some projects require limited investment but purport to have large significance, such as Ningbo's Central and Eastern European Consortium and Silk Road Maritime Index along with Chongqing's Yu-Xin-Ou Ecommerce. Some carry big names but serve to boost experimentation with new means, such as the China-Singapore Financial Park in Chongqing and the Zhejiang Belt and Road Experiment Site in Ningbo.

Many more projects and programs are a continuation of previously uncertain, or forestalled, projects. In this category, the Yu-Xin-Ou Railway in Chongqing is a good example. Due to the political downfall of its major benefactor Bo Xilai, the transnational railway was in an uncertain state, and its operation was on hold. The launch of the BRI injected new life – and considerable capital and resources – into the railway and enabled it to continue and expand operations to connect Chongqing with European markets. The key infrastructure in Hubei and Hunan provinces in central China was approved during the inflationary period of 2008–2012, and economic tightening after 2012 put that construction on hold. Again, under the Belt and Road, many of these projects were revived and received new financing. The BRI's *additive* effect is also clear in private power device-maker Safety Electric' decision to expedite and greatly enlarge its production in Xi'an, as well as state-owned Ningbo Port Group's decision to invest in the rail–water connection project in Hebei.

The second set of projects and programs under the BRI umbrella took place abroad but had significant domestic considerations. CDB's credit line to small and medium-sized enterprises in Central Asia in 2015 was to help foreign consumers buy Chinese vehicles made by Yutong. A new line of credit was also given to operators in Kashigar industrial zone under the pretense of connecting with the new Gwardar Port in Pakistan. Furthermore, China Ex-Im Bank started the "3+N" scheme in Chongqing, which helps the Chongqing Foreign Trade Group and other SOEs find overseas markets.

If these measures amount to state efforts to save struggling SOEs, then cases in railways, hydropower, telecommunications, and new energies are ways to help competitive Chinese companies expand global markets. Here, the business rationale was salient in these companies' overseas expansion. China Railways Construction, for example, planned to build headquarters in Malaysia that would cost $200 million; the plan was based on calculations related to Malaysia's own market value and potential to expand into rapidly growing infrastructure in Southeast Asia. In Pakistan's Karot hydropower plant that was reported to cost billions of U.S dollars to construct, the Chinese contracting company explained how this project presented reasonable medium- to long-term returns and in the meantime helps the company gain foreign presence (see Chapter 5).

Recent projects founded by China Ex-Im Bank also indicate strong connections between the BRI abroad and BRI-internal. It mostly supports Chinese companies to expand foreign markets. For example, it financed Russia's revamping of its "green-house agriculture," but the main contractor for this project was a Chinese building company based in central China. It also financed Xiamen University's construction of a campus in Malaysia, and in Bangalore its funding enabled the establishment of a fourth-generation Data Center, in which Chinese Telecoms was deeply involved. Investment by the Silk Road Fund was particularly calculated to spread risk and ensure mutual benefits. From 2015 to 2018, it acquired minority stakes in the Dubai Solar Power plant, the China-Kazakhstan Capacity Cooperation Fund, tourism in Uzbekistan, and a Russian gas and chemical company.[57]

The third set of projects under the BRI seems to have strong strategic and diplomatic implications for China's external power in the region. These projects support the various external arguments related to the BRI's imperialist intent. Chief among them are the infrastructure projects in connection with the CPEC, the highways linking Chinese borders with Lahore and Gwardar Port, as well as the construction of the deepwater port itself. Even in these strategically driven projects, the implementation has been more diversified than first impressions might have predicted. Take the CPEC as an example. The initial package amounted to $46 billion, and inside China it was seen as a strategic commitment that would not make a profit. Deep down, the package includes a variety of projects that display commercial considerations. Among them, CEIB financed the Lahore light rail, the Karakoram Highway, a solar plant near Punjab state, the Karot hydropower plant, a nuclear power facility, and another solar energy site. Behind these projects, the motivation to help Chinese manufacturers was clear. SRF's decision to acquire a minority stake in the Karot plant was also justified with long-term returns.

[57] Project compiled from Baidu and CEIB's website.

The Roadblocks

Now what about the roadblocks? The first thing to consider is state capital. How might state capital help or hinder the BRI's external implementation? In Chapter 7, the analysis demonstrates that Chinese state and state capital are in a long-term, repeated game structure. In this structure, the transactional-style project assessment is likely to be unhelpful because state capital may lose in one investment but gain in another, and it may lose in the near term but gain in the longer term. And because the players belong to a steady and codependent group, state capital may lose investments in some places but gain in others. Such repeated games can unravel, however, because the external environment of the "game" is different from that inside China. The external proportion of the CGG strategy has shown that different institutional contexts have unraveled these repeated game dynamics, such as in Brazil, Canada, and Malaysia.

Second, ambiguity and ambition – two characteristics of the strategy– are counterproductive abroad. Oversized rhetorical pledges generate unrealistic expectations of Chinese "generosity" in the receiving countries, which leads to disappointment, disillusionment, and resentment once the receiving countries recognize the commercial nature of the Chinese projects. Diplomatic disputes have ensued and will ensue in the future. In the CPEC, for example, in mid-2017, a mini crisis came when the first set of loans matured and a new round of financing was about to start. Pakistan expected the same concessionary rates; yet the Chinese financiers argued the concessionary rates applied only to Early-Harvest projects and asked to revise the terms for the second round of financing. Facing push-back and negative press in Pakistan, the Chinese conceded and renewed at the same concessionary rates. However, the damage was already done – it was sobering to Pakistan and alarming to the Chinese domestic audience.

Inside China, the nationalist rhetoric served to mobilize state and market actors to improvise measures of globalization and growth. Outside, however, ambitious rhetoric based on Chinese nationalism created diplomatic backlash at regional and global levels. In South Asia, India was an important partner and destination for commercial implementation of the Belt and Road. Yet when CPEC was announced and justified by its strategic and political significance, India became extremely wary. Responding to apprehension in Japan and US efforts to counterbalance China's actions, India became a prime member of the Indo-Pacific Grouping that seeks to countervail the Belt and Road as the strategy moves to this region. In Burma and Sri Lanka, Chinese projects in the Belt and Road face immediate counterbids from India. In Indonesia and Thailand, projects that China has pursued strongly are invariably resisted by counteroffers from Japan, which has had a significant social and economic presence there. Even friendly neighbors of China, South Korea and Singapore, have become wary and closely aligned with the United States while distancing themselves from China.

These external challenges are concerning, but the gravest dangers to the Belt and Road lie inside China. On the one hand, the BRI seems to delay structural reform in the Chinese economy. By mobilizing lower state units and state capital, even in a business-conforming fashion, the BRI thwarted the function of the market to overcome economic recessions and delayed rebalancing investment and consumption. It is clear in Wenzhou, which has a relatively weak local government, that the economy has been more quickly rebalanced from industrial overcapacity to consumption and service-based development. In Chongqing and Ningbo, one with capable state capital and the other with a "smart" local state, the investment-led growth model has yet to be changed.

On the other hand, mobilization of the BRI has greatly boosted the power of the autocratic leader in the Communist regime. In the past five years, the personalistic power of the individual leader has been strengthened; technocratic debates have been silenced; and fragmented ad hoc policy response has continued, if not intensified. How such trends are shaped by the BRI and will shape the BRI in the future remains critically unclear.

CONCLUSION

China has an authoritarian political system; in the past twenty years, this system has tightened power at the apex of the regime, as epitomized by the ascent of the strong leader Xi Jinping. China also has a state-controlled capitalist system, in which the state owns and manages the financial sector, major infrastructure companies, and powerful local governments. Situated in such a political–economic system, when the political leadership announced the Belt and Road strategy, it is natural and logical for foreign observers to attribute the strategy to the autocrat's nationalist ambitions and be deeply concerned about major disruptions by Chinese outward investment and lending in the name of the BRI.

This view is, however, woefully incomplete. It misses important domestic drivers and internal institutions that have shaped and will continue to shape the implementation and impacts of the BRI, in China and abroad. Research in this book adopts the SMG analysis and reveals that it was not so much the "vision" of the leader, but a combination of crises and state paralysis that gave rise to the BRI. Furthermore, after the leadership announcements, central agencies have "inserted" their policy ideas and practices into the strategy, state capital has leveraged it for its own commercial interests, and local governments have likewise reinterpreted the BRI to serve localized development priorities. Such diverse and decentralized implementation has made the BRI a reasonably effective "state intervention" in the marketspace and helped stabilize the high-growth economy inside China.

The SMG logic has also driven China's development and globalization experiences since at least 1998. In two prior nationalist strategies launched by the political leadership, the Western Development Program (CGG) and the China Goes Global (CGG) policy, the same drivers, processes, and outcomes have prevailed in China. In the case of CGG, however, the research finds that the SMG logic, while working in China, clearly failed outside the country because the external institutions and environment are incongruent with political mobilization and state-led investment from China.

From 2013 to 2019, China's the BRI has finished its first phase of implementation. It managed to present a more or less cohesive platform from Chinese capital to expand globally and garnered worldwide attention to globalizing China. Yet, much of its impact on Chinese diplomacy has been problematic. It is still a long way away from turning China's industrial overcapacities to lead the world's latest industrialization, achieving what China pledged "Win-Win" globalization.

In short, the mobilization state in China has worked during its own globalization because it combines nationalist ideology, powerful party politics, *and* robust market tendencies in the national economy. It has propelled China to leap from a middle power to the other superpower in just twenty years (1998–2018). Unfortunately, it is counterproductive as a driver of globalization *by* China. Time will tell. While the BRI can build a lot of roads abroad, it faces a lot of roadblocks too.

Appendices

Appendix 1

SAMPLE LIST OF INTERVIEWS

The project built on interviews with national agencies, government-affiliated think tanks, and university scholars, as well as corporate managers and media personnel, in Beijing and the localities in China. The overriding concern in arranging and selecting interviews was to unearth the real policy dynamics and actual motivations of business decisions. Here is a sample list.

Locale	Function	Experience	Venue	Discovery
BJ	Retired senior official (Agency 1)	Trade ministry, chief negotiator	Interviewer's home	Internal politics behind international negotiation
BJ	Retired official (Agency 2)	Development	Private lunch	Information/ideas available in bureaucracies
BJ	Scholar (Think tank 1)	Leading grand strategy studies	Institution conference room after work	Why BRI is important
BJ	Retired scholar (University)	Lifetime policy advising	Institutional office	Origin and problems with a policy proposal
BJ	Official (Agency 3)	20 years regional diplomacy	Office during lunch break	Origins and earlier proposals for BRI
BJ	Researcher (Think tank 2)	20 years regional experience	Institutional conference room	Why a particular policy was adopted

Locale	Function	Experience	Venue	Discovery
BJ	Researcher (Think tank 2)	15 years global finance	Cafes	Think tank–state relations and channels of policy input
BJ	Former official from (Agency 4)	Head of a private think tank	Institutional conference	Commercial drivers behind BRI policy
BJ	Policy advisor (Think tank 3)	Head of government think tank	Office	Leadership vision and scholarly input
BJ	SOE	20 years in the company	Office	History of globalization; BRI projects
BJ	Official (Agency 4)	15 years in the agency	Office	Planning process; priorities of BRI
SH	SOE	20 years work and director of BRI implementation	Corporate conference room	Communication with central actors; self-identified market
SH	Private company	Chief financial officer	Corporate conference room	Years of experience in risky market, new moves along BRI
SH	Private company	20 years management	Café	Challenge in globalization
SH	Scholar	15 years experience	Lunch	University's ideas of leveraging in BRI
HZ	Scholar	10 years	Office	Origin of WDP
HZ	Private firm	20 years	Office	Globalization
CQ	Official	30 years experience	Café	City's BRI plans
CQ	Provincial SOE	Senior manager	Corporate conference room	History of cross-border railways
CQ	SOE spinoff	CEO	Corporate office	Motivation of BRI projects
CQ	Official	15 years of work experience in the Bureau	Office	Ranking of types of capital in the city
CQ	Official	10–15 years of experience	Office	BRI projects and programs in the city and their origins
CQ	Retired scholar	30+ years	Lunch	WDP process

Locale	Function	Experience	Venue	Discovery
NB	Official	Economic planning	Institution conference room	Bottom-up industrial planning
NB	Official	10 years FDI promotion	Office	Challenges and priorities in FDI promotion
NB	Official/SOE	20 years of zone management	Institution conference	City's globalization history
NB	Provincial SOE	General manager	Conference room	Commercial interpretation of BRI
NB	City SOE	CEO	Conference room	Motivation and challenges of state business
NB	Scholar	Director	Office	Motivation of the program and activities
WZ	Official	Party affairs	Late night tea house	Challenges in local economy
WZ	Official	Urban planning	Café	De-industrialization
WZ	Private companies	Senior manager	Office after work	Companies' involvement in WDP
WZ	Private entrepreneur	Director	Office	Process and nature of BRI project
WZ	Official	Public relations	Café	State–corporate relations
WZ	Journalist	20 years	Many occasions	Different periods of growth
UQ	Official	30 years planning	On tour	Origin of BRI-related projects
UQ	Official	15 years PR	Office	Tourism

Keys: BJ, Beijing; SH, Shanghai; HZ, Hangzhou; CQ, Chongqing; NB, Ningbo; WZ, Wenzhou; UQ, Urumqi.

Appendix 2

SAMPLE ARCHIVES ON BRI

The second set of information comes from archival materials. I argue that it is important to read through the whole text of the reporting to get to the bottom of the projects, rather than using keyword searches. As examples, in the list below, you find the article title, but only with full text reading can we can identify the actors, sectors, and real motivations for their outbound projects. Further, to identify whether the actor is a state or private company, and if state, at which level, I conducted separate research to pin down their affiliations.

Article title	Actor	Sector	Motivation
Chinese Construction Bank Signs BRI MOU with Singapore's Investment Promotion Bureau	National Bank	Finance	Financial services and tech transfer
Southern Airlines Opens 179 Lines along one Belt and One Road	National SOE	Industry	Hollow pledge, no concrete steps
Unipay International: Multiple Means to Serve One Belt and One Road	Subnational Bank	Finance	Business expansion

Article title	Actor	Sector	Motivation
One Belt, One Road New Blue Sea: Chinese Net Companies Explores the Arabic World	Private company	Industry	Exploring markets
Power China Construction Post-Earthquake Restoration in Indonesia	National SOE	Infrastructure	Diplomacy/ foreign aid
Power China Construction Housing Project in Pakistan	National SOE	Industry	Diplomacy/ foreign aid
China Construction Highway Project in Pakistan	National SOE	Infrastructure	Diplomacy and business
China Rails Regional Headquarter in Malaysia	National SOE	Infrastructure	Business expansion
China Construction Landmark Building in Cambodia	National SOE	Infrastructure	Business expansion

Appendix 3

LIST OF CHINESE DOCUMENTS ON OUTBOUND INVESTMENT

1. 1989, SAFE, Jingwai touzi waihui guanli banhua [Regulation of Foreign Exchange Used in Overseas Investment], ended on January 8, 2011, available www.doc198.com/p-578751.html.
2. 1991, MOFTEC, Guowuyuan pizhun guojia jiwei guanyu jiaqiang haiwai touzi xiangmu guanli yijian de tongzhi [State Council Approval of State Planning Commission Notice on Enhancing Regulation of Overseas Investment], State Council Circular #13, available https://law.lawtime.cn/d606379611473.html?from=singlemessage.
3. 1997, State Planning Commission & SAFE, Jingwai jinxing xiangmu rongzi guanli zanxing banfa [Temporary Measures on Regulation of Raising Funds Overseas], available www.chinalawedu.com/falvfagui/fg22016/10012.shtml.
4. 1999, the State Counil, Guanyu guance luoshi guowuyuan guanyu guli qiye liyong yuanwai youhui daikuan he yuanwai hezi hezuo xiangmu jijin kaizhan jingwai dailiao jiagong zhuanpei yewu yijian [Implement the State Council Opinion on Companies Using Foreign Aid Concessionary Loans to Expand Manufacturing Assembly Business], State Council Circular #17, available www.mofcom.gov.cn/aarticle/b/e/200207/20020700032507.html.
5. 2001, Ministry of Finance, Duiwai chengbao gongcheng baohan fengxian zhuanxiang zijin guanli zanxing banfa [Temporary Measures on Regulating Overseas Contractual Infrastructure

Risk Funds], available www.mofcom.gov.cn/article/b/bf/200207/20020700031431.shtml.

6. 2001, MOFTEC, SPC, MOF, etc., Guanyu "shiwu" qijian jinyibu cujin jidian chanpin chukou de yijian [Opinion on Promoting Electronics and Machinery Exports during the 10th Five Year Plan], State Council Public Notice, #35, available www.gov.cn/gongbao/content/2001/content_61212.htm.
7. 2002, State Planning Commission, Guanyu cujin he yindao minjian touzi de ruogan yijian [Opinions on Promoting and Regulating Private Capital Investment], The State Council Public Notice #26, available www.gov.cn/gongbao/content/2002/content_61718.htm.
8. 2002, MOF and MOFTEC, Zhongxiao qiye guoji shichang kaituo zijin guanli shixing banfa [Experimental Measures on Regulating Small and Medium Sized Enterprises Overseas Exploratory Funds], available www.mofcom.gov.cn/aarticle/bi/200209/20020900042231.html.
9. 2003, SAFE, Guanyu jinyibu shenhua jingwai touzi waihui guanli gaige youguan wenyi de tongzhi [Notice on Further Deepen Reform of the Regulation of Foreign Exchange Use in Overseas Investment], State Council Public Notice #24, available www.gov.cn/gongbao/content/2004/content_62874.htm.
10. 2004, MOF and MOFCOM, Guanyu zuohao 2004 nian ziyuanlei jingwai touzi he duiwai jingji hezuo xiangmu qianqi feiyong fuchi youguan wenti de tongzhi [Notice on Financial Support of Resources Overseas Investment and Joint Projects in Early Stages], available http://project.mofcom.gov.cn/1800000121_23_65169_0_7.html.
11. 2004, NDRC, Jingwai touzi xiangmu hezhun beian zanxing guanli banfa [Temporary Regulatory Measures on Overseas Investment Project Approval], State Council Public Notice #20, available https://baike.baidu.com/item/境外投资项目核准暂行管理办法/7995090. Ended on May 8, 2014.
12. 2005, MOFCOM, MFA, and SASAC, Guanyu jiaqiang jingwai zhongzi qiye jigou yu renyuan anquan baohu gongzuo de yijian [Opinions on Protecting Staff and Employees of Chinese Companies Investing Abroad], available www.gov.cn/xxgk/pub/govpublic/mrlm/200803/t20080328_32462.html.
13. 2005, MOFCOM, Guanyu jingwai touzi kaiban qiye hezhun gongzuo xize [Approval Procedure for Companies Overseas Investment],

State Council Public Notice #28, available www.mofcom.gov.cn/aarticle/b/g/200511/20051100755581.html.

14. 2006, MOFCOM, NDRC, MOST, MOF, PBOC, et al., Guanyu "shiyiwu" qijian jiakuai zhuanbian jidian chanpin chukou zengzhang fangshi de yijian [Opinions on Expediting the Change of Export Contents in Electronics and Machinery during the 11th Five Year Plan], available www.gov.cn/xxgk/pub/govpublic/mrlm/200803/t20080328_32513.html.
15. 2007, China Bonds Regulatory Commission, Hege jingnei jigou touzizhe jingwai zhengquan touzi guanli shixing banfa [Experimental Measures on Regulating Overseas Bond Investment by Eligible Domestic Institutional Investors], available www.csrc.gov.cn/pub/newsite/flb/flfg/bmgf/jj/hgjn/201012/t20101231_189784.html.
16. 2009, MOFCOM, Jingwai touzi guanli banfa [Regulatory Measures over Overseas Investment], State Council Public Notice #29, available www.mofcom.gov.cn/aarticle/b/c/200903/20090306103210.html.
17. 2011, SASAC, Zhongyang qiye jingwai guoyou zichan jiandu guanli zanxing banfa [Temporary Measures to Monitor and Regulate Overseas Assets of Central State Owned Companies], available www.sasac.gov.cn/n2588035/n2588320/n2588335/c4258958/content.html.
18. 2012, NDRC, MOFCOM, MFA, et al., Guanyu jiakuai peiyu guoji hezuo he jingzheng xinyoushi de zhidao yijian [Guidelines on Expediting Development of New Advantages in International Cooperation and Competition], available www.doc88.com/p-7129545919450.html.
19. 2014, State Council, Guanyu cujin fuwu waibao chanye jiaokuai fazhan de yijian [Opinion on Expediting the Development of Services Export Industry], State Council Circular #67, available www.gov.cn/zhengce/content/2015-01/16/content_9402.htm.
20. 2014, NDRC, Guanyu xiugai "jingwai touzi xiangmu hezhun he beian guanli banfa" he "waishang touzi xiangmu hezhun he beian guanli banfa" [Decision to Revise the Regulation over Overseas Investment Project Inspection and Reporting and the Regulation over Foreign Investment Projects Inspection and Reporting], State Council Public Notice #8, available www.ndrc.gov.cn/zcfb/zcfbl/201501/W020150115578202458544.pdf.

Bibliography

Amsden, Alice. 1989. *Asia's Next Giant: South Korea and Late Industrialization.* New York: Oxford University Press.

2003. The Rise of "the Rest": Challenges from Late-Industrializing Economies. New York: Oxford University press.

Ang, YuenYuen. 2016. *How China Escaped the Poverty Trap.* Ithaca, NY: Cornell University Press.

Anonymous. 2002. "shishi zouchuqu zhanlue chujian chengxiao" [The Early Effect of the Go Out Strategy], *Liaowang*, May 6, No. 19.

Anonymous. 2005. "China's Railway Marvel Heightens Tibetan Fears," *Sydney Morning Herald*, October 1.

Anonymous. 2006. "Zhuanfang waihui guanliju juzhang huxiaolian" [Special Interview of SAFE Director Hu Xiaolian], *Caijing*, No. 9.

Anonymous. 2006. "Zhongguo qian chuhai" [Chinese Money Goes Global], *Caijing*, No. 9.

Anonymous. 2006. "Zhong yidong, fangqi de yiyi" [China Mobile: Significance of Giving Up], *Caijing*, No. 15.

Anonymous. 2007. "Retake the Test of Finding Overseas [chongkao haiwai tankuanglu] Ore", *Caijing*, No. 24.

Anonymous. 2012. "12nian xibu dakaifa: xibei jubianzhong de yu shi" [*Western Development at 12: The Gain and Losses in Western China*], *Economic* [*jingji cankao bao*], *Reference*, January 11.

Anonymous. 2012. "Zhongguo haiwai binggou bixiuke" [The Must Take Lesson of China's Overseas Acquisition], *Caijing*, No. 9.

Anonymous. 2014. "lunlun wenzhou moshi shengminli de neizai genju" [On Inner Vitality of the Wenzhou Model], *Wenzhou xuekan* [Wenzhou Journal],April, No. 2.

Anonymous. 2014. "yidai yilu wei dapeng chashang xin chibang" [Yidai Yilu, China the Roc's Two Wings], *Renmin Ribao*, May 7.

Anonymous. 2014. "yidaiyilu: Zhongguo waijiao xin siwei" [Yidai Yilu, China's New Diplomatic Perspective], *Guangming ribao* [Enlightenment Daily], June 7.

Anonymous. 2018. "China Set to Tackle Overseas Investment Risks," *Financial Times*, June 28.

Axelrod, Robert. 1984. *The Evolution of Cooperation*. New York: Basic Books.

Backaler, Joel. 2014. *China Goes West: Everything You Need to Know about Chinese Companies Going Global*. London: Palgrave Macmillan.

Bairoch, Paul, and J.-M. Limbor. 1968. "Changes in the Industrial Distribution of the World Labour Force, by Region, 1880–1960," *International Labour Review*, 98: 311–336.

Bernard, Mitchell, and John Ravenhill. 1995. "Beyond Product Cycles and Flying Geese: Regionalization, Hierarchy, and the Industrialization of East Asia," *World Politics*, 47(2): 171–209.

Borthwick, Mark. 2014. *Pacific Century: The Emergence of Modern Pacific Asia*. New York: Westview Press.

Brautigam, Deborah. 2009. *The Dragon's Gift: The Real Story of China in Africa*. New York: Oxford University Press.

Bremmer, Ian. 2010. *The End of the Free Market: Who Wins the War between States and Corporations?* New York: Portfolio.

Bromley, Patricia, and Walter Powell. 2012. "From Smoke and Mirrors to Walking the Talk: Decoupling in the Contemporary World," *Academy of Management Annals*, 10: 1–48.

Calder, Kent. 2012. *The New Continentalism: Energy and Twenty First Century Eurasian Geopolitics*. New Haven, CT: Yale University Press.

2017. *Circles of Compensation: Economic Growth and the Globalization of Japan*. Stanford, CA: Stanford University Press.

Calder, Kent, and Min Ye. 2010. *The Making of Northeast Asia*. Stanford, CA: Stanford University Press.

Chen, Derong. 2012. "renzhen guanche luoshi sheng dangdaihui jingsheng, nuli tuijing Wenzhou jianshe" [To Implement Provincial Party Committee's Principle and Implement Wenzhou Development], *zhengce liaowang* [Policy Outlook], No. 7: 10–12.

Chen, Ling. 2018. *Manipulating Globalization: Business and Local Governments in China*. Stanford, CA: Stanford University Press.

Chen, Ling, and Barry Naughton. 2016. "An Institutionalized Policy-making Mechanism: China's Return to Techno-Industrial Policy," *Research Policy*, 45(10): 2138–2152.

Chen, Nan. 2010. "zhuanfang yuan guojia shuiwu zongju fujuzhang xushanda: zhongguo maxieer jihua yu fazhanzhong guojia gongxiang fazhan" [Interview of former State Administration of Taxation Vice Minister Xu Shanda: China's Marshall Plan and Joint Development in the World], *Shangwu zhoukan*, January 20. http://news.sohu.com/20100129/n269914596.shtml

Chen, Yangyong. 2009. "Jiang zemin zouchuqu zhanlue de xincheng jiqi zhongyao yiyi" [The Formation and Significance of Jiang Zemin's "Go Out" Strategy], Party Archives, No. 1. www.wxyjs.org.cn/wxzj_1/dbzb/201305/t20130531_140005.htm

Chen, Yao. 2015. "yidai yilu zhanlue de hexin neihan yu tuijing silu" [The Core Meaning and Implementation of One Belt and One Road], *Zhongguo fazhan guangcha* [Chinese Development Observation], No. 1: 53–55.

Christensen, Thomas. 2015. *The China Challenge: Shaping the Choices of a Rising Power.* New York: W.W. Norton & Company.

Dickson, Bruce. 2004. *Red Capitalism in China: The Party, Private Entrepreneurs, and Prospects for Political Change.* New York: Cambridge University Press.

2007. "Integrating Wealth and Power in China: The Communist Party's Embrace of the Private Sector," *The China Quarterly*, 192: 827–854.

2018. *Dictators' Dilemma: The Chinese Communist Party's Strategy for Survival.* New York: Oxford University Press.

Dimitrov, Martin. 2009. "Popular Autocrats," *Journal of Democracy*, 20(1): 78–81.

Doig, Will. 2018. *High-Speed Empire: Chinese Expansion and the Future of Southeast Asia.* New York: Columbia Global Reports.

Downs, Erica. 2004. "The Chinese Energy Security Debate," *The China Quarterly*, 177: 21–41.

2019. "The Dragon Steps Out: What Became of China, Inc.?" www.brookings.edu/wp-content/uploads/2016/06/china-inc-erica-downs.pdf, accessed on March 20, 2019.

Economy, Elizabeth. 2018. *The Third Revolution: Xi Jinping and the New Chinese State.* Oxford: Oxford University Press.

Einstein, Katherine Levine, Maxwell Palmer, and David Glick. 2019. "Who Participates in Local Government? Evidence from Meeting Minutes," *Perspectives on Politics*, 17(1): 28–46.

Eisenman, Joshua and Eric Heginbortham (eds.). 2018. *China Steps Out: Beijing's Major Power Engagement with the Developing World.* New York: Routledge.

Evans, Peter. 1995. *Embedded Autonomy: States and Industrial Transformation.* Princeton, NJ: Princeton University Press.

1997. "The Eclipse of the State: Reflections on Stateness in an Era of Globalization," *World Politics*, 50(1): 62–87.

Fewsmith, Joseph. 2010. *China Today, China Tomorrow: Domestic Politics, Economy and Society.* Lanham, MD: Rowman & Littlefield Publishers.

Friedman, Thomas. 2000. *The Lexus and the Oliver Tree.* New York: Farrar, Straus and Giroux.

2005. *The World Is Flat.* New York: Farrar, Straus and Giroux.

Fukuyama, Francis. 1992. *The End of History and the Last Man.* New York: Free Press.

Gallagher, John, and Ronald Robinson. 1953. "The Imperialism of Free Trade," *Economic History of Review*, 6(1): 1–15.

Gallagher, Kevin. 2007. *Dragon in the Room: China and the Future of Latin American Industrialization.* Stanford, CA: Stanford University Press.

Gallagher, Kevin. 2016. *The China Triangle: Latin America's China Boom and the Fate of the Washington Consensus.* New York: Oxford University Press.

Gallagher, Mary. 2002. "Reform and Openness: Why China's Economic Reforms Have Delayed Democracy," *World Politics*, 54(3): 338–372.

2017. *Authoritarian Legality in China: Law, Workers, and the State.* New York: Cambridge University Press.

Gandhi, Jennifer, and Adam Przeworski. 2007. "Authoritarian Institutions and the Survival of Autocrats," *Comparative Political Studies*, 40(11): 1279–1301.

Gao, Boyang, Michael Dunford, Glen Norcliffe, et al. 2017. "Capturing Gains by Relocating Global Production Networks: The Rise of Chongqing's Notebook Computer Industry 2008–2014," *Eurasian Geography*. doi:10.1080/15387216.2017.1326312.

Gao, Zhigang. 2014. "Sichou zhilu jingjidai kuangjiaxia zhongguo yu zhoubain guojia nengyuan yu waimao hulian hutong yanjiu gouxiang" ["Research Ideas on" before Silk Road Economic Belt and China's Energy and Trade Mutual Connectivity], *Fazhan yanjiu* [Development Studies], No. 1: 46–51.

Garver, John. 2006. "Development of China's Overland Transportation Links with Central, South-West and South Asia," *The China Quarterly*, 185: 1–22.

Gilley, Bruce. 2003. *China's Democratic Future: How It Will Happen and Where It Will Lead*. New York: Columbia University Press.

Gilpin, Robert. 1996. "Economic Evolution of National Systems," *International Studies Quarterly*, 40: 411–431.

Goodman, David. 2004a. "The Campaign to 'Open Up the West': National, Provincial-Level and Local Perspectives," *The China Quarterly*, 178: 317–334.

2004b. "Qinghai and the Emergence of the West: Nationalities, Communal Interaction and National Integration," *The China Quarterly*, 178: 379–399.

Gourevitch, Peter. 1986. *Politics in Hard Times: Comparative Responses to International Economic Crises*. Ithaca, NY: Cornell University Press.

Guo, L.C. (ed.). 2017. *The Belt and Road: Official Documents*. Beijing & Washington, DC: ICP Intercultural Press.

Guo, Shuyong. 2008. "lun heping fazhan dazhanluexia de guoji jingji yu guoji anquan xietiao" [On International Economic and Security Coordination Under the Peaceful Development Grand Strategy], *Shehui kexue* [Social Sciences], No. 12: 17–22.

Haggard, Stephan. 1991. *Pathways from the Periphery: The Politics of Growth in the Newly Industrializing Countries*. Ithaca, NY: Cornell University Press.

2018. *Developmental States*. New York: Cambridge University Press.

Haggard, Stephan, and Robert Kaufman. 2008. *Development, Democracy, and Welfare States: Latin America, East Asia, and East Europe*. Princeton, NJ: Princeton University Press.

Haggard, Stephan, and Steven Webb. 1993. "What Do We Know about the Political Economy of Economic Policy Reforms?" *World Bank Research Observer*, 8(2): 143–168.

Hall, Peter and David Soskice (eds.). 2001. *Varieties of Capitalism: The Institutional Foundations of Comparative Advantage*. New York: Oxford University Press.

Hall, Peter. 2013. "The Political Origins of Our Economic Discontents: Contemporary Adjustment Problems in Historical Perspective," in *Politics in the New Hard Times: The Great Recession in Comparative Perspective*, Miles Kahler and David Lake (eds.). Ithaca, NY: Cornell University Press.

Hamilton, Alexander. [1791] 1991. *The Works of Alexander Hamilton.* www.gilderlehrman.org/content/hamilton's-report-subject-manufactures-1791

Harding, Harry, Ian Bremmer, Thomas Stewart, et al. 2006. "China Goes Global: Implications for the United States," *National Interest*, September/October. https://nationalinterest.org/article/the-gramercy-round-china-goes-global-implications-for-the-united-states-1046

Heilmann, Sebastian. 2018. *Red Swan: How Unorthodox Policy-Making Facilitated China's Rise.* Hong Kong: Chinese University Press.

Heilmann, Sebastian, and Oliver Melton. 2013. "The Reinvention of Development Planning in China, 1993–2012," *Modern China*, 39(6): 580–628.

Helleiner, Eric, and Jonathan Kirshner (eds.). 2014. *The Great Wall of Money: Power and Politics in China's International Monetary Relations.* Ithaca, NY: Cornell University Press.

Herbst, Jeffrey. 1990. "War and the State in Africa," *International Security*, 14(4): 117–139.

Holbig, Heike. 2004. "The Emergence of the Campaign to 'Open Up the West': Ideological Formation, Central Decision-making and the Role of the Provinces," *The China Quarterly*, 178: 335–357.

Hu, Angang, and Wang Shaoguang. 2001. *The Chinese State in Crisis: State Capacity and Tax Reforms in China.* London: Routledge.

Hu, Angang, Liu Shenglong, and Wang Yahua. 2009. "Xibu dakaifa chengxiao yu zhongguo jingji shoulian" [The Effects of Western Development Program and China's Economic Contraction], *jingji yanjiu* [Economic Research], No. 9: 94–105.

Hu, Bing, and Zheng Liansheng. 2015. "Yazhou hulian hutong: Zhongguo de zhanlue, zhengce, yu xingdong" [Asia's Mutual Connectivity, China's strategy, Policy, and Action], *Xueshu qianyan* [Academic Frontiers], No. 12.

Hu, Shuli. 1999. "long yongtu shentan rushi" [Minister Long Deep Talk on China's WTO Entry], *Caijing*, No. 12.

Huang, Peijian. 2003. "Huali: chuanyue waihui guanzhi pingjing" [Huali, Overcoming Foreign Exchange Restriction Bottle neck], *Caijing*, No. 4.

Huang, Yanhua. 2015. "xiqi dongshu guihua xijie" [Details on the Planning of Western Gas to East Project], *nanfang nengyuan guancha*, January 7. http://finance.sina.com.cn/chanjing/cyxw/20150107/080521241852.shtml

Huang, Yasheng. 1995. "Administrative Monitoring in China," *The China Quarterly*, 102: 203–233.

2002. *Selling China: Foreign Direct Investment during the Reform Era.* New York: Cambridge University Press.

2008. *Capitalism with Chinese Characteristics: Entrepreneurship and the State.* New York: Cambridge University Press.

Huang, Yukon. 2018. "Chinas Economy Is Not Normal. It Doesn't Have to Be," *New York Times*, March 13.

Hurst, William. 2012. *The Chinese Worker after Socialism.* New York: Cambridge University Press.

Jamil, A., S. Henny, and B. Farhan. 2018. "Pakistan Rethinks Its Role in Xi's Belt and Road Plan." *Financial Times*, September 9.

Jessop, Bob. 2010. "The 'Return' of the National State in the Current Crisis of the World Market," *Capital & Class*, 34(1): 38–43.

Jiang, Zemin. "Speech on the CCP Central Committee on January 20, 2000," in *Jiang Zemin Selected Works, Volume 2*, The Central Committee Compilation Office (ed.). Beijing: Renmin Publisher, 2006, pp. 519–582.

Jiang, Zemin. 2001. The CCP Central Committee Compilation Office, *Jiang zemin wenxuan* [*The Selected Works of Jiang Zemin*]. Beijing: Renmin Publisher.

[1995] 2006. "zhengque chuli shehui zhuyi xiandaihua jianshezhong de ruogan zhongda guanxi" [Correctly Deal with the Major Relations during the Construction of Socialist Modernization], in *Jiang Zemin Selected Works*, The Central Committee Compilation Office (ed.). Beijing: People's Publisher.

[1999] 2006. "bushi shiji de shishi xibu dakaifa zhanlue" [Seize the Moment to Implement the Western Development Strategy], in *Jiang Zemin Selected Works*, The Central Committee Compilation Office (ed.). Beijing: People's Publisher.

[1999] 2010. "Seize the Opportunity to Implement the Strategy of Large-Scale Development of the West," in *Selected Works of Jiang Zemin*, Vol. 2, pp. 331–338. Beijing: Foreign Languages Press.

[2002] 2013. "Hold the Initiative in Fierce International Competition," in *Selected Works of Jiang Zemin*, Vol. 3, pp. 429–446. Beijing: Foreign Languages Press.

Jin, Zhongxia. 2012. "Zhongguo de maxieer jihua tantao zhongguo duiwai jichu jianshe touzi zhanlue" [The Chinese Marshall Plan and China's Outbound Infrastructure Investment Strategy], *Guoji jingji pinglun* [Commentary on International Economy], 6: 57–65.

Johnson, Chalmers. 1982. *MITI and the Japanese Miracle: The Growth of Industrial Policy, 1925–1975*. Stanford, CA: Stanford University Press.

Kahler, Miles. 1988. "External Ambition and Economic Performance," *World Politics*, 40(4): 419–451.

Kang, David. 2003. "Getting Asia Wrong: The Need for New Analytical Frameworks," *International Security*, 27(4): 57–85.

2007. *China Rising: Peace, Power, and Order in East Asia*. New York: Columbia University Press.

Kaplan, Robert. 2018. *The Return of Marco Polo's World: War, Strategy, and American Interests in the Twenty-First Century*. New York: Random House.

Kastner, Scott. 2009. *Political Conflict and Economic Interdependence Across the Taiwan Strait and Beyond*. Stanford, CA: Stanford University Press.

2016. "Buying Influence? Assessing the Political Effects of China's International Trade," *Journal of Conflict Resolution*, 60(6): 980–1007.

Kennedy, Scott. 2008. *The Business of Lobbying in China*. Cambridge, MA: Harvard University Press.

Kissinger, Henry. 2011. *On China*. New York: Penguin Press.

Kohli, Atul. 2004. *State-Directed Development: Political Power and Industrialization in the Global Periphery*. New York: Cambridge University Press.

Kong, Bo, and Kevin Gallagher. 2017. "Globalizing Chinese Energy Finance: The Role of Policy Banks," *Journal of Contemporary China*, 26(108): 834–851.

Kroeber, Arthur. 2016. *China's Economy: What Everyone Needs to Know.* New York: Oxford University Press.

Kurlantizick, Joshua. 2016. *State Capitalism: How the Return of Statism Is Transforming the World.* New York: Oxford University Press.

Lampton, David. 2014. *Following the Leaders: Ruling China, From Deng Xiaoping to Xi Jinping.* Berkeley: University of California Press.

Lardy, Nicholas. 1998. "China and the Asian Contagion," *Foreign Affairs*, 77(4): 78–88.

2014. *Markets over Mao: The Rise of Private Business in China.* Washington, DC: Peterson Institute for International Economics.

2019. *The State Strikes Back: The End of Economic Reform in China?* New York: Columbia University Press.

Li, Qiang. 2002. "nuli ba Wenzhou jiancheng quanguo zuiju huoli de chengshi" [Strive to Develop Wenzhou into the Most Vibrant City in China], *jingri Zhejiang* [Today's Zhejiang], No. 23: 12–13.

2003. "shishi haishang Wenzhou jainshe, jianshe haiyang jingji qiangshi" [Realize Oceanic Wenzhou and Develop a Strong Maritime Economy], *Zhejiang jingji* [Zhejiang Economy], No. 16.

Li, Shufeng, and Huang Peijian. 2003. "Jingwai touzi waihui guanli gaige chushi shenshou" [Outward Investment Foreign Exchange Experimental Reforms], *Caijing*, No. 3.

Li, Xiangyang. 2014. "lun haishang sichou zhilu de duoyuanhua hezuo jizhi" [On Multilateral Cooperation Mechanisms of the Maritime Silk Road], *World Economics and Politics*, pp. 2–17, November.

Li, Xiaojun. 2012. "China's Geoeconomic Strategy: China as a Trading Superpower," *IDEAS Report*. http://eprints.lse.ac.uk/44204/

Li, Yubao. 2005. "Qiguan changhong: xiqi dongshu gongcheng jianshe jishi" [Daring Act: The Real Record of the West to East Pipeline]. Beijing: Petroleum Industry Publisher.

Li, Zhiguo. 2012. "PS: yinnan ershang mou zhuanxing fazhan" [Precious Steel: Strive to Self-Restructure and Develop in Face of Difficulties], *Jingri ribao* [Economics Daily], February 27.

Lieberthal, Kenneth, and David Lampton (eds.). 1992. *Bureaucracy, Politics, and Decision Making in Post-Mao China.* Berkeley: University of California Press.

Lieberthal, Kenneth, Michael Oksenberg, and David Lampton. 1988. *Policymaking in China: Leaders, Structures, and Processes.* Princeton, NJ: Princeton University Press.

Lin, Li. 2014. "xin changtai, xin Wenzhou" [The New Normal, the New Wenzhou], *Wenzhou* Xuekan [Wenzhou Research], No. 3, June, 19–25.

Lin, Qiping. 2002. "Zhongguo rushi hou de 'sange bu zhenglun' he 'sange guanjian'" [Three "No Disputes" and Three "Critical" after China's WTO Membership], *Guoji Maoyi Wenti* [Issues in International Trade], No. 12: 1–4.

Lin, Yifu. 2012. "yong xinjegou jingjixue kan weilai quanqiu he zhongguo de jingji zengzhang" [Use New Structural Economics to Examine the Future Growth in China and in the World], *Xin jinrong pinglun* [New Financial Commentaries], No. 2, 1–17.

List, Friedrich. 1996. *Outlines of American Political Economy*. Paul & Co Pub Consortium. www.openlibrary.org.

Liu, Jianchao. 2014. "yidai yilu jianshe shi yazhou guojia de gongtong shiye" [The Belt and Road Is the Common Project of Asian Nations], *Guangming Ribao* [Enlightenment Daily], May 28, 8.

Liu, Weidong, Tian Jincheng, and Ou Xiaoli. 2017. *Yidai yilu zhanlue yanjiu* [Study of the Belt and Road Strategy]. Beijing: Shangwu yinshuguan.

Liu, Weidong, Michael Dunford, Song Zhouying, and Chen Mingxing. 2016. "Urban-Rural Integration Drives Regional Economic Growth in Chongqing, Western China," *Area Development and Policy*, 1(1): 132–154.

Magee, Darrin. 2006. "Powershed Politics: Yunnan Hydropower under Great Western Development," *The China Quarterly*, 185: 23–41.

McNally, Christopher. 2004. "Sichuan: Driving Capitalist Development Westward," *The China Quarterly*, 178: 426–447.

2012. "Sino-Capitalism: China's Reemergence and the International Political Economy," *World Politics*, 64(4): 741–776.

Mertha, Andrew. 2009. "Fragmented Authoritarianism 2.0: Political Pluralization in Chinese Policy Process," *The China Quarterly*, 200: 995–1012.

2010. *China's Water Warriors*. Ithaca, NY: Cornell University Press.

Miller, Tom. 2017. *China's Asian Dream*. London: Zed.

Milner, Helen. 1988. *Resisting Protectionism: Global Industries and the Politics of International Trade*. Princeton, NJ: Princeton University Press.

Minzner, Carl. 2018. *End of An Era: How China's Authoritarian Revival Is Undermining Its Rise*. New York: Oxford University Press.

Mishra, Pankaj. 2018. "The Rise of China and the Fall of the Free Trade Myth," *New York Times*, February 7.

Naughton, Barry. 2009. "Understanding the Chinese Stimulus Package," *China Leadership Monitor*, 28. www.hoover.org/research/understanding-chinese-stimulus-package

Naughton, Barry, and Kellee Tsai (eds.). 2015. *State Capitalism, Institutional Adaptation, and the Chinese Miracle*. New York: Cambridge University Press.

Naughton, Barry. 2017. "Is China Socialist?" *Journal of Economic Perspective*, 31(1): 3–24.

2018. *The Chinese Economy: Adaptation and Growth*. Cambridge, MA: MIT Press.

NDRC. 2014. "xin silu zhanlue de jingji zhidian" [The Economic Anchor of the New Silk Road], *Zhongguo jingji zhoukan* [China Economics Weekly], July 7.

2015. "fagaiwei: woguo zhengzai zhiding guoji channeng hezuo sannian xingdong jihua" [NDRC: We Are Making Capacity International Cooperation Three Year Action Plan], *zhongguo jingji wang* [China Economics Network], December 25.

NDRC and CBRC. 2015. "yidai yilu rongzifa" [One Belt and One Road Financing Method], *Caixin Weekly*, 43: 36–39.

NDRC, MFA, and MOFCOM. 2015. "tuidong gongjian sichou zhilu jingjidai he ershiyi shiji haishang sichou zhilu" [Vision and Action Plan to Promote the Joint Construction of the Silk Road Economic Belt and the 21st Century Maritime Silk Road], www.mofcom.gov.cn/article/ae/ai/201503/20150300928878.shtml.

Nicolas, David. 2015. *Chinese Infrastructure in South Asia: A Realist and Liberal Perspective*. Middletown, DE: Progressive Management.

Norris, William. 2016. *Chinese Economic Statecraft: Commercial Actors, Grand Strategy, and State Control*. Ithaca, NY: Cornell University Press.

Oakes, Tim. 2004. "Building a Southern Dynamo: Guizhou and State Power," *The China Quarterly*, 178: 467–487.

Oi, Jean. 1995. "The Role of the Local State in China's Transition Economy," *The China Quarterly*, 178: 467–487.

Pan, Feng. 2015. "Zhongguo yu 21 shiji yazhou jichu sheshi hulian hutong jincheng" [China and the 21st Century Asia Infrastructure Mutual Connectivity], *Guoji yanjiu cankao* [International Studies Reference], No. 8: 23–28.

Pan, Shifu. 2009. "Zhongguoban maxieer jihua xiaoguo chunyi" [China's Marshall Plan Is Doubtful], *Zhengquan shibao* [China Stocks], 22 July, 3.

Pearson, Margaret. 2015. "State-Owned Business and Party-State Regulation in China's Modern Political Economy," in *State Capitalism, Institutional Adaptation, and the Chinese Miracle*, Barry Naughton and Kellee S. Tsai (eds.). New York: Cambridge University Press.

Perry, Elizabeth. 1992. "Moving the Masses: Emotion Work in the Chinese Revolution," *Mobilization: An International Quarterly*, 17(2): 111–128.

2008. "Playing by the Rule," in *China Today, China Tomorrow*, Joseph Fewsmith (ed.). Lanham, MD: Rowman & Littlefield.

Qiu, Lin. 2009. "Maxieer jihua bu fuhe zhongguo guoqing" [Marshall Plan Does Not Work for China], *Zhonghua gongshang shibao* [Chinese Commerce Daily], 17 August.

Ray, Rebecca, and Kevin Gallagher. 2013. *China-Latin America Economic Relations Bulletin*. Working paper, Boston University Global Economy and Governance Initiative (GEGI). https://ase.tufts.edu/gdae/Pubs/rp/wg/WG_ChinaLA_Bulletin_2013.pdf.

Reilly, James. 2013."China's Economic Statecraft: Turning Wealth into Power," Lowy Institute for International Policy, University of Sidney, November. www.lowyinstitute.org/sites/default/files/reilly_chinas_economic_statecraft_web_0.pdf

Rein, Shaun. 2014. *The End of Copycat China: The Rise of Creativity, Innovation, and Individualism in Asia*. Hoboken, NJ: John Wiley & Sons.

Rogowski, Ronald. 1989. *Commerce and Coalitions: How Trade Affects Domestic Political Alignments*. Princeton, NJ: Princeton University Press.

Rolland, Nadege. 2017. *China's Eurasian Century? Political and Strategic Implications of the Belt and Road Initiative*. Washington, DC: The National Bureau of Asian Research.

Ruggie, John. 1982. "International Regimes, Transactions, and Change: Embedded Liberalism in the Postwar Economic Order," *International Organization*, 36(2): 379–415.

Schmidt, Vivien. 2009. "Putting the Political Back into Political Economy by Bringing the State Back in Yet Again," *World Politics*, 61(3): 516–546.

Shahbaz, R. 2017. "Pakistan Stops Bid to Include Diamer-Bhasha Dam in CPEC," November 15, https://tribune.com.pk/story/1558475/2-pakistan-stops-bid-include-diamer-bhasha-dam-cpec/

Shambaugh, David. 2013. *China Goes Global: The Partial Power*. New York: Oxford University Press.

2018. "U.S-China Rivalry in Southeast Asia: Power Shift or Competitive Coexistence?" *International Security*, 42(1): 85–127.

Sharma, Bal Kishan, and Nivedita Das Kundu (eds.). 2017. *China's One Belt One Road: Initiative, Challenges, and Prospects*. New Delhi, India: Vig Books India PVT.

Shen, Xiaoxiao, and Kellee Tsai. 2016. "Institutional Adaptability in China: Local Developmental Models under Changing Economic Conditions," *World Development*, 87: 107–127.

Shih, Victor. 2008. *Factions and Finance in China: Elite Conflict and Inflation*. New York: Cambridge University Press.

2004. "Development, the Second Time Around: The Political Logic of Developing Western China," *Journal of East Asian Studies*, 4(3): 427–451.

Shirk, Susan. 1993. *The Political Logic of Economic Reform in China*. Berkeley: University of California Press.

2007. *China Fragile Superpower*. New York: Oxford University Press.

Skowronek, Stephen. 1982. *Building a New American State: The Expansion of National Administrative Capacities, 1877–1920*. New York: Cambridge University Press.

Solingen, Etel. 1998. *Regional Orders at Century's Dawn: Global and Domestic Influences on Grand Strategy*. Princeton, NJ: Princeton University Press.

State Council. 1993. "guojia jiwei guanyu xibei diqu jingji guihua wenti baogao" [State Planning Commission Report on Issues in Economic Planning in Northwestern China], No. 19, March. www.gov.cn/zhengce/content/2010-12/30/content_2152.htm

1996. "guojia jiwei guanyu xinan he huanan bufen shengqu quyu guihua gangyao de tongzhi" [State Planning Commission Notice on Regional Planning Issues in Southwestern and Southern Regions], State Council (SC) #56.

2000. "guajia jiwei guanyu shishi xibu dakaifu de tongzhi" "[Notice on Policies Implementing the Great Development of Western Region]," State Council Circular #33. www.gov.cn/gongbao/content/2001/content_60854.htm

2004a. "guanyu jinyibu xibu dakaifa de ruogan yijian" [Opinions on Further Implementing Western Development], State Council Circular #6.

2004b. "guanyu xibu diqu liangjian gongjian jihua de tongzhi" [Notice on Two Basic Plans in Western China], State Council Circular #20.

2005a. "guanyu jinyibu fangsha zhisha gongzuo de jueding" [Decision on Further Conducting Sand Prevention and Control], State Council Circular #29.

2005b. "guanyu weihe liuyu zhili guihua de pifu" [Approval on the Plan to Improve the Wei River Region], State Council Circular #99.

2007. "guanyu wanshan tuigeng huanlin zhengce de tongzhi" [Notice on Perfecting the Policy to Return Agricultural Cultivation to Forestry], State Council Circular #6.

2008. "guanyu jinyibu cujin ningxia jingji shehui fazhan de ruogan yijian" [Opinions on Further Promotion of Social-Economic Development in Ningxia], State Council Circular # 29.

2009a. "guanyu jinyibu cujin guangxi jingji shehui fazhan de ruogan yijian" [Opinions on Further Promotion of Social-Economic Development in Guangxi], State Council Circular #42.

2009b. "guanyu yingdui guoji jinrong weiji baochi xibu diqu jingji pingwen jiaokuai fazhan de yijian" [Opinions on Maintaining Steady and Reasonably Fast Economic Growth in Western China as Means to Confront the Global Financial Crisis], State Council Circular # 55.

2010. "guanyu jinyibu zhichi gansu jingji shehui fazhan de ruogan yijian" [Opinions on Further Support of Social-Economic Development in Gansu], State Council Circular #29.

2011a. "Guanyu zhichi yunnansheng jiakuai jianshe mianxiang xinan kaifang zhongyao qiaotoubao de yijian" [Opinions on Supporting the Expedition of Yunnan Province's Openness to the Southwest], State Council Circular #11.

2011b. "guanyu jinyibu cujin neimenggu jingji shehui youhao youkuai de ruogan yijian," [Opinions on Further Development of Inner Mongolia Faster and Better] State Council Circular # 21.

2012. "guangxi haiyang gongneng quhua," [Regional Planning in Maritime Functions] State Council Circular # 166.

2014a. "guanyu tongyi sheli shaanxi xixian xinqu de pifu." [Approval to Establish Xixian New Zone in Shaanxi] State Council Circular #2.

2014b. "guanyu tongyi sheli guizhou guian xinqu de pifu." [Approval to Establish Guian New Zone in Guizhou] State Council Circular #3.

2014c. "guanyu tongyi sheli neimengu erlian gaote zhongdian kaifa shiyanqu de pifu." [Approval to Establish Erlianhaote Experiment Zone in Inner Mongolia] State Council Circular #74.

2015. "guanyu lanzhoushi chengshi zongli guihua de pifu." [Approval on Comprehensive City Planning in Lanzhou], State Council Circular #109.

Steinfeld, Edward 2010. *Playing Our Game: Why China's Economic Rise Doesn't Threaten the West.* New York: Oxford University Press.

Stern, Rachel. 2014. *Environmental Litigation in China: A Study in Political Ambivalence.* Cambridge: Cambridge University Press.

Sun, Yat-sen. 1922. *The International Development of China.* New York & London: G.P. Putnam's Sons.

Swaine, Michael. 2014. "Chinese Views and Commentary on Periphery Diplomacy," *China Leadership Monitor*, 44: 1–43.

Tan, Zhenyi, and Zhao Linyun. 2013. "Historical Assessment of China's Western Development Program" [zhongguo xibu dakaifa jincheng de lishi shenshi] *Yun nan minzu daxue Xuekan*, [*Journal of Yunnan Nationalities University*], 30(2): 101–107.

Thelen, Kathleen. 2019. "The American Precariat: U.S Capitalism in Comparative Perspective," *Perspectives on Politics*, 17(11): 5–27.

Thun, Eric. 2008. *Changing Lanes in China: Foreign Direct Investment, Local Governments, and Auto Sector Development.* New York: Cambridge University Press.

Tsai, Kellee. 2007. *Capitalism without Democracy: The Private Sector in Contemporary China*. Ithaca, NY: Cornell University Press.

2015. "The State of China's Economic Miracle," *Asia Policy*, 20: 144–148.

Wade, Robert. 1990. *Governing the Market: Economic Theory and the Role of Government in East Asian Industrialization*. Princeton, NJ: Princeton University Press.

Wang, Huiyao. 2016. *China Goes Global: How China's Overseas Investment Is Transforming Its Business Enterprises*. New York: Palgrave Macmillan.

Wang, Jisi. 2011. "China's Search for a Grand Strategy: A Rising Great Power Finds Its Way," *Foreign Affairs*, 90(2): 68–79.

Wang, Yichao. 2002. "tianranqi shidai kaiju" [The Natural Gas Era Opens], *Caijing*, No. 10: 21–41.

Wasserstrom, Jeffrey. 2013. "China & Globalization," *Daedalus*, 143(2): 157–169.

White, Lynn T., III. 1998. *Unstately Power: Local Causes of China's Intellectual, Legal and Governmental Reforms*, 2 vols. Armonk, NY: M.E. Sharpe.

Wolf, Martin. 2004. *Why Globalization Works*. New Haven, CT: Yale University Press.

Wu, Ming. 2011. ["New Thinking on Reform and Openness in the Context of Western Development Program", shenru shishi xibu dakaifa zhanlue beijingxia de xibu diqu duiwai kaifang xin silu], *Research on* [Jingji Wenti Tansuo] *Economics Issue*, 11: 6–9.

Wyn, Grant and Graham K. Wilson (eds.). 2012. *Consequences of the Global Financial Crisis: The Rhetoric of Reform and Regulation*. New York: Oxford University Press.

Xi, Jinping. [2012] 2014a. "Achieving Rejuvenation Is the Dream of the Chinese People," in *The Governance of China*, Xi Jinping (ed.), pp. 37–39. Beijing: Foreign Languages Press.

[2012] 2014b. "Work Together to Build the Silk Road Economic Belt," in *The Governance of China*, Xi Jinping (ed.). Beijing: Foreign Languages Press.

Xu, Shaoshi (ed.). 2015. *Guojia xibu kaifa baogao* [National Western Regional Development Report 2015]. Hangzhou: Zhejiang University Press.

Xu, Sitao. 2006. "shentan waihui chubei touzi zhanlue" [Be Careful with Strategic Investment of Foreign Exchange], *Caijing*, No. 3. http://opinion.caixin.com/2006-02-06/100304495.html

Yao, Wang. 2006. "Zhongguo 'zouchuqu' zhanlue huanjing yanjiu" [The Study of Strategic Environment of China Goes Global Based on SWOT-PEST Modeling], *Jingji luntan* [Economics Forum], 22: 54–57.

Ye, Min. 2009. "Policy Learning or Diffusion: How China Opened to Foreign Direct Investment?" *Journal of East Asian Studies* 9(3): 399–432.

2014. *Diasporas and Foreign Direct Investment in China and India*. New York: Cambridge University Press.

2014."China Invests Overseas: Regulation and Representation," *Modern China Studies*, 21(1): 173–204.

2015. "Competing Cooperation in Asia Pacific: TPP, RCEP, and the New Silk Road," *Asian Security*, 11(3): 206–224.

2016. "Utility and Conditions of Diffusion by Diasporas: Foreign Direct Investment in China and India," *Journal of East Asian Studies*, 16(2): 261–280.

2019. "Fragmentation and Mobilization: Domestic Politics of China's Belt and Road Initiative," *Journal of Contemporary China*. doi:10.1080/10670564.2019.1580428

Ye, Zi. 2016. "Wenzhou dianzi shangwu yanjiu" [Wenzhou Ecommerce], *Wenzhou xuekan* [Wenzhou Journal], No. 2, April, 12–13.

Yip, George, and Bruce McKern. 2016. *China's Next Strategic Advantage: From Imitation to Innovation*. Cambridge, MA: MIT Press.

Yu, Keping. 2008. *Globalization and Changes in China's Governance*. Boston, MA: Brill.

Zeng, Peiyan. 2010. *Xibu dakaifa juece huigu* [Reflections on the Process of Western Development Program Policy Making]. Beijing: Zhonggong dangshi chubanshe.

2013. "Yazhou jichu sheshi hulian hutong shizai bixing" [Asian Infrastructure Mutual Connectivity Has to Be Done], *Boao Review*, October 13, 38–40.

Zhang, Jiwei. 2000. "Zhongguo shiyou: guoqi qijian nan xiashui" [China Petroleum: Flagship SOE Had Difficulty in Going Global], *Caijing*, No. 5.

Zhang, Lin. 2012. *Venture Capital and the Corporate Governance of Chinese Listed Companies*. New York: Springer.

Zhang, Monan. 2009. "Jiji zhudong de chuangzhao waixu shishi zhongguoshi maxieer jihua" [Actively and Proactively Create External Demand and Implement the Chinese Marshall Plan], *Zhongguo jingji daobao* [China Economic Herald], June 27.

Zhang, Xiangdong. 2013. "PS xin liunian guihua jiedu" [How to Read Precious Steel's New Six Year Plan], *Jingji guancha wang* [Economics Observation Network], June 25.

Zhang, Yansheng. 2012. "cong yinjinlai dao zouchuqu de kuayue" [The Leap from "Attract In" to "Go Out"], *Liaowang* [The Outlook], August 22, 35–37.

Zhou, Xiaoqian. 2016. "xidian dongsong, quangguo daju" [Western Electricity to the East Is the National Priority], *Zhong guo nengyuan bao* [*China Energy Newspaper*], November 6.

Zhu, Caihua. 2013. "Dongya jichu jianshe hulian hutong rongzi" [Financing for East Asia Infrastructure Development Mutual Connectivity], *guoji jingji hezuo* [International Economic Cooperation], No. 10, 2013.

Zhu, Rongji. 2001. "shiying xin qingkuang xin renwu, nuli ba liyong waizi gongzuo tigaodao xinshuiping" [Adapt to New Conditions and New Tasks, Strive to Improve the Utilitization of Foreign Capital in China], in *15da yilai zhongyao wenxian xuanbian* [Important Central Documents Since the 15th Party Congress]. Beijing: Central Party Compilation Office.

Zhu, Yuchao, and Dongyan Blachford. 2012. "Economic Expansion, Marketization, and Their Social Impact on China's Ethnic Minorities in Xinjiang and Tibet," *Asian Survey*, 52(4): 714–733.

Index

For EU product safety concerns, contact us at Calle de José Abascal, 56–1°, 28003 Madrid, Spain or eugpsr@cambridge.org.

www.ingramcontent.com/pod-product-compliance
Lightning Source LLC
LaVergne TN
LVHW091528200926
848483LV00002B/332
* 9 7 8 1 1 0 8 4 7 9 5 6 1 *